Holding
the Home Front

The men must take the swords,
And we must take the ploughs,
Our Front is where the wheat grows fair,
Our Colours, orchard boughs.

Come out of the towns
And on to the downs
Where a girl gets brown and strong,
With swinging pace
And morning face
She does her work to song.

The children shall not starve,
The soldiers must have bread,
We'll dig and sow and reap and mow,
And England shall be fed.

From the Land Army Song.

Holding
the Home Front

*The Women's Land Army in
the First World War*

Caroline Scott

PEN & SWORD
HISTORY

First published in Great Britain in 2017 by
PEN AND SWORD HISTORY
an imprint of
Pen and Sword Books Ltd
47 Church Street
Barnsley
South Yorkshire S70 2AS

ISBN 978 1 78383 112 8

Printed and bound in England
by CPI Group (UK) Ltd, Croydon, CR0 4YY

Typeset in Times New Roman by
CHIC GRAPHICS

Pen & Sword Books Ltd incorporates the imprints of Pen & Sword
Archaeology, Atlas, Aviation, Battleground, Discovery,
Family History, History, Maritime, Military, Naval, Politics, Railways,
Select, Social History, Transport, True Crime, Claymore Press,
Frontline Books, Leo Cooper, Praetorian Press, Remember When,
Seaforth Publishing and Wharncliffe.

For a complete list of Pen and Sword titles please contact
Pen and Sword Books Limited
47 Church Street, Barnsley, South Yorkshire, S70 2AS, England
E-mail: enquiries@pen-and-sword.co.uk
Website: www.pen-and-sword.co.uk

Contents

Illustrations

ILLUSTRATIONS

Introduction

In recent years the Women's Land Army has received some long-overdue formal recognition, firstly with the issue of a commemorative badge to veterans and a reception at Downing Street in 2008, and then with the unveiling of a statue at the National Memorial Arboretum in 2014. On both occasions women who had been members of the Land Army during the Second World War reflected that it had felt like their contribution had been 'forgotten' after the 1940s.

The Land Girl might well have been out of sight and out of mind through much of the second-half of the twentieth century, but popular culture discovered her around the turn of the millennium. Over the past fifteen years films, television series and novels have seen Land Girls pushing their way into our line of sight. That gutsy girl, winning over the sceptical farmer and stolid rustics with her charm and chat, has become almost a cliché. Veterans of the Second World War have, understandably, sometimes reacted angrily to these over-coloured retellings of their experiences. Indeed, it's been observed that they have little basis in truth; this is a phoney war with far too much flirting and not nearly enough dirt and hard graft. The authenticity of the on-screen Land Girl is certainly doubtful, her exploits much romanticised, and she's frequently to be found with anachronistic values falling out of her lipsticked mouth, but there's no danger of the public forgetting about her. (There's no danger that she'll let us forget.) We might be misremembering her, we might have distorted her image into one that suits a twenty-first century audience, but we haven't forgotten. Other things have been forgotten, though. One could be forgiven for supposing that women first stepped out into the fields in 1939, but it's a much older and more complicated story.

Even in histories of the Women's Land Army, the First World War doesn't get too much of a look-in. The period of 1917-19 is generally quickly précised, condensed into an introductory chapter to set the

INTRODUCTION

scene for the Second World War. And perhaps understandibly so. The Landswomen of the First World War are rather more difficult to get to know than the Second World War's Land Girls.[1] Alas, they've all gone now and haven't left enough of themselves behind. Their experiences exist in scraps and snippets and fragments of voices. They didn't mean to fade away, though. As soon as the war was over, women began curating their own history, committing their experiences to paper and to museums. In 1920, invited by the new Imperial War Museum, they posted off badges and certificates and accounts of their wartime lives to London. The museum wanted to create a permanent record of the work performed by women during the war and land workers responded readily to the invitation to participate. In 1920 they wanted to have their voices heard. But time nudged on and the prevalent mood wasn't one for lingering in reminiscence. The women themselves were making homes and families, and social and economic forces were testing the resolve of those who tried to cling on and make a career on the land. Then, all too soon, another war was eclipsing the story of the Landswoman. Have we unfairly undervalued the contribution of the First World War's female land workers, then? Has history short-changed them?

Within days of the start of the First World War there were calls for women to come to the fields, but it would be almost three years before the Women's Land Army was established. In that time though, various private and public initiatives would be launched to pull women onto the land. The Women's Land Army would be shaped as much by the successes and failures of these earlier enterprises as by the precise requirements of 1917. It was a process of evolution, not revolution, and agricultural policy had also evolved over the course of the first three years of the war. By the spring of 1917 farmers were being called upon to plough out, to push back the borders and extend the cultivated acreage back to the highs of the 1870s. Agriculture would thus need most labour just as it had least available. Britain's food security had never looked most precarious than it did at the start of 1917.

A year on, in the spring of 1918, Miss May Kemble ('a land worker') addressed a demonstration in Chelmsford. She said,

There was a world shortage of food. England alone of the belligerent countries had not only maintained her pre-war production, but had increased it. (Cheers.) Farmers had done this in spite of very great difficulties, one of the greatest being the scarcity of labour. Farmers were sending in more and more applications for women workers, but, alas! There were so few to send them.[2]

It wasn't just a girl's vain boast. Having come through a 'great national emergency', British wartime agricultural policy was held up as a success story; domestic food production was higher at the end of the war than at the start, the average calorific value of the British diet barely changed and bread never had to be rationed. By comparison, in continental Europe, agricultural output had declined by around one third. As the press reported starvation and food riots on the other side of the Channel, British agriculture looked like it had been victorious. Rowland Prothero, President of the Board of Agriculture, called this 'one of the great achievements of the War' – and Lloyd George would go further, stating in his memoirs that 'The food question ultimately decided the issue of this war.'[3]

1917 was the darkest hour, the danger point, and it was at that moment that Lord Selborne, formerly President of the Board of Agriculture, observed, 'If it were not for the women agriculture would be absolutely at a standstill on many farms.'[4] Is that true? Were women really keeping the wheels turning? Or was that statement loaded with political purpose – rhetoric targeted to induce women to come forwards and to persuade farmers to accept their offered labour? This book is an attempt to understand how the return of women to the fields and farmyards impacted agriculture – and, in turn, an examination of how that experience affected them.

Chapter 1

'Such Dirty Work'

In February 1915 the *Liverpool Daily Post* reflected: 'We know that female labour is very extensively employed in Germany, France, and Italy. But with us the day when women took their part on the land and in the stockyard is gone – probably for good. And few of us have regretted the change.' England thus patted itself on the back. The fact that its womenfolk were 'long estranged' from toil in the fields was held up as progress, a sign of a civilised society. It might be alright for Continentals to let their women muddy their hemlines, but this really was not British behaviour.

But, the *Post* was contemplating 'A National Problem' (that was the headline above this text). A shortage of labour now threatened to eclipse in gravity all other difficulties which farmers faced. In the spring of 1915 fields were unploughed and unsown, the paper reported, and a huge amount of work was in arrears.[1] Could it be time to think again about women playing their part on the land, perhaps to take something from the Continental example? Could they be persuaded? Could they be capable? It was time to find out.

Agriculture had come through a great convulsion over the past fifty years and, while some areas were still struggling to shake that off in 1914, others had seen a pick-up in fortunes. Poor weather and disease had combined with an increasingly competitive import market to plunge British agriculture into depression from the 1870s. With the advance of the railroads across America, cheaper shipping and the progress of agricultural and refrigeration technology, foreign food had poured into Britain. While other countries had reacted to these developments by imposing or increasing tariffs, Britain had stuck to its free trade commitment. By the 1870s imported grain was arriving in such volume, and at such low prices, that British farmers started to throw their hands up in defeat. In 1894 wheat hit its lowest price for 150 years. Insolvencies multiplied, investment in the land retracted, only the best wheat fields were kept. Between 1871 and 1901 the corn growing area of England and Wales shrank from 8.2 million to 5.8 million acres.[2] Despite the nation's addiction to bread, by the eve of the First World War only around three per cent of farming land was producing grain for flour.[3]

Opportunity had been the flip-side of disaster, though. While some farmers had gone under by 1914, others were prospering. With the price of wheat having fallen, and general wages stable, bread took up a diminishing portion of urban workers' expenditure and there was thus more to spend on other foodstuffs. Meat and milk consumption increased and market gardening flourished as diet broadened. Successful farming was now about diversity and detail. Writing in 1912, Rowland Prothero observed:

> *The development of the milk trade, dairying, pasture-farming, flower-growing, market-gardening, poultry-keeping is characteristic of the new period... Instead of the large stake and open-handed expenditure of the old-fashioned corn-grower, there are many small stakes and a careful attention to minute details. The eggs are not crowded into one basket, but are distributed in many baskets.*[4]

In general, compared with circumstances at the turn of the century, agriculture was looking more comfortable by 1914, but not every farm had innovated and expanded its scope. Not every farm was doing well. While some areas were modernising, others were still profoundly traditional. Prosperity was as varied as practice. The fact that there was this diversity at the start of the war would mean that there would be a great variety in experience over the next four years.

Changes in land use, the increase in affordability of tools and machinery and the persistence of low wages caused the agricultural labouring population to fall by around a third in the last quarter of the nineteenth century. Women had outnumbered men in the rural exodus, the negative factors pushing them from the land combining with the pull of the greater opportunities and freedoms of urban employment. While the overall number of women in work was increasing (the 1911 census showed that about one third of women now did some paid work), the number employed in agriculture was going down. Milkmaids and female field workers weren't quite extinct by 1914, but they were well advanced in their decline.

Female employment in agriculture in 1914 can be roughly broken down into four categories: women farmers; female relatives of farmers; female farm servants (whose duties were both within the household and extended to the barns and the fields), and seasonal workers. In terms of the numbers within each category the 1911 census recorded 94,722 women engaged in agriculture in England and Wales (as such they represented eight per cent of the total farm workforce) and of these 20,027 women were working as farmers or graziers in their own right, 56,856 were relatives of farmers assisting in work and 13,245 agricultural labourers.[5] It's frustrating that the census statistics are so very different from those of the 1908 *Report on the Agricultural Output of Great Britain*, which recorded 244,000 female agricultural workers.[6] The discrepancy (much greater than the inclusion of Scotland and Ireland in the latter figure would explain) draws attention to the difficulties with census statistics, both in their consistency and their reliability.[7] The very nature of much female employment in agriculture (casual, seasonal, low-status and typically combined with other jobs) meant that women weren't necessarily likely to give agriculture as their trade when asked by census enquirers. It is pretty certain that the 1911 census significantly understates the number of women working in farming, and it was remarked on at the time that the picture presented by the census didn't reflect reality on the ground. All of the above said, the trend in female agricultural employment is beyond doubt; the number of women working on farms (particularly the number of labourers) was heading down.

Census year	Number of women employed as agricultural labourers
1871	57,988
1881	40,346
1891	24,150
1901	12,002
1911	13,245

Source: *Report of the Sub-Committee Appointed to Consider the Employment of Women in Agriculture in England and Wales* (1919), p. 25.

The 1911 census report remarked on the 'extraordinary variations in different counties in the degree to which women are employed on farms.' It surmised: 'Evidently the nature of the crops, as well as local custom, has much influence upon the extent of female employment.'[8] The county data in the table below is ordered by the percentage of women in the overall population of agricultural labourers:

County	Number of female agricultural labourers in 1911 census	Women as percentage of agricultural labour force (male and female)	Average weekly earnings of labourers in county (1907)
Northumberland	1,864	23%	21s. 10d.
County Durham	690	11%	22s. 9d.
Middlesex	242	6%	20s. 10d.
Kent	1,357	4%	19s. 4d.
Cheshire	433	3%	19s. 9d.
Cumberland	191	3%	20s. 5d.
Yorkshire, West Riding	531	3%	20s. 11d.
Lancashire	494	2%	21s. 7d.
Cambridgeshire	468	2%	17s. 2d.
Westmorland	52	2%	21s. 8d.
Worcestershire	216	2%	17s. 2d.
Surrey	188	2%	9s. 9d.
Shropshire	247	2%	18s. 10d.
Herefordshire	152	2%	17s. 11d.
Dorset	174	2%	16s. 6d.
Lincolnshire	607	2%	19s. 3d.
Devon	326	2%	18s. 1d.
Huntingdon	96	2%	17s. 2d.
Cornwall	158	2%	18s. 5d.

County	Number of female agricultural labourers in 1911 census	Women as percentage of agricultural labour force (male and female)	Average weekly earnings of labourers in county (1907)
Yorkshire, North Riding	173	1%	20s. 6d.
Derbyshire	107	1%	21s. 1d.
Yorkshire, East Riding	180	1%	20s. 1d.
Staffordshire	159	1%	19s. 4d.
Essex	401	1%	17s. 7d.
Hertfordshire	126	1%	18s. 3d.
Berkshire	116	1%	17s. 9d.
Hants & Isle of Wight	202	1%	18s. 1d.
Gloucestershire	145	1%	17s. 6d.
Norfolk	351	1%	16s. 6d.
Monmouthshire	31	1%	19s. 1d.
Wiltshire	159	1%	16s. 9d.
Buckinghamshire	92	1%	17s. 9d.
Nottinghamshire	76	1%	20s. 6d.
Warwickshire	83	1%	16s. 6d.
Sussex	156	1%	18s. 9d.
Leicestershire	56	1%	19s. 7d.
Rutland	9	1%	17s. 10d.
Suffolk	166	1%	16s. 7d.
Oxfordshire	62	1%	16s. 11d.
Northamptonshire	68	1%	17s. 10d.
Bedfordshire	47	0%	17s. 5d.
Wales	1,368	4%	
Scotland	14,927	17%	

Source: *Report of the Sub-Committee Appointed to Consider the Employment of Women in Agriculture*, p. 117.

The figures above illustrate that, while in a few counties female employment clung on, be it in field work, milking, or in a specialised area, in most counties it was now exceptional. This would have an impact on how female workers would be regarded when they arrived on the land in increasing numbers during the war.

While female labour had almost disappeared from many of the southern counties, in the north – and particularly in the north east – the practice of employing women on farms continued. In the far north there had been a tradition that male agricultural labourers were engaged on the understanding that they brought their wife's labour into the bargain. Something of this 'bondager' system still clung on in 1914. In Northumbria and Durham there were large, isolated farms where women were employed to do all varieties of work, while in Cumberland and Westmorland there was a tradition of female farm servants undertaking both household and farmyard duties. What's also noticeable in the table overleaf is that women were generally most frequently employed in the counties where agricultural wages were highest; they're taken on where labour is scarcest (be it on account of the remoteness of farms, or the fact that agriculture was competing for workers with industry) and therefore more expensive. Further south women tended to be employed particularly in districts where potatoes (Cambridgeshire, Lincolnshire and Norfolk) and other vegetable and fruit crops were grown (Kent and Worcestershire) and in the market-garden zone around London (Middlesex, Surrey, Essex and Hertfordshire).

In Wales, as in England, things had been changing. While in some counties women continued to work as farm servants (Carmarthenshire, Pembrokeshire and particularly Cardiganshire), over much of the country the custom of using female labour in agriculture had significantly declined. In 1871 women represented twelve per cent of agricultural wage earners in Wales; by 1911 the figure had fallen to four per cent. Welsh girls in search of employment had been attracted to towns, had 'bettered' themselves as domestic servants and shop girls, as clerks, dressmakers and milliners, and firmly turned their backs on agriculture. In Carmarthenshire it was observed that women had developed a 'repugnance' of farm work. The difficulty in attracting farm servants was attributed to girls having had 'too much education'. 'Girls now, they say, all want to be "genteel,"' a Board of Agriculture investigator was told. They wanted '"to wear slippers instead of clogs," and those who do not go away to work in shops aspire to become dressmakers.' A Board of Agriculture investigator recorded much the same attitude in Glamorganshire: 'During recent years a feeling has grown up that it is derogatory for a woman to undertake dirty work of any kind, and especially work connected with animals.' The women of Monmouthshire, meanwhile, were said to think themselves above farm work. 'They are too proud to do farm work,' said one farmer's wife. 'They say it's such dirty work attending to the beasties.'[9] This pejorative attitude to farmwork wasn't confined to Wales.

Understanding why women were leaving the land prior to 1914 will help to explain why many of them were reluctant to return to it during the war. This trend is attributable both to developments in agriculture and also due to expanding opportunities elsewhere. From the 1870s expanding adoption of planting, harvesting and threshing machinery eroded some of the traditional female roles. Moreover, male agricultural workers often did not want women there. The widespread employment of women and children in harvest gangs was seen as likely to depress overall agricultural wages. As women generally did the lighter jobs in field work, and were often paid piecework rates, everywhere they earned significantly less than men. A War Cabinet report observed:

> *In Lancashire, where men received up to 25s a week, women might get as much as 20s, while in Wiltshire and Berkshire, 9s to 12s for women would correspond to 12s to 15s for ordinary male labourers. In the Eastern Counties at haymaking, men in 1914 would receive 3s to 3s 6d per day of 10 hours, and women 1s 6d to 2s 6d per day of eight hours.*[10]

Women were seen as a wage suppressant and, as male agricultural labour became more organised through the 1870s and 1880s, female employment was discouraged. Joseph Arch, first President of the National Agricultural Labourers' Union, had advocated that instead of working on the land, women should be 'minding their houses… in domestic service, or working at some trade suited to women.'[11] The fact that agricultural unions did not necessarily welcome women onto the land would be significant during the war – as would the fact that farmers expected female labour to be cheap.

Perhaps the most important factor though, was that the women themselves no longer wanted to be on the land. In the 1860s Reverend James Fraser's opinions were recorded in the *First Report from the*

Commissioners on the Employment of Children, Young Persons and Women in Agriculture. Fraser wrote that agricultural work was likely to 'unsex a woman in dress, gait, manners, character, making her rough, coarse, clumsy, masculine.' Such work was 'social mischief', taking women away from their 'proper duties at home'.[12] To see women working on the land wasn't quite nice. It wasn't quite civilised. While it might be alright for the Germans and the French, it was not something that Englishwomen ought to be doing. Field work, in particular, was seen as demeaning labour. It's no accident that when Thomas Hardy's Tess sinks to her lowest point, he places her in a field grubbing up turnips. These values were communicated to rural women by the clergy and the rural elite and field work seemed more and more lowly.

As early as 1843 farmers were attributing the difficulty in hiring dairymaids to their 'over-education, which makes girls anxious to become housemaids, nursery-maids, dress-makers, &c.'[13] It was the subject of some amusement that farmers' wives were donning lace and feathers and giving their daughters piano lessons – and the improvement in male agricultural wages, toward the end of the nineteenth century, made it possible for increasing numbers of wives to remain at home embroidering cushions and for increasing numbers of daughters to have options. And those daughters opted to be anywhere other than working on the land. With the improvement in transport and general education, alternative opportunities became more realistic and accessible. Working as a domestic servant, or a dressmaker, or a shop girl was more respectable, more remunerative and offered greater variety and freedom. Thus only the women who had few other options were left to do the milking and the field work – and general opinion of this employment declined further. By 1914 the idea that work on the land was degrading was well engrained. Wartime landworker Kathleen Gilbert said that in the countryide of her childhood 'women stopped at home, and girls went to service in the houses.' She went into domestic service herself at fourteen, because 'all the girls did that.' Although she loved working with horses ('it was in my blood to be with horses'), farm work was not an alternative that she had really even considered until the war. It just was not done.[14]

In 1916 Viscountess Wolseley observed that countrywomen would 'prefer to undertake any other work', rather than go back on the land. They were convinced that 'work upon farms is derogatory to women, that it may be injurious to their health and that their children and homes will be neglected in consequence.' Like other women of her class, she saw an answer to this problem in using educated women to set an example. She wrote:

> The daughters of Army and Navy officers and of other professional men should fully realise what inestimable good they could do, if they became gardeners and thus showed others, by their example, that working for the land is by no means a degrading occupation and is in no sense unfeminine.[15]

By such women demonstrating patriotic energy – and saying that they felt valued and proud to be so doing – it was hoped that rural women could be persuaded to get over their prejudices. They would take a lot of convincing, though.

In July 1914 the supplementary report analysing the breakdown of occupations recorded in the 1911 census was published. The overall increase in the number of working women attracted a lot of attention, as did their apparent migration from the country to towns. Many viewed the diminishing numbers of women employed in agriculture as a sign of progress. On 1 August 1914 the *Essex Newsman* reported that the corn harvest was in full swing in the county ('the swish of the scythe and the rattle of the self-binder being heard everywhere'). The author observed how the advance of technology was positively impacting on farming – and one particular 'favourable sign of the times' that the author identified was 'the diminishing number of female workers in the fields.' The article went on:

> To bring the women out from their homes to work in the fields all day is bad for themselves and bad for the men. The

conditions of field labour are too exacting for women, and the onerous nature of the men's work in the summer time demands that they shall receive more personal attention from their woman-folk, and not less. The wives and mothers should be in their own homes looking after the food and drink side of the men's life during this laborious season, and paying increased and not diminished attention to the bodily requirements of their husbands and sons.[16]

But, within a few months, there would be a large number of vacancies in 'men's work' and the female role would have to be reassessed.

Chapter 2

'The New Woman and
the Old Acres'

A peculiar turnstile was in motion by the 1890s: just as working-class women were leaving the fields, women of a different social class were being drawn to the land. 'Agriculture as a career for women would have been looked upon as an impossibility and an absurdity half a century ago,' a newspaper article reflected in 1910. But things were changing: 'Now after centuries of artificiality and suppression women are once more permitted and encouraged to go "back to the soil," and to-day they may study Nature from the scientific standpoint.'[1] Increasing numbers of educated women had been hearing the call of the land and agricultural and horticultural training initiatives had developed to give them a leg-up to that scientific standpoint. As all such schemes were at fee-paying colleges, only a narrow demographic of women could take advantage of these opportunities, but these ground-breaking gentlewomen would lead the charge during the war. It was these pioneers who would determine how women in agriculture were perceived and recruited and trained. As such, these pre-war training colleges were effectively like an O.T.C. for the lady lieutenants who would marshal the Other Ranks back on to the fields.

The Horticultural College and Produce Company Ltd, near Swanley, Kent, founded in 1889, was Britain's first horticultural college. Women were admitted in 1891, initially partly in a move to shore up the institution's ailing finances, but while the number of female students increased, the number of male students declined, and from 1903 the college ceased to admit male students altogether. Fanny

Rollo Wilkinson, formerly landscape gardener to the Metropolitan Public Gardens Association, headed an institution which took a scientific approach to horticulture and offered practical training. Eighty-five women were enrolled at Swanley in 1914.[2]

Swanley was quickly followed by Studley. In 1897 Frances Evelyn 'Daisy' Greville (as in *Bicycle Built for Two*), Countess of Warwick, famous socialite and long-term mistress of King Edward VII, was making herself conspicuous in other areas; she was chairing conferences on Women's Work at the London Victorian Era Exhibition and writing articles about agriculture. In a piece for *The Land Magazine* Lady Warwick said that an agricultural training college ought to be established specifically for women – and, sure enough, the next year she made it happen. In 1898 she took on a property in Reading, which would become known as the Lady Warwick Hostel. University College Reading had set up a Department of Agriculture in 1893, partly funded by the Sutton seed company, and in 1896 the British Dairy Institute had relocated to Reading to become part of the same teaching institution.[3] Lady Warwick's plan was that her students would attend classes at the university and then apply the theories they were learning within the grounds of the hostel.[4]

Complimenting her efforts at Reading, Lady Warwick had also launched the Agricultural Association for Women and started editing a monthly magazine, *The Woman's Agricultural Times*. The opening article of the first issue, penned by Lady Warwick herself, was entitled *The New Woman and the Old Acres* and was a 'rallying cry for women of "Back to the Land."' She stated the motive for her efforts thus:

> *If we look at the melancholy, colourless and monotonous existence of so many educated women, who drift upon any marriage, however contrary to their better judgement, because marriage alone offers them a possible chance of escape, we cannot help admitting that a project that may with careful provision offer a career to large numbers of such women, is a project that should attract our whole sympathies.*[5]

Her articles promoted *'petite culture'* as an occupation for women (i.e. the lighter sort of farm work – growing fruit and flowers, bee-keeping and poultry farming), but she also advocated the establishment of agricultural settlements ('consisting of six or eight cottages, two women in each cottage, cultivating their own plot of land, but forming a co-operative society for buying and selling').[6] Having gone public with her ideas, Lady Warwick said that she was inundated by letters. These could typically be summarised as:

> *We are the daughters of professional men or of farmers, brought up in the country. Our parents are dead; we have £500 in funds; we have been forced by poverty into lodging in big cities where we are eking out the sad span of life on £15 a year, recognising in the dreary seclusion of our tiny city tenement that there is a green world beyond the gates, with woods and streams, from which we are shut out for want of opportunity.*[7]

While she saw definite opportunities for women in agriculture and horticulture, Lady Warwick believed that such endeavours shouldn't be entered casually. 'Thoroughness of work was essential,' she said. 'They must train, train, train, so that everything they did – whether the growing of a cabbage or the milking of a cow – should be done as well as it could be done.'[8]

With growing numbers of applications, and possibly on account of a cooling in relations with the University of Reading, a decision was made in 1901 to look for a larger property, 'with sufficient land contiguous thereto for farming purposes'.[9] Unable to find a sponsor (adverts placed in *The Times* failed to lure a benefactor), Lady Warwick bought Studley Castle in Warwickshire. She expressed the hope that the new Studley College would send forth women who, 'with intellects trained by scientific methods of study, and kept clear and vigorous by healthful occupation, in contact with nature, would contribute a little to the satisfactory solution of the great questions of land and labour.'[10] Despite her ambitions for it, Lady Warwick became less involved with the college after the move to

Warwickshire. She was a woman of various crusades, all initially fierce in their conviction, but not all of them lengthily-sustained, and by 1905 she was focussing her energy on the Social Democratic Federation.

In 1911, Dr Lillias Hamilton leased Studley Castle from the Warwick Estate and became its principal. The following year the College received a £1,000 grant from the Ministry of Agriculture. It was now offering a training course for women who wished to farm in the colonies, a 'housewife's course' and a general course in agriculture. Lillias Hamilton advocated that women could do well in this career 'provided they set about it in the right way'; though they might lack brute strength, they could make up for it with 'skill, power of organisation, and business knowledge and ability.'[11] One young woman who seemingly possessed all those qualities was Emily Ekins, who was the first woman from the college to be awarded the National Diploma in Horticulture in 1913. She went on to get a BSc in Horticulture from the University of London and would return to Studley as its principal in 1924.[12]

A 1905 newspaper article reflected:

Nowadays it is not so much a question: What shall we do with our boys? As what shall we do with our girls? Those with a taste for rural pursuits could certainly not do better than take up gardening under such pleasant and systematic conditions as obtained at Miss Wolseley's school.[13]

Viscountess Frances Wolseley had established the Glynde School for Lady Gardeners the previous year. As well as instructing women in horticulture (whatever its promises of pleasantness, Glynde had a reputation for iron discipline), Viscountess Wolseley also wrote extensively about the subject. She would go on to publish seven volumes on gardening and horticultural education, including *Women and the Land,* which came out in the spring of 1916. 'Physical strength and activity are increased by work in the health-giving atmosphere of the countryside, which is so replete with nerve-soothing influences,' she promised.[14] But, by 1916, work on the land was not just about self-improvement and pleasure. Viscountess Wolseley's text bristles with urgency and imperative. By 1916 the back-to-the-land rallying cry had reached a higher pitch.

In 1899 an International Congress of Women, held in London, brought together a group of land workers. Discovering that they had values and ambitions in common, they resolved to establish an association – the Women's Agricultural and Horticultural International Union – through which they might share information on methods, training and employment opportunities, endeavour to secure adequate wages and promote the reputation of women's work.[15] A newspaper article described the Union's ethos thus:

The union does not hold with women merely dabbling in agricultural science. It is workers who are needed; women of resource, who do not expect that farming shall be adapted to them. As the union makes clear in one of its admirable leaflets, women who do not mean to put their shoulders to the wheel had far better let the work alone.[16]

By 1910, when the association's name was changed to the Women's Farm and Garden Union (WFGU), many of the members were women of considerable resource. Mrs Chamberlain, the honorary secretary, farmed 700 acres in Sussex and employed seventeen men. One member was farming 174 acres in the Midlands, including a dairy and herds of cows, pigs and sheep, and another in Suffolk was managing 160 acres.[17] This was not an association for 'dabblers' and it meant to put its shoulder to starting a social movement. One of those admirable leaflets stated:

Social movements spread from the top downwards. If, presently, girls and women of the less educated classes find that a country life, and work on farm or garden, is not without charm for the more educated classes, they will not be so anxious to get away to towns and shops… When it is seen that ladies are healthy, happy and contented working on the land, the rustic damsel will begin to think it may be worthwhile to acquire knowledge of the primitive industries they have so neglected.[18]

That approach and understanding would have a significant influence on how women were recruited for work on the land during the First World War.

Chapter 3

'Keeping Calm'

The harvest not yet won, the empty bin,
The friendly horses taken from the stalls,
The fallow on the hill not yet brought in,
The cracks unplastered in the leaking walls.

Yet heard the news, and went discouraged home,
And brooded by the fire with heavy mind,
With such dumb loving of the Berkshire loam
As breaks the dumb hearts of the English kind.

From *August 1914* by John Masefield.

On 4 August 1914, as Britain entered the First World War, the President of the Board of Agriculture, Lord Lucas, told the House of Lords that there was 'no occasion whatever for public alarm over food supplies.'[1] An official notice from the Board of Agriculture followed this up. It stated: 'It may be said with confidence that there is actually in the United Kingdom at the present time, including the home crop now being harvested, five months' supply of breadstuffs. This is additional to the wheat and flour on passage and due to arrive shortly.' The National Farmers' Union backed up the Board with a statement to the press: 'Farmers can render assistance to the nation by keeping calm, and as far as possible conserving their supply of foodstuffs, both grain and cattle, and not rushing them to the market for the sake of high prices. Such a policy would be both unpatriotic and short-sighted.'[2] Panic was not deemed to be an appropriate reaction. Agriculture was told to keep its nerve, to 'play the game' and to carry on. 'It is reassuring to know that the best informed are the least apprehensive about the security of our food supplies,' the *Sussex Agricultural Express* reflected. 'In official and other circles familiar with the facts there is complete tranquillity.'[3]

The weather had been kind through the summer and the harvest of 1914 was the earliest for many years. 'That war should have broken out just before the fields of England were whitening to harvest seems like one of those instances in which this country has been so strangely fortunate in times of a great crisis,' the *Northampton Mercury* reported. 'Had the choice of the "selected moment" been left to ourselves, we could not possibly have fixed on a better for our own interests, so far as the food of the people was concerned.'[4] In most areas there was no shortage of hands to bring the harvest in, but Army Reserves were now being called up. Several men of the thousand-strong Yorkshire Farm Wagoners' Reserve were handed their mobilisation papers as they worked in the fields. 'The mobilisation of the force is a heavy blow to the farmers,' the *Yorkshire Evening Post* observed, 'inasmuch as their services are required for the harvest, which is imminent.'[5] Within two days of Britain entering the war, the Wagoners were mobilised and the sudden departure of their labour was the main subject of discussion amongst farmers attending Malton market the following weekend. Young men were called upon to help and a meeting of shop assistants resolved to offer their labour to local farmers in the evenings.[6]

There was much willingness to help. After the secretaries of the Farmers' Club and the Central Chamber of Agriculture addressed a joint statement to the press, on 8 August 1914, inviting the public to assist in the harvest fields, they were inundated with letters – from both men and women. Many of the volunteers were people 'of the better class, and are offering their services purely out of patriotism,' the Central Chamber of Agriculture reported. It therefore issued a letter to farmers, again through the press, offering the services of these keen volunteers.[7] However, the response came back that 'no help is wanted'; less than one percent of the farmers who contacted the Central Chamber of Agriculture stated that they needed assistance. In most areas the hay was already in and where the corn harvest was on-going farmers were confident that they could get through without the help of well-meaning Londoners (and, heaven forfend, women).[8]

Farmers dismissed 'highly coloured' newspaper stories about labour shortages, but still many unaccustomed hands found themselves in the harvest fields in 1914.[9] In Northumbria, Durham and Derbyshire, miners, who had gone on to short-time, assisted.[10] In Buckinghamshire artist brothers John and Paul Nash sweated in the fields ('novel amusement for me and great fun,' Paul Nash wrote), as did writers Edward Thomas and Robert Frost in Gloucestershire.[11] Troops of London Boy Scouts were made available to farmers within thirty miles of Westminster.[12] There was pleasure and purposefulness and money to be had on the land in the summer of 1914. And women wanted to be part of it too. The 'Woman's World' column of the *Western Daily Press* appealed:

> *Already the Boy Scouts have been enlisted by the farmers in considerable numbers; but why should our girls not turn to and help gather in the golden grain? In the Old Testament history we read of Naomi and her daughters-in-law going out into the fields with the reapers, and I am quite sure the English country maidens would make splendid workers, and while saving the harvest, be enabled to put much-needed money into the family purse.*[13]

Many women were not content with rolling bandages and knitting socks. They indeed wanted to show themselves to be splendid workers. As Britain entered the war, the National Union of Women's Suffrage Societies (NUWSS) had declared that it would transform itself 'into a relief organisation'. As Millicent Fawcett, leader of the NUWSS put it, it was now time for 'resolute effort' – and an opportunity for women to show themselves to be 'worthy of citizenship.' 'It is on the women of the European countries which are now at war that will fall the work in the fields and the harvesting of the year's crops,' the NUWSS stated and British women wished to play their part in that. Members were encouraged to make contact with local farmers and to ascertain whether they needed assistance.[14] Rallying cries were issuing from other quarters too. In mid-August retired Civil Service doyenne Mary Mason submitted letters to the provincial press with suggestions of 'How Women Can Help With The Harvest'. She wrote: 'In some places women are already working in the harvest, but it does not seem to have occurred to them generally.' She proposed: 'Women could bind the sheaves where necessary and set them up into stooks, and do other light work, as they did before the invention of machines… tedious as this might be, it would be better than letting the crops spoil on the ground.'[15] Women 'responded nobly' to Mary Mason's appeal and, impressed by this example, she next suggested that they should be formed into a fighting corps – 'not only to shame the men, but because it will be necessary if the men will not enlist.'[16] At the end of August *The Sketch* published picturesque photographs of women in white dresses working in the harvest fields of Buckinghamshire. They were captioned: 'How Women are Filling the Gaps in the Ranks.' The paper reported:

Owing to the scarcity of male labour in many parts of the country, due to the calling up of Reservists for the War, women are now actively helping in getting in the harvest. In thus taking up the work of the men who are fighting for them at the front they are following the example of their French sisters.[17]

Like Mary Mason's call for a women's fighting corps, these pictures look more like propaganda than practicality.

As summer turned to autumn those gaps started to become more apparent. Rural young men, largely fitter and healthier than their urban counterparts, were good material for the army and for them there was an attraction in escaping low and irregular wages and a humdrum country life. The eyes of recruiting officers scanned the agricultural districts. Moreover in the early months of the war the county elite, many of whom had links with the local regiments, were encouraging the men in their employment to demonstrate their mettle. And it was more than just encouragement in some places; both Lord Rothschild in Hertfordshire and the Earl of Lonsdale, who owned a goodly expanse of Cumberland and Westmorland, threatened to dismiss men from their estates if they did not enlist.[18]

At the end of August, Captain Sir Charles Bathurst told the House of Commons:

A large number of farmers are ready and anxious to facilitate the enlistment after harvest of the younger men in their employ if they could have the temporary services of boys between eleven and fourteen years of age to assist them in the necessary farm operations during the autumn and winter.[19]

The Education Acts of the 1870s had taken children out of the fields, but farmers wanted them back now. With the mobilisation of the Wagoners' Reserve, a serious labour shortage was being felt in East Riding and at a meeting of the Yorkshire Union of Agricultural Clubs a resolution was passed calling on the local education authority to allow boys of 12 and over to be released from school.[20] There were similar requests all over the country. Thus local authorities began to pass by-laws granting blanket exemption from school attendance. Between the start of September 1914 and the end of January 1915 thirty-four education authorities released 1,413 school children for work on farms.[21]

More men did choose to enlist after the harvest was in. A private's pay (of 6*s* 8½*d* per week) was even less than most agricultural labourers earned, but at least it was regular. As workers looked at the prospects for the autumn there was some pull in that. By June 1915 around 150,000 men were estimated to have left agriculture, either for the army or other employment, representing eighteen per cent of the permanent male workforce.[22] Horses were going too. Within days of Britain entering the war, army remount officers were approaching farmers. Around eight per cent of the heavy horses used on farms would have been requisitioned by June 1915, and around twenty-five per cent of saddle horses, further exacerbating the sense of labour shortage.[23]

The harvest of 1914 was got in without too much worry, but agriculture must plan its year well in advance and, even as the war was still in its first weeks, thoughts were already turning to 1915. At the end of August, Viscount Milner raised a question in the House of Lords. He observed that, as more than half of the world's total wheat and rye supply was produced in the countries now at war, it seemed an absolute certainty that production would contract in 1915, resulting in rising prices. 'The pinch will come,' Milner forecast. Other members of the Lords suggested that, in talking of a potential shortage, he was encouraging panic. 'There is nothing "panicky" in my attitude,' Milner retorted, but he observed: 'the state of the supplies in this country under our own control may have the most momentous effect upon the course of the struggle in which we are engaged.'[24]

Whatever the cautions of his fellow Lords, at the start of September, Milner addressed a letter to the press, wishing to alert farmers to the likelihood of a wheat shortage in 1915 and appealing to them to increase their autumn sowing. 'The present harvest is an abundant one,' he wrote, 'but it seems impossible to hope that the European harvest of 1915 can be abundant or adequate.' Rather, shortage would make itself felt, he said, by the second half of 1915 at the latest. And he went further than he had in the Lords – so far as to use the f-word: 'We may hope that our own country will be better placed than its neighbours to obtain, at some price or other, a sufficient quantity of wheat to avert famine. But there can be no certainty of this.' Milner then issued an appeal to farmers' patriotism – and their pockets – stating that not only did they have the power to save the country from 'imminent catastrophe', but also 'greatly to benefit themselves, if they will only act with promptitude.'[25]

Importation of foodstuffs was disturbed in the first few months of the war, as exchange of goods with enemy nations ceased and trade with allies was disrupted. New sources had to be established and thought was newly focussed on Britain's dependency on imported food supplies. Ever since the repeal of the Corn Laws, in 1846, the free trade consensus had dominated British politics, but it was not the case that this commitment had not been challenged or debated. Britain was not blindly ignorant of its dependency. For years opinion was expressed that increasing reliance on foreign food could make Britain vulnerable; in the event of war, opponents said, disruption in food imports would quickly bring the country to her knees.

As refrigeration and packaging technology had improved through the nineteenth century, so the varieties of foods which could be imported had broadened. Thus it was not just wheat that was being shipped to Britain on a large scale, but also categories of goods that were formerly 'perishables' – fruit, eggs, butter, cheese and bacon. In terms of volume, by 1913 forty per cent of the UK's food was sourced from overseas. But, in terms of calories, with cereals providing such a big constituent of the average diet, foreign imports represented fifty-eight per cent of consumption. Eighty-one per cent of the wheat in Britain's bread was imported.[26]

Average UK annual calorie consumption (1909-13):

	Energy value	Millions of calories		Percentage of
	Millions of calories	Home produced	Imported	calorific value imported
Cereals	17,712,000	3,705,000	14,007,000	79%
Meat	8,890,000	5,369,000	3,521,000	40%
Dairy produce	8,253,000	4,715,000	3,538,000	43%
Sugar	6,633,000	-	6,633,000	100%
Other	9,536,000	7,504,000	2,032,000	21%
	51,024,000	21,293,000	29,731,000	58%

Source: *The food supply of the United Kingdom. A report drawn up by a committee of the Royal Society at the request of the President of the Board of Trade* (1917), pp. 3, 6.

In 1914 Britain was the only major European power dependent on foreign imports for the bulk of its food. With the flooding in of cheap grain from the American prairies, Germany and France had reacted by imposing tariffs, and while Britain's acreage under wheat had decreased thirty per cent over the past thirty years, that of France had increased seven per cent and Germany twenty-five per cent As a result, the UK's production of bread grain per capita was 90lbs, while France's was 500lbs and Germany's 485lbs.[27] Consequently, of the belligerent nations, Britain was the one whose larder was least prepared for war. She trusted the freedom of the seas, the supremacy of her navy and the open markets. But shipping would soon be turned over to military transport, supply and support for the navy and, as well as preparing its war larder, Germany had also been building U-boats.

For the moment, though, Britain seemed to be sitting fairly comfortably. The yield of the 1914 harvest was slightly up on the previous year and, as Milner had hoped, with wheat having increased sharply in price, a greater acreage was sown in the autumn and winter. The weather had been on the farmers' side too. It was a mild autumn and the cattle remained out in the fields until a late date. 'All this has done much for the farmer and the gardener,' Arthur Nicholson wrote in his 'Country Diary' for the *Manchester Guardian*. But at the Michaelmas hiring fairs in the north of England a shortage of agricultural labour was starkly apparent. 'From time immemorial, it has been always possible to meet with able and expert farm servants if you were prepared to pay the market price,' Nicolson wrote, however this year 'none was present'. He went on:

Many of the men have enlisted, and the few who remain at farm work have been re-engaged and did not trouble to attend. In other places a few put in an appearance, but prices asked were very high, and many farmers attended the second fair, still without engaging any help. The supply of women servants, old and young, and boys was also very small and prices high.[28]

It wasn't just the male labour supply that was contracting. Despite the voices rallying women to the land, the overall number regularly employed in agriculture had declined through 1914, as they were drawn to more lucrative or attractive roles. But they would need to be drawn back. When the WFGU held its annual meeting, at the end of December, it expressed the view 'that for the next few years women and girls with practical knowledge of agriculture and horticulture would be very much needed, and there need be now no hesitation about those naturally fitted for it taking up this work.'[29]

Chapter 4

'Lilac Sunbonnets' and the 'No-Corset Brigade'

Most people have in their mind's eye pretty pictures of gleaners, and regard harvest work as a charming, poetic occupation. That is because they have never done it. It is by no means a question merely of sun-bonnets and shady elms and cool, refreshing drinks. It is not a question merely of picturesque costumes and pretty attitudes. It is very plain, very hard work.

'Hints For The Amateur Worker In The Fields',
Manchester Guardian, 2 August 1915.

In January 1915 the Board of Trade's *Labour Gazette* observed: 'Scarcity of agricultural labourers is beginning to be felt as the season advances.'[1] Certainly Arthur Nicholson could feel it. When Nicholson was not writing the *Manchester Guardian*'s 'Country Diary' column, he was a Cheshire farmer. Now, at the start of 1915, he could see the impact of war in his district: 'New Year's Day has never in our generation brought with it to those who live a country life such novel conditions,' he wrote. 'The necessities of war have taken from us most, if not all, our able workers on the land; in many cases every man in the district of military age has gone.'[2] It was being felt further south too. At the end of January a farmer wrote to the *Leamington Spa Courier:*

Skilled agricultural labour is getting scarce. I wanted extra hands for threshing this week and could not get them – the first time this has occurred during all the years I have been here. My neighbours, too, are complaining of the same difficulty. I have had the Board of Agriculture's leaflet advising the farmers to increase the acreage of wheat, but don't see how it is to be done if the best skilled labourer leaves the country districts.[3]

Prior to the introduction of conscription in 1916, the numbers of men enlisting varied considerably by county, depending on local conditions (wages, type of contract and attitude of employers). Particularly on small owner-occupied farms, it was more urgent to get the necessary work done and on larger properties employers in many cases were willing to offer monetary incentives to keep good workers at home. A diminution in labour supply was, however, obviously being felt in many areas by the spring of 1915 and this was now causing an appraising eye to be cast over other potential labour sources. The *Spectator* wrote:

A considerable number of well-to-do women have been organizing themselves into Volunteer Corps and parading the streets in a quasi-uniform of khaki. They would be far better employed if they were setting their poorer sisters an example of how to assist their country by doing agricultural work. There is very little agricultural labour in which women cannot help. Throughout France the autumn harvest was gathered in, and the ground prepared for next year's crop, largely by women. In England women practically do next to nothing upon the land. There has grown up, it appears, a, social prejudice among the wage-earning classes against women doing any agricultural work, and if only that prejudice could be broken down the existing shortage of labour for farm work could largely be relieved. We suggest that well-to-do women of the leisured classes could do no more useful service at the present moment than by themselves undertaking a certain amount of farm work, if only to serve as an example to their less well-to-do sisters. Only this week we saw a lady—a nurse in a hospital—helping to cut down a tree, and greatly enjoying the use of axe and saw.[4]

It was not an entirely obscure observation. In February a letter was published in the press signed by several agricultural experts, significant landowners and politicians (a former President of the Board of Agriculture amongst them). It stated: 'In order that a start may be made, we have decided to do all we can to bring agriculturalists and women seeking employment together.'[5] That former President of the Board of Agriculture, Henry Chaplin, then spoke out on the subject in the House of Commons. He said that 'there was no doubt that the shortage of farm labour in some districts had become very serious, and that the time had arrived for farmers to take concerted action.' He was reported to have continued:

In his younger days there used to be a saying, "Where are you going to, my pretty maid?" And the pretty maid would often reply, "I'm going a-milking, sir." Now-a-days, pretty maids wanted to play the piano. (Laughter.) That was the kind of education he complained of, and it was nothing but sheer mischief as compared with the technical education which could be given.

But not everyone was quite so keen to see the milkmaid's return. Harry Verney, replying on behalf of the Board of Agriculture, put forward suggestions as to how the labour shortage might be alleviated: first, he proposed, town labourers could be induced to come to the countryside on the promise of better wages; secondly, he suggested 'tapping' Belgian, Danish and Dutch labour; thirdly, Irish labourers might be encouraged to come over sooner in the season; fourthly, boys from reformatory schools could be employed. 'Supposing all these sources of labour were tapped and there was still a shortage, then he suggested the employment of women.'[6]

In March, women who were prepared to do paid war work were asked to register at the Labour Exchanges. 'Any woman,' it was urged, 'who by working helps to release a man or to equip a man for fighting does national war service.'[7] Miss Dean, of the Board of Trade, told a Truro meeting: 'The agricultural need appeared to be the immediate one and it was in this connection that they must make their strongest appeal to women .'[8] By May, 70,000 women had registered for war work and, of these, 8,000 for agricultural work, but most would remain just names on paper as there was little organisation for actually getting the women off the lists and into work.[9] And, like Harry Verney, farmers put women far down their lists of ideal labour.

The Women's Social and Political Union welcomed the idea of the national register. This was women proving their worth, their equality, their practical patriotism, and surely that would have consequences? One unexpected short-term consequence was that, in June 1915, Lloyd George, then Minister of Munitions, requested a meeting with Emmeline Pankhurst. Suddenly it seemed they had something in common and might be useful to one another. They discussed organising a mutually beneficial demonstration, along the lines of a suffrage rally, which would encourage women to volunteer for work and create a patriotically-charged atmosphere that would make it difficult for unions and employers to reject their offered labour. Lloyd George put £3,000 on the table, out of his propaganda fund, to cover the costs. It was a meeting of two practical politicians. On 17 July 1915 then, despite the rain, 40,000 women marched through London under the banner 'We Demand the Right to Serve.' After the two-hour procession, a deputation, headed by Mrs Pankhurst, formally presented the case of women to Lloyd George at the Ministry of Munitions. Lloyd George was reported to have said: 'It will not be possible effectively to organise the resources of the nation until you mobilise the women as well as the men.' Both parties had delivered their message.[10]

With the formation of Asquith's first coalition government, in May, William Waldegrave Palmer, Second Earl Selborne, was appointed President of the Board of Agriculture. Selborne now convened a committee to examine how food supplies would be impacted if the war was prolonged beyond the harvest of 1916. Chaired by Viscount Milner, the committee's members included Rowland Prothero, who would succeed Selborne as President of the Board of Agriculture. The interim report of the Milner Committee, made public after just a month, suggested that the area under cultivation ought to be extended and farmers needed to be given some financial incentive to make this happen. The Committee also made recommendations on food distribution and advised that bodies should be set up to recruit female labour. But Asquith's government saw this as all too interventionist – and an over-reaction. In the summer of 1915 threats to shipping seemed to be abating, good supplies of grain were being secured from North America and prospects for the home harvest were excellent. The acreage planted with wheat had increased significantly without any government compulsion. Why, then, the need for exceptional measures? Once again Milner was deemed to be looking 'panicky'.

In July, Selborne put out a statement:

> *It looks as if the farmers will be able to get through their harvest operations this year, but with difficulty. In some districts the want of labour does not seem yet to be acutely felt; in others it is already acutely felt; but I cannot help suspecting that in many cases farmers will not realise all their difficulties in respect of labour until the harvest is actually upon them. In 1916 the shortage of agricultural labour will be felt much more seriously and universally.*

On that note, he issued a request to women – of every class – to come to the assistance of farmers. In so doing, he assured them, they would be contributing to the war effort 'as surely as her husband or son who is guarding the North Sea or fighting in the trenches.' And he directed an appeal to farmers:

> *To the farmers I would say, "Do not reject a form of labour to which you are unaccustomed, because you have not proved its value. If your need is not urgent now, it may very well become so next year, and the earlier the organisation of women's labour in each county is completed, the sooner will that labour become efficient."*[11]

Meanwhile, haymaking time had come around again and this year there was khaki in the fields. While they remained in camp in England, soldiers who wished to work on the land could be granted two weeks' furlough. This was initially a pretty loose arrangement, terms (including pay) being negotiated between the individual farmer and the soldier, however agricultural employment of military personnel would become more regulated as the year went on. From the autumn, farmers could appeal to the nearest Labour Exchange for assistance with specific seasonal tasks if there was a shortage of labour in the district. Soldiers could be released for up to four weeks but rates of pay were now fixed by the War Office.[12] Those farmers who got the drafts requested were not always delighted by the quality the work, though, and this labour source was now expensive; soldiers had to be paid 4½s per day (even if rain stopped work), considerably more than most farmers were accustomed to pay for their labour, and the cost of transport and accommodation had to be found by farmers too. In addition, soldiers only tended to work a nine-hour day, while at harvest time regular labourers might expect to put in twelve or thirteen hours. Despite these disadvantages, around 12,525 soldiers were used during the haymaking and wheat harvest of 1915. Farmers had applied for over 19,000 men.[13]

Mary Mason, who had summoned women to the fields in 1914, was not pleased to see soldiers on the land. 'Surely recruits have enough to do in training for fighting without being set to agricultural work?' she wrote to the papers. Instead, she asserted, the work ought to fall to women. 'There would be plenty of women to gather in the hay and harvest,' she wrote and 'the farmers' wives and daughters were not too grand nowadays to work themselves, and to get their labourers' wives and daughters to do so.' Mason proposed:

> *Ladies of well-known local position are needed to lead the way for the farmers' and labourers' wives and daughters in each county, and are usually quite ready to show that "noblesse-oblige" by working themselves. They are also needed to persuade the farmers to dismiss their prejudices and to depart*

31

from their usual routine by employing women for, in my experience, there is far more red tape among farmers than in the Board of Agriculture.[14]

In places it was already happening. In Cumbria the wives and daughters of 'quite well-to-do farmers' were reported to be assisting with the haymaking. This was one of the 'pleasantest times of the year', the *Manchester Guardian* encouraged, 'there generally being plenty of banter and laughter going round to lighten the task.'[15] Sporting types were encouraged to come forwards too. 'Those who are likely to prove physically unsuitable for the work are politely warned off,' the *Aberdeen Journal* reported, 'but the athletic type, the golfing, hockey playing, and swimming girl – or, as one enthusiast has described them, the "no corset" brigade – are being readily accepted to work in teams for the binding of the hay, which is urgent war work required for the Army at home and abroad.'[16] William Hawk, chairman of the Cornwall County Council Agricultural Committee, told a meeting in Saltash:

The girl that could swing a hockey club could handle a pike or a hoe, and the one who refused to do so was an enemy to herself and her country. (Hear, hear.) The person in this country who refused to do anything except eat the food which was becoming scarce was really a sponger on the country. (Hear, hear.) He would urge upon all that the battle could be won at home as well as on the battlefield, and he appealed to the women of Saltash to "bend your backs, maidens, for the glory of Old England."[17]

At the start of August the *Manchester Guardian* published an article giving practical advice for 'The Woman Harvester'. The piece was matter-of-fact as to sunburn and itches and sweat and insects. Sun bonnets ('though pretty') weren't deemed appropriate attire. Rather, 'workmanlike' clothes were called for – old tweed skirts, hessian aprons and large, strong boots. The piece concluded:

It will take at least a fortnight's labour for the work to become poetic. The poetry of harvesting will come out during the rest hours, when, after the longest possible drink and a solid feed – for harvesting makes for hunger as much as for thirst – it is permissible to throw oneself on the grass under the hedge and to sleep such sleep as one has not slept for years; or, when weary and soaked with perspiration, one goes home in the cool to bed, and, if one is lucky, to a heaven-sent bath. The seeming shortness of the rest hours is part of their fascination, and by degrees the harvester will realise as well the dewy morning hours, the long evening shadows – the alpha and omega of a hard day's work.[18]

Increasing numbers of women were getting to sample those pleasures and hardships. The *Labour Gazette* observed that their contribution was starting to become significant by August. 'In agriculture harvest operations were successfully carried on,' it was reported, 'the shortage of male labour being met by the employment of women and soldiers.'[19]

Children were still playing their part too. In March 1915 a circular from the Board of Education had been issued to local authorities. It stated that children of school age could be exempted for 'light' and 'suitable' agricultural employment, but only when no other labour was available. Between the start of February and the end of April 1915, 3,811 children were exempted. The policy of employing children was strongly opposed by the agricultural labourers' union, who accused farmers of using child labour in order to keep down wages, and it did not win farmers many fans generally. Harry Verney told the House of Commons that in Wiltshire, where there was a great demand for labour, only one per cent of agricultural workers were female. He went on:

This being the case, where was the necessity for child labour? (Ministerial cheers.) What was it that a boy could do that a woman could not do? Surely a woman could milk a cow better than a boy of 12. The real argument for the farmer was that it was more convenient to have little boys. They were on the spot, they had more suitable clothes, and they could be kicked to make them hurry up.[20]

On the 5 August 1915, 40,000 canvassers knocked on the doors of British households. A National Register was being prepared in order to gauge the number of men potentially available for military service. In the preparation of the Register certain occupations had been 'starred', as being vital for the continuance of normal economic life and the war effort, and a list of reserved occupations was prepared. The Derby Scheme was then introduced in October 1915. Every eligible man was now required to either enlist immediately or publically 'attest' that he was prepared to join the forces and be registered with the Army Reserve. As per the National Register, certain occupations were starred and, in the case of agriculture, these roles included bailiffs, carters, dairymen, stockmen and wagoners. Starred men would remain in Reserve until it was deemed to be in the national interest for their exemption to end. In November 1915 Selborne issued a statement to the press strongly advising that if men were really indispensible to the cultivation of the land they should not enlist for immediate service, but should offer themselves for the Reserve. They could thus continue in their present occupation and, if called up later, could make their case before a local tribunal. This arrangement, he assured, would mean that farmers would keep their essential men and 'give them some time to engage and train women or other subsititutes.'[21] The Derby Scheme, with its seeming respect for, and protection of, skilled agricultural workers initially looked like it might be a cause for optimism among farmers. However, as conscription was introduced in January 1916 and the definition of starred men was repeatedly pared back, that goodwill was not to last.

With a view to addressing the challenges that agriculture was facing, Selborne pressed for County War Agricultural Committees (CWAC) to be established in September 1915. Set up by county councils, these bodies were tasked with assessing the needs of farmers and formulating means of assisting them. The CWACs were voluntary and self-elected. Members typically included representatives of the county council, larger farmers and farmers' associations, local MPs, education authorities and county ladies. District sub-committees were expected to take practical steps – registering farms, surveying land and co-ordinating labour. They would be particularly encouraged to look at options for using female labour.

In an effort to inspire them to develop training initiatives for women, Selborne addressed a Circular Letter to the CWACs in November, showcasing schemes that were being tried in various parts of the country. The first case highlighted was that of Cornwall, where experienced women had been appointed as instructresses and were providing classes in such subjects as milking, caring for stock and field work. Farmers were assisting by allowing some of the instruction to take place on farms. In Nottinghamshire different arrangements were being tried out: the Nottingham County Council Advisory Labour Committee had taken on a farmhouse in which eight women could be accommodated and trained. The students, selected by the Labour Exchanges, were being given three weeks of instruction on the farm. In the third initiative highlighted, the Board of Agriculture was paying for girls to attend two to four week long courses at agricultural colleges and farm schools. The Labour Exchanges undertook to place the women out on farms on completion of their training. Thus far 218 women had been coached in this way and of these 199 were now in employment.[22]

There was, in particular, a need for extra dairy workers to be trained. Through 1915 the press were printing stories describing how farmers were selling their dairy herds because they no longer had the hands to milk them. A representative of Reading University's dairy school warned:

Reduction in our milk supply would be nothing short of a national calamity, and we are informed by the Dairy Farmers' Association that the dairy stock in the country is already greatly diminished. We appeal therefore to those who can assist our attempt towards preventing further disaster to come forward without delay.[23]

Such reports lent momentum to the efforts to train women for dairy work. From milking the cow to selling the end product, dairying had traditionally been a female domain. Women had milked as part of their role within a farming family, or as farm servants, and generally, on most small farms, butter and cheese-making was just an extra task done in the farmhouse kitchen. As in all other areas of agriculture though, the numbers of women working in dairying had decreased through the second half of the nineteenth century.

Over the period 1871–1914 the value of imported dairy products had increased by 270 per cent.[24] Britain couldn't compete with the price of foreign butter and cheese, and had pretty much stopped trying. As a result, in the years before the war, eighty per cent of the cheese consumed was imported and sixty-four per cent of butter.[25] By 1914 the butter and cheese produced on British farms tended to supply a local or a premium market. Britain had continued consuming its own liquid milk however, and this had emerged as a profitable area in the last years of the nineteenth century, demand increasing with the growth of urban population and prosperity. The thirsty London market drew in milk from the counties all around and wholesalers brought it in by rail from as far north as Lancashire. Milk was then big business and much of the market was being supplied by large commercial dairy farms.[26]

Women had traditionally combined milking with other roles, but where it existed now as a discrete job, combined with stock management, it was generally done by men. But it wasn't just that commercialisation of milking had driven women out; increasingly, as elsewhere in agriculture, women just had not wanted to do this type of work any longer. Milking by hand was laborious, required commitment at the start and end of the day, and was badly paid. Dr Lillias Hamilton, of Studley agricultural college, was reported to have observed:

In her younger days a man was never seen milking a cow. Now there seemed to be prejudice against women milking because it was said to be hard work. Milking was not hard work. The

36

*trouble was that the women did not learn to milk early enough…
she believed that the milkmaids had disappeared in consequence
of the low wages paid to them. In Gloucestershire she
understood that as little as 3s 6d per week had been paid for
morning and evening milking extending over three hours per
day, seven days a week.*[27]

There were some parts of England where female milkers were
unknown by 1914.

Dairy schools had first been set up in the 1880s, mostly through
local initiative to begin with, but dairy education – teaching modern
hygienic methods of producing and processing milk – had developed
over the ensuing years, with funding from central government, county
councils and agricultural societies. The Technical Instruction Act of
1889 gave the newly established county councils the responsibility for,
and powers to support, technical education, including agricultural
instruction. As counties developed their own schemes, there was
considerable variation in how dairying was taught; cheese-making
instruction was often run from a farm, several areas established
peripatetic courses and specialised dairy schools were set up. In 1891
Cheshire County Council took over the running of the Worleston Dairy
Institute, near Nantwich, which had opened eight years earlier and
claimed to be the first specialist institute training women in cheese
making.[28] Newton Rigg Joint Dairy School and Farm, near Penrith,
was also opened in 1896 and free studentships were offered through
the county councils of Cumberland and Westmorland. The pupils were
generally the 'daughters of working farmers or the better class of farm
servants.'[29] While there were some successful experiments, these were
exceptions rather than the rule.

The first few months of the war saw a flurry of new dairy schools
being set up in order that the departing male milkers could be replaced.
Devon, Staffordshire and Warwickshire County Councils acquired
farms at which teaching was to be given, and set up peripatetic dairy
schools.[30] The county of Gloucester did the same but also inaugurated
milking classes in schools for both girls and boys. By 1915 ten schools

were part of the scheme and as a result 100 extra 'junior milkers' were now working in the county. Like Henry Chaplin, the Gloucester Chamber of Agriculture looked forward to the return of the milkmaids:

> *In the past girls were employed much more largely on the farms than now, and one of the greatest delights of the rural districts had disappeared, namely, those buxom, merry milkmaids. If by extending their elementary school curriculum they could bring back into rural life the charming, merry milkmaids, who could not only milk but rear livestock, a source of agricultural wealth which was becoming more difficult of acquirement of late years, and from the lack of which they were suffering very extensively, would be brought again into their accounts.*[31]

Existing institutions also began to extend their courses. In March 1915 the Board of Agriculture offered to finance the tuition and maintenance of women attending the milking courses being launched at Reading University's College Farm.[32] Cornwall's County Council Dairy School was already training around 300 pupils per year, but a cheese school was added in 1914 and instruction widened to include calf-rearing, and the management and feeding of cows. By mid-1915 these efforts were supplemented by a travelling dairy school and the introduction of short courses on farms.[33] The county of Somerset, meanwhile, decided that it was more economical to offer scholarships for courses at the Midland Dairy College (Derby) and the Lancashire Dairy School.[34] Lancashire was particularly proud of what it was doing in the way of dairy education. Practical instruction was offered through the county council's Demonstration Farm and Dairy School at Hutton and via peripatetic training. A Board of Agriculture investigator was told that the quality of dairy training in Lancashire resulted in a higher price being achieved for the county's butter and cheese 'and would alone justify the whole cost of the instructional establishment.'[35]

The Board of Agriculture was also trying to get women to encourage each other into the dairy. A leaflet, *War Agricultural Service for Women*, issued at this time, stated:

If, for instance, women and girls of high standing socially, who live in a dairying district, will at once learn to milk, and will let the other inhabitants see them going, in suitable working-dress, to and from their work day after day – then their social inferiors will not be slow to follow their example, and employers of labour will take them seriously.[36]

Bessie ('Cuckoo') Ziman was a dairymaid of particularly high social standing. Bessie was 19 when the war broke out, living in Holland Park Gardens, London, and aspiring to become a concert pianist. She wanted to do her bit though, and managed to secure a position working at the Royal Dairy Farm at Windsor. As a pianist Bessie had been taught to take good care of her hands and, whether she was now working on a dairy farm or not, always carried a nail file in her pocket. Unfortunately, one day this item turned up in the cow's bran. 'Who owns this?' the head dairyman demanded. Bessie, 'pink with embarrassment', owned up. 'She was mortified,' her daughter later recounted. Bessie was reprimanded and, as punishment, was no longer allowed to deliver milk to the King and Queen at Windsor Castle, which had previously been part of her duties. While Bessie was at the Royal Dairy Farm she sang in the choir at Windsor Castle. Her daughter added: 'On Sundays the choir members were sometimes invited to take tea with the King and Queen at the castle.'[37] Not all of 1915's new milkmaids would have such a genteel experience.

1915 also saw various private initiatives seeking to bring women on to farms. The National Land Council had been established in 1914, 'to provide employment for women who have been thrown out of work in consequence of the war.'[38] By June 1915 its attention was focussed on agriculture. That month, newspapers carried accounts of an occurrence in Carlton Terrace. Here Lady Cowdray had set up a model farm in the garden of her London town house with a view to attracting funding, volunteers and attention for the National Land Council. It certainly achieved the latter. 'A passer-by in the Mall that runs from Buckingham Palace to Trafalgar Square might imagine he were near a country farmhouse,' one article reflected. It went on:

> *In the garden of Lady Cowdray's house, a tall stately building backing on to the Mall, a cow stands idly by and a couple of goats are tethered to a tree. There is a small haystack with women and pitchforks close by, and farm implements, such as butter-making machines, are stored in one or two of the bedrooms.*[39]

In addition to the model dairy, there were demonstrations of milking (on a model cow) and fruit picking (from model trees).[40] *The Sketch* carried a full page of photographs illustrating this '*rus in urbe*', picking out the curious mingling of top hats and pitchforks and dairymaids ('Milking a Cowdray Cow in the purlieus of Pall Mall.')[41] By October 1915 the Land Council was offering 'all-round practical farm training' and claiming that it had placed 300 women in work. Mary Adelaide Broadhurst, chairman of the Land Council, now issued an appeal for 100,000 women to come forward 'to help in the vital work of increasing the food production of the country', while Lady Denman (Lady Cowdray's daughter and vice-chairman of the Land Council) petitioned farmers to come forwards to assist with training.[42]

Another organisation calling for volunteers in 1915 was the Women's Defence Relief Corps. This body had also been formed with the aim of bringing women into 'home front' jobs in order to release men to join the army. In the summer of 1915 the Corps placed adverts in newspapers offering to supply 'gangs of five or ten strong young women as harvesters'.[43] The Corps' workers were 'of all sorts, from the Cockney woman of leisure who didn't know wheat from oats, to the shop assistant who had never so much as planted nasturtium seeds in a suburban garden.'[44] Despite the sincerity and determination of their instigators, neither the National Land Council nor the Women's Defence Relief Corps managed to place significant numbers of women in agricultural work, or to really attain much in the way of credibility. Similar initiatives multiplied at local level and had similar results. *The Field* magazine observed that there seemed to 'be no end to the number of leagues, societies, and such like bodies all working for the same object.' So many well-meant committee speeches; so much earnest letter writing; so few women actually working. *The Field* suggested:

One strong central institution, broad enough to embrace the various societies, and with ramifications spreading into all counties, would be more effective, and at the same time conduce more to economy of effort and money, than a continuance of the present system of separate and disjointed action.[45]

Though these early initiatives failed to achieve any scale, lessons (both good and bad) would be learned from them and applied to later, more concerted, endeavours.

There was much dubiousness among farmers as to the potential value of female labour and some of the initiatives launched in 1915 didn't do anything to persuade them otherwise. Lloyd George wrote that these women were 'jocularly hailed' as the 'lilac sunbonnet brigade'. The idea that such women could actually do the ordinary work of a farm 'called forth bucolic guffaws' and 'crude merriment'. Government efforts to encourage farmers to take women on were accordingly met with 'a good deal of sluggish and bantering prejudice and opposition.'[46] Mr P. L. Browne, Gloucestershire representative of the Association to Promote the Employment of Women in Agriculture, said that he was constantly asked by farmers, 'What good are they?' He reflected:

If farmers could only make up their minds and give the women a fortnight or a month to get used to the work, to help and encourage up, and treat them sympathetically, the difficulty would be overcome and it would ultimately be found that women would prove a great boon to them.[47]

But it would take a while for that difficulty to be overcome, particularly in those southern counties where female agricultural labourers had all but disappeared. In April 1915 Miss Dean, of the Board of Trade, spoke at a meeting in Cornwall. She was reported to have remarked that: 'As they came down through the counties the prejudice against women working on the farms seemed to grow… There was, she found, a greater prejudice in Cornwall and Devon than in Somerset and Gloucester.'[48] Many farmers, particularly in the south, just did not 'hold with women'.[49]

Farmworkers' unions were not enthusiastic either. They hadn't been keen on women working in agriculture before the war, and the prospect of them returning to the land now did not please them. Women had always been paid less than men in agriculture – and if they were now supposedly doing men's jobs, didn't that de-value men's work? What sort of wages would agricultural labourers return to after the war? Male farmworkers felt undermined and affronted. At the annual general meeting of the National Agricultural Labourers' and Rural Workers' Union a resolution was proposed, stating: 'That this council should strenuously oppose the introduction of child and women labour into agricultural industry.' George Edwards, the union's founder, thought that the wording was too strong and appealed to the meeting to consider the question 'from a patriotic standpoint.' In his opinion, with more and more men being taken from the land, 'the time had come, or would shortly arrive, when the work of women on the land would be absolutely necessary.' He moved an amendment to the resolution suggesting an alternative wording:

> *'That the employment of women should only take place when and where a shortage of male labour, owing to the withdrawal of such labour to military duties, has been proved. Further, when women are employed, that they should be paid the same rate of wages as prevails for men in that particular district.'*

On a show of hands Edwards' amendment was defeated and the original motion carried by thirty-six votes to two.[50] The Methodist church had similar concerns. In the spring of 1915 a document issued by the United Methodist Social Service Union warned against the resumption of 'the old practice' of employing women. It said;

We want to be assured that there is need for this expedient, and that adequate safeguards from grave and obvious dangers will be adopted. Those old times when women did much of the work on the land which men alone do now were times of little home comfort and heart-breaking toil, and resulted in the keeping down of the wages of the adult male worker. Would it mean that again?[51]

If the government wanted to convince farmers to try female labour, it needed to demonstrate willingness to employ them itself. And so it did. Early in 1915 the Army's Forage Department made a decision to no longer occupy men in jobs that women could do. With a massive demand for horse fodder for the army, by the summer of 1915 the department was handling 20,000 tons of hay per week and around 160 steam balers, transported and powered by traction engines, were operating throughout the country.[52] Colonel H. Godfrey Morgan, the chief administrator of the Forage Committee wanted to get the number of steam balers increased to 250 and was in favour of bringing in female labour to perform as much of the process as possible. Morgan was advised that this idea was 'impracticable and unworkable, that it was not fit work for women and that it was seeking disaster, moral and departmental', but he did not agree.[53] It was on his initiative, then, that in May 1915 appeals were published in the press offering women the opportunity to take on this 'agreeable and remunerative occupation'.[54] Thus while male labourers generally continued to control the engines, women were now taken on to pitch the hay from the rick into the baler and to operate the needle threaders which wired and tied the bales. The baling girls travelled from farm to farm with their tackle as hay became available. Generally they worked in gangs of six, with the assistance of two or three soldiers under a staff sergeant. Whatever the promise of agreeable occupation, this was hard graft and required workers who were prepared to put up with discomfort and inconvenience. It was something of a gypsy existence and securing adequate accommodation could be challenging.

Colonel Morgan also appointed women to work in the railway stations where forage was despatched, consigning and accounting for the movement of the trucks. One of these women, joining the Forage Department in November 1915, was Cicely Spencer. She was 28 when war broke out and working as a teacher in Norfolk. After a serious bout of pneumonia, a doctor advised her that she should change occupation for the sake of her health and work in the open air. Having been brought up to appreciate nature (her father had been fond of taking the family on country walks 'pointing out any special beauties of nature'), this was not unappealing. So, when a friend mentioned that the army was recruiting women for forage work, she decided to try. Cicely bought herself a tweed suit and went along to the HQ 'and had an interview with a Lieutenant who thought I was a farmer's daughter.' This move did not, however, go down well with her family. 'When I returned to the breakfast table, I announced that I was enlisting in the army, and had to go immediately. I was met, as I had expected, with strong opposition, but nothing daunted me, and off I went to HQ.'

After completing a considerable quantity of paperwork, she was given a badge.

> *Just a circular disc not much more than an inch in diameter, but the thrill it gave me as I pinned it on the lapel of my jacket comes back to me even now after fifty-six years. In my imagination it was as large as a dinner plate. I have it still, a very dear treasure.*

She was now a Forwarding Supervisor, dealing with the logistics of transporting hay. Sent to Norwich, Cicely began overseeing the loading of bales of hay onto wagons. She was supervising and keeping records – and finding that she liked the work. 'I felt sure I have made a good choice, and determined to do anything I might be asked to do, and to the best of my ability.' Later she dealt with the bagging, weighing and loading of oats in Great Yarmouth and distribution of grain on the Norfolk coast. She was soon travelling around the county by motorbike, overseeing baling teams, and staying in billets. 'I was enjoying every minute.'

Everyone that Cicely met was 'very co-operative' and she received much kindness from the people with whom she was billeted – and cabbages: 'As a parting gift I was presented with a large red cabbage, which took a great deal of handling with my luggage. My father met me at the home station and was a bit non-plussed when I handed it to him, but he gallantly carried it home.' They also seem to have given her quite a bit of alcohol. Billeted on the Essex–Suffolk border, she stayed with a shoemaker and his family. Her evenings were spent playing whist with his sisters and drinking homemade wines. ('They would give me a glass of wine which I had never tasted previously and try to make me guess what it was. I never could.') And in Norfolk farmers offered her cider.

> *It was deliciously cool and I drank it down… The moon had risen by this time, but to my amazement I saw not one moon but long lines of moons strung from tree to tree. I found myself singing a popular song of the time. "Let the great big world keep turning." And it certainly was turning alright… I slept the sleep of the righteous. I told the people at my billet about the cider and they were amazed that I had got home safely as they said that farmer was noted for his strong cider, into which he put twice as much brandy as anyone else.*[55]

Rates of price inflation looked rather tipsy by this time too. By the end of the year the retail price of food was on average forty-five per cent higher than it had been in July 1914. The war was now having an impact on the food that women could put in front of their families. It was in their lighter purses and their shorter shopping lists. They were having to economise and innovate and invest more time and thought in the day-to-day running of the home. It was in this climate that the Women's Institute (WI) took root. Several similar organisations had been active here before the war, but the WI really came into being after Margaret 'Madge' Watt relocated to England in 1913. The movement had been established in Canada in 1897, and, having been an active member in British Columbia, Madge Watt now sought to replicate it here. To that end she spent a couple of years determinedly trying to get something off the ground, variously giving talks on rural life and women's future within it. She was, by all accounts, an excellent public speaker and she caught the ear and imagination of John Nugent Harris, General Secretary of the Agricultural Organisation Society (a body founded in 1901 to encourage co-operation within the agricultural community). At a meeting in Bangor he had found Mrs Watt 'so absorbingly interesting' that he had missed his train home. Taken by her enthusiasm, and by what she had said about the Canadian movement, he booked her to speak at an up-coming agricultural conference and requested a meeting to discuss formally setting up the WI in the UK. Nugent Harris quickly appreciated the potential of the movement, both for co-ordinating women's war effort and for the long-term health of rural life.[56]

While housewives might be feeling the pinch, farmers' pockets were getting heavier. The rising price of wheat had encouraged farmers to increase the acreage and, with the weather also favourable, production was up by nearly twenty per cent year-on-year. But things were about to turn. It was a bumper year on farms in North America too. Indeed the worldwide crop of wheat would be so large in 1915 that prices would subside again. British farmers had achieved a higher wheat output by switching from barley (the overall cultivated acreage had actually declined slightly) and, as the price now started to fall, they would revert back to barley again. By the autumn of 1915, the weather was not looking quite so friendly either. The harvest of potatoes and late root crops was slowed down by heavy rain, and damp and frost would hold back the sowing of winter wheat. A shortage of labour was holding work back too. At the end of November Arthur Nicholson's 'Country Diary' observed that it was rapidly becoming 'impossible for any farmer to lay out work for the coming season,' but he added, 'Many women are coming forward to the aid of the farmer, and it is well that they are.'[57]

The number of women regularly working on the land had actually decreased through 1915, as they were drawn to other occupations which offered better pay, shorter hours, friendlier conditions and more sense of contributing to the war effort. But other women, who were willing to replace those leaving the land, had their offered labour rejected. In November Selborne expressed frustration about his seeming inability to convince farmers to consider alternative labour sources. He was reported to have said: 'He could issue leaflets by the million and make speeches for hours, but only a very small proportion of farmers would pay any attention.'[58] The case needed to be convincingly made at a local level – but this was starting to happen. In December 1915 West Kent Women's County Agricultural Committee sent out a letter to its members. Rallying them to 'draw up their plan of campaign' for the county, it stated: 'All women in the Country are asked to help. We have been called the SECOND LINE OF DEFENCE. By ORGANISATION we can justify this title.' It went on: 'Personal interest and willing help must be the key-note of the movement, because the Call has come to EVERY Woman, rich or poor, gentle or peasant, strong or weak, to do something, and to do it NOW.'[59] This was just the sort of thing that Selborne wanted to see replicated throughout the country. On 31 December 1915 he addressed a conference of representatives of CWACs which had been convened to discuss employing women on the land. Selborne opened by stating that 'on the solution of this question depended whether agriculture was or was not going to rise triumphantly over its difficulties in the coming year.' He thus sent a call out to the county organisers: he asked them now, if they had not already done so, to recruit committees of women who could take on the task of organising local female labour. As a start, he instructed, they must organise a canvass of women 'just as there had been a canvass of the men for the Army', but that administrative exercise was not sufficient. They must also arrange meetings at which the need would be 'forcibly put before women' – and they must also forcibly make the case to farmers.[60]

Chapter 5

'From the White Hands of Strapping Girls'

The harvests of East Anglia
This year old maids must reap;
This year young boys in Cumberland
Must dip the struggling sheep.
And in the pails of Lunedale
This year the milk must foam
From the white hands of strapping girls,
Whose sires are gone from home.

Verse by Francis Acland, Parliamentary Secretary
of the Board of Agriculture, published in the
Lincolnshire Echo, 24 May 1916.

By the spring of 1916 it seemed as if the weather had ceased to do its bit for the war effort. Hours of sunshine were seasonally low and the earth was saturated. On many farms last year's root crops were rotting in the ground. Snow was still falling in March. It was against this bleak backdrop that farmers learned that they were about to lose another raft of their workforce. In January 1916 the first Military Service Bill, aiming to conscript all single men and childless widowers aged between 18 and 41, was introduced to parliament. As under the Derby Scheme, men engaged in certain trades ('certified occupations') would be exempted from enlistment, and, in the case of agriculture, these included drivers, mechanics and attendants of agricultural machinery, bailiffs, foremen, stewards, stockmen, carters, ploughmen, horsemen, shepherds and thatchers – that is to say, all of the more senior and skilled agricultural roles. It exempted farmers too, if their presence was deemed indispensable for the cultivation of their land. Men in these occupations must now apply to the local Military Service Tribunal by the start of March for a certificate of exemption. The newspapers of 1916 are full of reports of farmers making cases before the tribunals as to why their workers must be retained, and it seems as if the tribunals had a thorny job, their decisions picked over by the press and often seeming to be contentious. In particular there was much accusation that farmers' sons were managing to dodge the draft. There was a lot of perceived unfairness, undue influence and bitterness. There was a sour atmospere to the spring of 1916.

This was the context in which Sir Hugh Bell, Lord Lieutenant of North Riding, issued an appeal to the women of Yorkshire. He said: 'Unless the farmers are amply provided with help before the early spring, the consequences to the nation may be serious.' This was a national emergency, he urged, and the women who came forward to assist would be of as much service to their country as men they were replacing. At the same time Lady Sykes was summoning the women of East Riding. She said:

Some people might say that women could not work on the land, but times were not normal, and there was no doubt about the shortage of male labour. The time might come when every man would be wanted to end the war, and it was necessary to have women to be ready to do the men's work.[1]

Many women were ready to do just that (even if the farmers were not quite so ready for them). Olive Hockin arrived on a Dartmoor farm in January 1916. She was 35 years old and had trained as an artist before the war. She had also applied her artistic skill to suffrage banners and magazines. And gone further. In 1913 Olive had been on trial at the Old Bailey, charged with 'having conspired to set fire to the croquet pavilion and furniture belonging to the Roehampton Club, Limited, Surrey; to damaging plants in the orchid house of the Royal Botanical Gardens, to cutting telegraph wires, and to placing fluid in a letter-box in Ladbroke Grove, London.' Olive was found guilty and sentenced to four months in Holloway Prison.[2] But she also had a love of nature and animals and in 1916 she wanted to do her bit. Having seen an advertisement for 'a capable man to drive his horses and to work the land', she had sent in a letter of application. Receiving no reply, Olive just turned up. Her qualifications, as she summed them up, were: 'some months experience on another farm; a great love of horses, and indeed of every other animal tame or wild (not even excepting pigs); and further, an unbounded confidence in my own ability to do any mortal thing I wished to do.'[3] Olive's account of her year on Dartmoor, published in 1918, is romanticised and fictionalised to a degree; she turned her experience into a story – accentuating the colour and tugging it into a satisfying shape – and it is told in retrospect. There are no place names (her setting is 'By-the-Way' Farm) or names (Olive takes on her nickname 'Sammy', and the other woman working on the farm is 'Jimmy'), but the attitudes and practices that the account documents have some value.

The initial reaction of the farmer's wife ('The Missus') to Olive's arrival is shock and hilarity:

Well, really! You must come in and tell me about it. Do you know, we've been reading such a lot in the Daily Mail about 'Ladies on the Land.' We were looking at the pictures of them only last night. But I am afraid my husband only laughs at the idea. He says that a woman about the place would be more trouble than she is worth, and we quite made up our minds that no woman could possibly do the work![4]

But, though, 'evidently sceptical as to the power and uses of the (normally) skirted sex,' the farmer ('The Maester') takes Olive on. The Maester is 'a jovial good-natured sort of fellow, and was easy enough on the whole to get on with', but he's also portrayed as 'somewhat cotton-woolly in the brain'. He is a bit of a buffoon, in truth – all empty-headed bluster and self-importance and certainly a skinflint. Though he shows some kindness to his female workers, he also expects a lot for his money. Olive wrote: 'The idea that it could be anything but a favour to allow anyone, be it man, woman, or child, to work for ten or twelve or fourteen hours a day for a munificent daily dole of two shilling and sixpence had never yet occurred to the Devonshire agricultural potentate.'[5]

Farming is less clean and compassionate than Olive expects it to be:

When, partly because of my interest in animals, I went to work on a farm, I was under the impression that one could in some way make it up to them by keeping them comfortable and clean and well-fed; that one could keep cows for their milk, living in comfort and ease like luxurious ladies (the ideal of the old anti-suffragists); sheep for their wool, and pigs – not at all.[6]

Instead, farming is a business, with little room for sentiment, and very much hard, heavy and dirty work. But whatever the long hours, the filth and drudgery of the life, it is also evident that she was deriving pleasure and inspiration from her surroundings. Olive had a long-held interest in nature, in the spiritual and in folklore and it is evident that something in the landscape of Dartmoor spoke to her. She wrote:

Dartmoor is a country all by itself. The very formation of the land is unlike anything else in England; it has a grandeur of its own that does not vie with the grandeur of mountains, yet is almost more beautiful; and to come upon it after agricultural country is like some big, simple, soul-stirring strain of music ringing out above the complexity of an orchestra.[7]

Olive's book is full of such rapturous nature observation. Whatever the long hours and aches and damp, the book resonates a love for the country (and for *writing about* the country). It's apparent that Olive had found what she wanted to do.

Viscountess Wolseley also knew what she wanted to do. In January

1916 this was to call women back to the fields. Her book, *Women and the Land*, which came out at this time, begins:

> *The call of the Land rings out loudly. It comes now with a vigour which no-one can overlook, although for over a hundred years it has called in vain. Do not let it be lightly disposed of or swept aside this time; do not allow the words "Too late" to be even whispered in connection with it.*

Viscountess Wolseley's long-term ideal was to settle educated women in colonies on the land and for Britain to thus become self-sustaining in food supplies, but for the moment, what she wanted was to see women working on farms. In particular she believed that it was vital that rural women should re-connect with the land. It was not plucky middle-class spade-wielders who were needed right now; patriotic novices were not enough. 'Some few, if urged on by speakers and moved by what they see on posters, may come forward in the spirit of wishing to do "their bit"... but their numbers will scarcely suffice for the requirements of future months,' she wrote. What was wanted was 'the real countrywoman'. *Women and the Land* is pitched at educated women, though, because Viscountess Wolseley believed that they did have their part to play. She wanted to see a government scheme, pulling women on to the land just as Lord Derby's scheme had drawn their menfolk into the army. At the local level upper-class women could recruit, rally and administrate. They could give financial and moral support. Wolseley proposed that, having drummed up recruits, they would need to be put through 'a formulated system' of training: 'They will need training in the same way that Lord Kitchener's New Army was trained,' she wrote.[8]

Some of the initiatives that Viscountess Wolseley was calling for were actually happening by the time that her book was published. Following on from Selborne's speech at the end of December 1915, a circular was sent out to all CWACs ordering the formation of Women's War Agricultural Committees (WWACs). The success of the these bodies would be mixed, as much depended on levels of local initiative and energy, but a register of women willing to undertake agricultural work was started and by June 47,860 volunteers had signed up.[9] The county with the highest number of women registered by this date was Durham, which had 4,893 women on its roll, of whom 2,438 had experience, 2,678 were prepared to work full-time and 360 were prepared to leave home to work.[10] A large proportion of women (the vast majority in most counties) could only commit to work part-time, sometimes just for a few hours per week, and wanted to work locally. It is evident that reluctance to make a greater commitment, and fear of being moved away from their home village, put many women off registering. Both workers and farmers often preferred to keep the relationship informal. This was particularly true in some of the areas where women were still regularly working in agriculture before the war. In Pembrokeshire, for example, registering was widely considered to be an 'unneccessary fuss'.[11] In the Kesteven Division of Lincolnshire 2,041 women were apparently working on the land in 1916, of whom only 599 were on the register.[12]

In February 1916 recruitment efforts cranked up a gear. It was stated that 250,000 men had already left agriculture for the forces and a further 100,000 would soon be called up. The public were warned that, if agricultural production was not to drop, 'it is essential than an army of at least 400,000 women should be mobilised.'[13] In order to heighten the sense of importance of land work, a decision was made to give land workers some collective sense of identity – an identity with some military trappings. All women registered with the WWACs received a certificate emblazoned with Royal arms and stating: 'Every woman who helps in agriculture during the war is as truly serving her country as the man who is fighting in the trenches or on the sea.' Moreover, women who had worked for thirty days (or 240 hours) were now entitled to wear a khaki armlet. During 1916 72,000 certificates and 62,000 armlets were issued.[14]

It was also announced that a full land workers' uniform had been agreed ('as distinctive and as important as the familiar Voluntary Aid Detachment outfit') and would now be made available through the Co-operative Wholesale Society.[15] But, as women had to pay for it themselves, the outfit's adoption would be purely voluntary. Prices and details were published in April ('Drabbett coat, with band 9s 11d, drabbett skirt, 5s 11d, knickerbockers in soft drill, 2s... overall pinafore in drabbett, with band, for summer wear, 5s 11d (all the above being washable), black leather nailed boots 6s 8d').[16] Despite the attempts of the Board of Agriculture to negotiate low prices, it was beyond the budget of many women farmworkers – and for some those knickerbockers were beyond the pale.

The discussion as to the appropriate clothing for women doing agricultural work would take up many newspaper column inches over the course of the war. Putting them into male jobs was one thing, seeing them in trousers was quite another. Wearing breeches might be practical, but was it respectable? Was it irretrievably damaging their femininity? The case of Mrs Easterbrook was discussed at a public meeting in Totnes; after her son had enlisted, she had taken over the running of his farm, but going out into the fields wearing breeches and leggings had caused her to be 'blackguarded by the farmers around'.[17] The adoption of masculine clothes just was not seen as right. 'Should women wear trousers in war time?' asked an article in the *Daily Mirror*. The piece went on: 'This is not a mere academic question: it is a question of practical and even topical interest.' The paper highlighted the case of a number of women farm trainees who had recently caused consternation by walking around Aberavon in dungarees. Margaret Milne Farquharson, of the National Land Council, responded that 'it struck her as unreasonable when a woman works a ten-hour day, and has only an hour or so leisure, that more than half of it should be spent in changing her gown.' She said that the clothing denoted 'work for one's country. True, in peace time officers get into mufti; but, then, this isn't peace.'[18]

It wasn't just men who objected to the sight of women's trousered legs, though. Ellen Walshe had signed up to do a season as a fruit picker in the summer of 1916. She and her friends had dressed in clothing which they judged to be appropriate for the task, but the local women working in the fields jeered:

"I'd be ashamed to go about dressed like them. Not decent, I don't call it." They called such remarks to each other in a loud voice as we passed. "They're the sort as is called 'well-brought up,'" they explained to each other in tones of scorn... They were specially angry at the breeches of two or three of the younger ones. They had no objection at all to gym dress, which really showed more leg than breeches and a smock.[19]

It is perhaps not surprising then, given attitudes and the cost, that the Board of Agriculture's scheme to get women farmworkers into knickerbockers failed. The arrangement with the Co-operative Wholesale Society was terminated at the end of 1916.[20]

A further innovation of the spring of 1916 was the creation of the Women's National Land Service Corps (WNLSC). Discussions between Selborne and the WFGU resulted in the decision to recruit a body of women to work as 'officers' to oversee local female workers. Educated women were to be recruited, who, it was hoped, would demonstrate resourcefulness, self-sufficiency and patriotism. Rates of pay were deliberately set low, and recruiting emphasised that women must have their own private means. They were meant to set an example to village women, to show that work should be about more than just wages, and that it was not demeaning. Louisa Wilkins of the WFGU was appointed Chairman of the Executive Committee of the WNLSC. She was often introduced to meetings as 'a practical lady farmer' and drew on her own experience.[21] Through the WNLSC she was determined to get rural women working. She wrote: 'Every effort should be *made at the start* to hit on some method of making them feel *real war workers.*' A sense of 'corporate effort' had to be stirred up. It needed to be something 'appealing and sensational.'[22] In June she sent a letter to *The Times*:

One educated woman, by her mere example and encouragement and powers of organisation, has been the means of making available 20 village women, at the same time as she herself is doing farm work. As it is on the village women that we must

55

depend for the bulk of necessary labour, the inference is obvious.
We want more educated women of the right type to take this up.
We want 2,000 women, not merely to work for 2,000 farmers,
but to be the means of making available the labour of 40,000
village women.[23]

The WNLSC sought to recruit women aged 18 to 35, in good health, who had had secondary education and were prepared to go wherever in the country their services were needed. A great emphasis was put on character and attitude, on selecting that 'right type' ('not those who are merely doing it for the sake of a country holiday').[24] One WNLSC trainee described her fellow recruits thus:

The students were mostly well-educated and refined. One of our
number was a society woman, and her trunk held beautiful ball
dresses and splendid opera cloaks, whole worlds removed from
the heavy boots, leggings, knickers, and short overalls of her
working costume. (Long skirts are an abomination after the
freedom of overalls and knickers.) This lady, a generous and
loyal comrade, professed her intention of remaining on a farm
and never going back to her London society life again.[25]

In recruiting for the WNLSC, Louisa Wilkins addressed meetings all over the country and circulars were sent to female societies, girls' schools and hockey and lacrosse clubs. In two months, 4,500 letters were sent out from headquarters, posters were displayed around the London area and professional speakers were hired.[26]

Arrangements for training the WNLSC recruits were made by the WFGU, which was granted £500 by the government for this purpose (Wilkins publically called it 'a miserable grant').[27] Women were brought on to the WFGU's training farms and facilities lent by county authorities and colleges and land owners. WNLSC recruit, Anne Farewell-Jones, was sent to a large private estate in Berkshire and trained on the job: 'We were taught, by going with her usual farm staff, to handle the horses, plough, harrow, and to milk by hand a herd of small black Kerry cows.'[28] By the end of 1916 it was estimated that the WNLSC had trained nearly 1,000 women and placed 1,500 on farms.[29]

As well as rounding up the village women, the WNLSC was tasked with convincing farmers to take them on. Louisa Wilkins told the Herts WWAC:

In one county 2,000 women had put their names on the register, but not one farmer had applied for their services… It was the work of the Women's National Land Service Corps to act as the connecting link between the farmers and the registered workers, and to get the women off the paper on to the land.[30]

In its efforts to recruit women land workers, and to persuade farmers to take them on, the WNLSC orchestrated a series of demonstrations through the spring and summer of 1916. The first was staged at Launceston, in Cornwall, with women exhibiting their ploughing and manure-spreading skills – tasks deliberately chosen because they were not normally performed by women. As this event attracted interest, a second was then arranged in Truro and soon this was being copied across the country, with the encouragement of the Board of Agriculture.[31] The women's ploughing demonstration was a particularly popular spectacle at the Royal Agricultural Society's Royal Show, held in Manchester, in June 1916. Farmers from all over the country attended and were said to have watched the 'fair farm workers with critical eye,' but they made 'good offers to those whose methods they fancied to go to their farms'.[32] In August 1916 the *Illustrated War News* reported:

Many prejudices have been laid aside during the last twenty months or so and there has now sprung up in the country a corps of land Amazons armed with hoe and rake, and scythe and pruning-knife, ready to go where duty and the farmer calls, and their usefulness is not by any means limited to waging war on dock and nettle, "or doing a little weeding," or keeping flower-

beds tidy. The land army is out for "business" in the strictest sense of the word.[33]

The Board of Agriculture estimated that 250,000 men had left agriculture for the army by February 1916 and a real shortage was being felt in some districts. The Kent CWAC estimated that in some parts of the county the agricultural labour force was down by twenty-five to thirty per cent. In the Faversham area mangolds were rotting in the field because there wasn't the labour to pull them. 'The question is not how to increase production, but how to maintain the present production,' the *Kent & Sussex Courier* reported. 'Normal crops will be harvested with extreme difficulty.'[34] The Essex CWAC estimated that twenty-four per cent of the county's agricultural labourers had left and, with those now called up, the deficit would increase to about a third of the workforce. The *Chelmsford Chronicle* printed a statement from Selborne:

Women of every class must assist – the squire's wife, and the parson's, and the farmer's, and the wife and daughters of the labourer. Each in turn can make a contribution to agriculture, and so work for victory, just as a husband, son, or brother in the Fleet or in the trenches. Women must do their part just as the men. They must go on the land.[35]

There was some insinuation that the labourer's wife was not responding quite as keenly to the call as the squire's wife. At a meeting of the Berks and Oxon Chamber of Agriculture it was stated that wives of former agricultural labourers, now in receipt of separation allowances, were reluctant to work 'as they were in considerable comfort and preferred to stay at home.' As a comparison, the example of the Duke of Marlborough's women workers was raised. He had several 'well-bred ladies living in a cottage at Woodstock, who were doing splendid work at an average of £1 per week.' It was observed: 'If women as well-bred as the Duke could "buckle to", put on breeches and gaiters, drive beasts into Oxford market, and work a pair of horses, surely there must be thousands of women willing to do similar patriotic work.'[36]

Also 'buckling up' was the London Lady who sent a letter to the *Western Times*: 'Three of my woman servants have volunteered to work on any farm or a well-managed estate from early May until after the harvest,' she wrote. And she was throwing herself into the package:

> *Should my servants find employment, I propose to live in a hut caravan or inn upon or near the farm, so as to be at hand if required. Many of my friends in the same position as I am are waiting to see if I succeed, as if so, they hope to send out some of their people as well. We shall, of course, pay their regular wages throughout as now.*[37]

In Lancashire the wives of Lords and the Bishops were putting their backs into it; it was reported that Lady Derby had been helping to gather potatoes and the wife of the Bishop of Whalley was learning to plough.[38]

With labourer's wives not flocking back to the land in the numbers hoped for, there was some debate as to why this was the case. The issue of the separation allowance reoccurs. Soldiers' wives received 12*s* 6*d* per week, plus 5*s* for their first child, 3*s* 6*d* for the second and 2*s* thereafter. This provided an income not far off normal for some rural families, leaving women with no monetary incentive to work. In other cases household incomes had increased as their husbands had found work in better paid non-agricultural occupations. With the countryside full of army camps women were also making money from billeting and doing laundry for soldiers and, if they did want to go out to work, there were other jobs offering much better pay than agriculture. In particular there had been a considerable movement of agricultural workers (both male and female) into munition factories. The issue was raised in the House of Commons in May. Laurence Hardy, MP for Ashford, told the House that women could not be found in sufficient numbers for the fruit and hop districts:

> *We have munition works all along the Thames, and they have taken a large part of the available supply of women's labour.*

The difficulty at the present moment is not so much that of employing more women, but to get the same number that has been employed in previous years.[39]

It was the same case in Cumbria. The Board of Agriculture investigator for the area was told that the cordite factory at Gretna was a big pull for local women and had had an impact on the availability of the women who would normally do dairy work. 'I will call attention to the strongly expressed complaints I received from a meeting of farmers at Carlisle with regard to the lack of co-ordination between the Ministry of Munitions and their own industry,' the investigator noted. 'The Ministry of Munitions, by offering excessive wages, have, they say, made farm maids impossible of obtaining.'[40] And in Wales, Parish Councils were struggling to find candidates for dairy training, as women preferred to take munitions jobs instead – prompting the *Newcastle Journal* to quip: 'The second line of the old nursery rhyme, "Where are you going to my pretty maid? I am going a milking, sir, she said," will have to be altered to "I am going a munitioning."'[41]

If agriculture paid wages comparable with 'munitioning', more women might have been inclined to go milking. *The Woman Worker* magazine wasn't impressed by government attempts to woo women back to the fields, and its attitude probably mirrors what many women felt:

Now, work on the land is useful work and much of it is suitable to women; but there are points about this scheme which we should do well to look at. It is said that a representative of the Board of Trade at a meeting at Scarborough, said that the wages would be from 12s to 1 pound. Twelve shillings is not a proper living wage for a woman; and our masters seem to know this… The farmers are doing very well. The price of corn is higher than has ever been known before. Why should women be deprived of "any really adequate reward"? Why should women assist in keeping down the miserably low wages of agricultural labourers?[42]

The wages were miserable and many women believed the work was too. Having been told for decades by their 'betters' that field work was degrading, that learning was not easily reversed. Acknowledging that this was the case, the government appealed to their patriotism. Selborne urged that village women must 'have their imaginations touched, and must be convinced that by going over the neighbouring hedge to hoe turnips they were doing as good service for the country as if they were making shells in a munitions factory, or as their husbands and brothers were doing in the trenches.'[43] But the long-established prejudice against field work would take some time to erode. Olive Hockin observed a distaste amongst Devon women for farm work and a resentment of outsiders taking on that degrading work:

> Some of the local women were not so generous, for they opined that we ought to be thoroughly ashamed of ourselves for undertaking such dirty work as milking – "going down about in the yard with the men!" One woman I came across, an "assistant" in a farmhouse, when asked to empty something away out of a bucket, refused to do so on the ground that someone might see her carrying a bucket in the yard. If such was the conventional view, it can be readily believed that we, who spent half our time carrying buckets and things about, must have sunk very low![44]

'The counter, the restaurant, the workshop, the laundry, the factory, even the scullery, is preferred to work on the land,' wrote the *Exeter and Plymouth Gazette*. The paper reported that Cambridge University had recently debated 'Does Farm Work Cause a Deterioration in Women?' and reflected:

> The answer that Girton girls do not find anything derogatory in the farm work, which many of them have done in their vacation, or that a few university women have adopted farming as a career, is scarcely the best answer. What the ordinary

Lincolnshire and Holderness woman shirks from doing is going into the fields under the same conditions as many of their grandmothers went. They have a misconception of the present-day conditions of labour for the land worker. It is this misconception that will have to be overcome, and the conditions and remuneration made as liberal as possible before the Board of Agriculture's idea can be carried into general practice.[45]

With farmers reluctant to pay higher wages, efforts had to be made to inspire women, it was concluded. In March Viscountess Wolseley issued an 'urgent call' through the press, appealing to the women of Britain to follow the example of the French and Belgians.[46] From the start of the war regular reference was made to the heroic efforts of the French and Belgian women on the land. While the men had gone to defend the country, the women were preserving the crops, it was said, 'ploughing the fields on which German shells were falling'.[47] It was thought that there was currency in using this example to inspire women on this side of the Channel, and it was on this understanding that a plan was hatched in the spring of 1916: a party of Englishwomen was to travel to France in order to observe the women farmworkers in action and, on their return, they would tell English audiences what they had witnessed. The party of eight included Gladys Pott (treasurer of the Berkshire Committee of Women and Farm Labour and the organiser), Bertha La Mothe (Women's Agricultural Advisor of the Board of Trade), Mrs Sutherland (representing the WFGU), Mrs N Stocks (of Reading Women's Liberal Association), Mrs Saint (of Staffordshire Education Committee), Mrs Boyce (an advocate of Tariff Reform), Miss Chillingworth, (a farmer's daughter from Berkshire) and Professor Salmon (of University College, Reading).[48] The trip attracted considerable newspaper coverage. The party left Paris on the day that the battle of Verdun began ('We were within sound of the big guns of Verdun all the time', Gladys Pott told journalists) and they went over the battlefield of the Marne ('the rolling, open arable country dotted over in every direction with the graves.')[49]

Gladys Pott said: 'Our special object in taking them out was that they might return equipped to rouse our own village women to a sense of their duties in connection with labour on the land. This was the real point of the expedition.'[50] And, to some degree, the travellers do seem to have delivered. The party came back 'with some pungent lessons for our women' and in the months that followed they would pass those lessons on to audiences throughout the country.[51] Mrs Stocks spoke at meetings in Norfolk and Miss Chillingworth gave a lantern-slide lecture in Berkshire, showing images taken on her trip.[52] But it was Mrs Sutherland who was most active, addressing meetings from Thirsk to Penzance.[53] She was recorded as giving 'graphic descriptions' of what she had witnessed and the efforts of the French women: 'Although not out of the sound of the guns, they ploughed, harrowed, rolled, sowed, reaped, attended to the vines, and many other things, besides attending to cattle and live-stock.' Meanwhile, she said, 'In England we sauntered about leisurely.'[54] She told a Cornish audience:

The loss of so many ships by enemy submarines was becoming a serious matter to England, and the lessening of shipping and transport meant shortage of food, and shortage of food meant famine. Because they wanted to stave off that awful shadow they asked the women to do what their sisters in France did, to carry on the work on the land where no man sowed or reaped or cultivated, but where the countryside smiled and where it was never so beautiful as when watered by the blood of her sons. They wanted the cry of victory, they wanted to stave off famine, they wanted women to say, "Here am I."[55]

Francis Acland, Secretary of the Board of Agriculture, was meanwhile making speeches to farmers. He told a Stafford meeting:

Whatever farmers might think of employing women, they had got to do it and keep their feelings to themselves. After all, when women tackled a job they could generally do it, whether it was managing a husband or milking a cow. (Laughter.) All women could plough some sort of land with some sort of horses. For light work women would be very suitable, and it would be a thousand pities if farmers did not come forward and take advantage of the women's offer to work.[56]

But farmers were not coming forwards. In March 1916 a farmer told the Wetherby and District Chamber of Agriculture that: 'He had teamed for a gang of women who were "potato scrattin'," and declared, "Rather than have another week I would go to Germany and be shot." (Laughter.) Unless, he added, they could get a better type of women they had better leave the female question alone altogether.'[57] This – 'bantering prejudice', as Lloyd George put it – was the tone of this period.

There were exceptions, but many farmers simply did not believe that women were physically up to the work. Every aspect of supposed feminine frailty was aired in their objections; women were weak, or squeamish, or ill-disciplined, or empty-headed. A farmer told the Bucks Chamber of Agriculture that 'they as working farmers were in doubt as to whether women were physically and constitutionally strong enough to take the place of men.'[58] A shepherd told a Northamptonshire tribunal that: 'he had only heard of one woman shepherd and that was Little Bo-Peep and she lost her sheep. (Laughter.)'[59] In Somerset, land worker Mary Lees (definitely no Little Bo-Peep) found herself 'tested' by a farmer. He instructed her to shear a ewe that had been dead for several weeks. The beast was so putrid, though, that she was simply able to pull the wool away. With the task completed, she asked the farmer for a spade so that she might bury the carcass. He expressed amazement that she had completed the challenge. '"Gor," he said. "You done it?" He said, "I were testing you. Will you shake hands?"' (Mary recalled the incident in a taped interview and her eye-roll is audible).[60] A Mr E. J. Keeble, a farmer, told the Essex WWAC that he had employed women for several years in the summer, but had 'great difficulty' with their discipline. 'It was no use for the women to run off home when a shower of rain came,' he said.[61] Mary Adelaide Broadhurst, of the National Land Council, wrote an exasperated letter to the press on the subject of fair-weather farm work. Women were 'accused of being too "flighty" for farm work. She is branded as a frivolous, "fair weather" individual, unsuited to country life. Are these accusations true? My answer is, emphatically, No!'[62] The next month a newspaper headline exclaimed: 'Hairpins in the pig trough!' A farmer, it was said, alleged that a National Land Council worker had left hairpins in the pigs' feed. The National Land Council denied that the incident had taken place. A statement said that 'no agriculturalist has yet reproached them with this crime on the part of their protégées', but the mischief was done.[63]

Sometimes objections were dressed up in chivalry. Fear was expressed for ladies tender sensibilities. It was thought that breeding farms might push corrupting sights at their eyes and early morning starts were 'conducive to moral laxity.'[64] An article in the *Aberdeen Weekly Journal* said that, while women might be capable of light farm work in summertime, they were not suited to the harder, rougher work of winter. And Little Bo-Peep was not the only fictional female held up as an example; 'For illustration', the writer quoted from *Tess of the D'Urbervilles*, citing a passage of happy harvest workers and the grimness of winter in the fields. 'It is very good of our womenfolk to undertake all the duties they possibly can in this time of excessive stress,' he reflected, 'but the sooner they are relieved from the coarser and rougher work on farms, the better for everyone.'[65] In a similar tone, the *Stirling Observer* reflected:

> *In Germany it is no unusual sight to see women yoked to a plough, but the British have an inborn repugnance of employing women on work requiring great physical strength and endurance. We are proud of what women are doing in the time of need, and accept their services in vital tasks with gratitude, but it must be admitted that a good deal of the work on the land is unsuited to their capacities.*[66]

Farmers in Cumberland and Westmorland were concerned about what type of woman might arrive on their farms. Would she be the sort of women who would expect to be invited 'into the sitting room for a cup of tea with his wife'? The CWAC debated whether it would be appropriate to keep groups of women workers apart 'to avoid mixing classes'.[67] The *Yorkshire Post* was thinking along the same lines: 'Another cause of popular prejudice arises from the roughness in tongue and talk of the women who ordinarily work in the fields – a roughness from which the sensitive girl, reared in a nice home shrinks with horror.'[68]

Hilary Crowe observes that, though the farmers of Westmorland and Cumberland objected to paying for imported female labour, women in farming families (i.e. unpaid) certainly had to do more work now.[69] Farmers were accustomed to wives and daughters working on the farm, and even local women – they were cheap, convenient and farmers knew what they were getting – what they objected to was paying strangers. A lot of the prejudice seems to boil down to territorial prickliness (why should the government tell them how to run their own farms?) and money. A further ground for objection was that, despite repeated assurances to the contrary, many farmers were convinced that if they took women on, they would have their skilled male labourers taken away. Why should they accept that their men could be replaced by so many incompetent, hairpin-scattering Little Bo-Peeps? They did not want women on their farms. They feared what the wider consequences would be. And they particularly objected to having women forced upon them.

In Devon, farmers were particularly dubious about women's worth. At a meeting of the Devon Farmers' Union, in January 1916, the chairman set the theme, stating: 'A woman on a farm was about a quarter the use of a man.' Another farmer followed up that 'a boy of twelve was worth two women on a farm.'[70] The same sentiments were voiced when the Wrangaton and Totnes branch of the Union met in February. Here again it was said that it wasn't possible to 'get so much out of' women as it was boys of twelve.' Another farmer reflected: 'People who started the business of getting women to work on the farms knew absolutely nothing about business.'[71] The WWAC here were always going to have an uphill struggle. In February, Sylvia Calmady-Hamlyn, Honorary Secretary of the Devon WWAC,

66

addressed a meeting convened in Barnstaple to discuss 'Women for Service in Agriculture'. She told the audience that she had started work on a register of women, but farmers were reluctant to take them on. This was evidently the case; as two farmers entered the meeting they were reported to have said: 'It will only be twaddle'.[72] When the Dartmouth Branch of the Devon Farmers' Union met shortly afterwards, Calmady-Hamlyn was the subject of discussion. One farmer reflected:

If farmers had to be dictated to, and had to be told the price they had to pay for their labour, the sooner they gave up their farming to Miss Calmady-Hamlyn the better. (Hear, hear, and a voice, "Let her farm it herself.") Miss Calmady-Hamlyn could, he thought, better employ herself at home doing her domestic affairs and liberate some of her servants. Farmers must be thought to be some of the biggest fools in the world if they needed to be told by ladies what they had to pay for taking up their mangolds or anything else. There was a lot of that talk going on, and it was very detrimental to farmers.[73]

It wasn't a good basis to be starting from. Only a few weeks into the existence of the Devon WWAC, there was a lot of ill feeling and this antagonism would rumble on through the year. By May the hostility between the Devon WWAC and the county's farmers was being aired in the House of Commons. Francis Acland explained how Alice Mildmay, President of the Devon Women's War Service Committee, had been confronted at a public meeting. A farmer had challenged her to find any women who would be willing to spread manure.

She promptly took his name and address, and the next day and following days took her house party of ladies to his farm and spread the manure, charging the farmer for the work done, and giving the money to the Red Cross Fund. That ought to make a really considerable impression in that county.[74]

By October 2,254 women had registered as willing to work on the land in Devon, but of these, only 835 had secured work during the past quarter. 'There were numbers of women ready to work, but there was no demand for their labour,' Calmady-Hamlyn told a meeting of the Devon WWAC. It her opinion it came down to wages. She told the meeting that 'women's work was hampered by the very absurd wages offered by the farmers in some of the districts of the county.' She said that farmers in South Devon were paying women 7s 6d per acre for pulling mangold. By comparison, in West Devon, farmers paid 12s per acre. She commented: 'Seven and sixpence per acre was practically sweated labour so far as she was able to see.' She went on: 'It should be strongly put to the agriculturalists that if they wanted women to work for them they must be prepared to remunerate, at least, fairly.' Devon's farmers were being insular and unpatriotic, she said, and this was 'a type of mind very difficult to deal with.'[75] As might be expected, this provoked an angry reaction. In December 1916, at a meeting of the Totnes Farmers' Union, they hit back. And it got personal. It was alleged that Alice Mildmay had men in her service that ought to be serving in the Army.[76]

At the other end of the country different objections were aired, but the outcome was the same. At a meeting of Rydale Agricultural Club a Mr Hebron said that women were only coming to farms on a 'spooning expedition' – they were just there 'trying to catch husbands'. Women's labour on the land was 'a farce', he said. A woman's 'proper place' was in the home not the fields.[77] Farmers in West Riding clearly felt similarly if the figures are anything to go by. At a meeting of West Riding WWAC in May 1916, it was disclosed that 1,009 women had thus far volunteered for farm work in the district, but there had been only thirty-two applications from farmers.[78] So much effort, so much rallying of the women, and the reception was indifferent at best.

The newspapers of 1916 are full of farmers making a case for why they wouldn't employ women. But, as the year progressed, and more women were seen on the land, acceptance started to creep in. At Nantwich Farmers' Club, opinion was expressed that employing women was 'distasteful' but, the speaker said,

The war had disturbed the home life of most people. It had disturbed church life, social life and commercial life, and farmers had to ask themselves whether, in those disturbing circumstances, they should not ask women to help them… He did not like it himself, but when circumstances compelled them he said, "Let us avail ourselves of this labour with a good grace."[79]

And as some farmers tried female labourers, positive examples started to be picked up by the press. The government urged them on. In May, Francis Acland told the House of Commons: 'At present all who have tried women are pleased and swear by them; all who have not tried them do not believe in them, and, it may be, continue to swear at them. This ought to be altered, and there is no time to waste.' Putting time into training women was a good investment, Acland urged: 'Women will be of very little use, of course, when they first come, but if they have good intelligence, good will, and good health and strength—and there are plenty who have all four—they will be wonderfully useful after a few weeks spent in adjusting themselves to farm work.' He went on to make the point that if women were not given a chance they would stop offering their services and likely take more highly paid jobs in munitions – and then 'the chance of using them to maintain our food supplies will be gone.' He concluded:

To summarise the position: It is no longer now a question of saying to farmers, "We think we can get women; we think they may be useful to you; will you try them?" The position is: "The women are here; we know they are useful—that is proved up to the hilt; you must try them. If you do not you are doing the Kaiser's work, not the King's.[80]

In an effort to encourage farmers to try women workers, WWACs had started training them. The Board of Agriculture was of the opinion that on-the-farm training was the best option, where possible, but several educational institutions had also begun to offer instruction and, from May 1916, the government offered 400 free scholarships at colleges and farm institutes. After a training of four-to-six weeks, scholarships girls were usually required to commit to work on a farm for a period of three to six months.[81] Mary Lees, from Somerset, was one of these women. She had just left school as war broke out and, when her mother pronounced that she must now take over care of household ('She'll do the shopping and the cooking'), Mary decided to get out. 'Blow me,' Mary recalled, 'you will not! Mary's *not* going to do the cooking and the shopping.' She resolved to sign up for the first agricultural training course that she could get on. Mary's godfather knew the director at Seale-Hayne Agricultural College, and with his assistance, she managed to secure a place. 'There they taught us to do everything, you see,' Mary said. 'They taught us to plough, to milk, to make cheese.' Regarding the attitude of her fellow Seale-Hayne students, she remembered: 'There was an extraordinary spirit of fighting amongst those women. There's no doubt about that.'[82]

Seale-Hayne Agricultural College, in Devon, had been scheduled to start taking students – both male and female – in 1914, but with the outbreak of war its opening was put on hold. In 1916 the governors of the College decided to make their facilities available to women students from Devon and Cornwall. A four-week practical training course was launched, offering instruction in milking, butter-making, calf-rearing, pig-feeding and field work.[83] Bernard Wale, Principal of the college, disclosed that the students included nurses, artists, musicians and women off the stage. Generally they were all 'above the average in education and intelligence', but 'refined as they were, they murmured not at the unpleasant work they had instantly to undertake. For instance, the job of cleaning out the pig-houses before breakfast the day after arrival did not in any way damp their spirit of determination.' In his opinion, town girls made better students than country girls. 'The more highly educated the girl, the more adaptability she possesses for learning and taking to the work,' he reflected 'The women who come from the towns are the better students. Some have never been on the land before, and consequently they are desirous of learning all they can. We don't find so much difficulty in getting them to do as they are told.' He told the *Western Times* that he regularly received letters from former students. 'I am getting strong, and find it good to live,' one girl had recently written to him.[84]

The Board of Agriculture also formally recognised the training work of the WFGU. The Union had been lent two farms in Essex by Lord Rayleigh in 1915 and training efforts here were hailed to be a success. With this experiment having gone well, the programme was to be extended. Viscount Hood was now offering a large farm on his estate at Barton Seagrave, Kettering. This was a 'most up-to-date' farm and here the women would have chance to become acquainted with 'practically every form of agricultural motor machinery.'[85] A demonstration farm at Cambridge University was also placed at the disposal of the WFGU during the university vacation. Boarding and lodging at Girton College, the women would be trained in 'the most up-to-date methods of modern farming.'[86] Francis Acland acclaimed the efforts of the WFGU as 'work of the utmost national importance.'[87]

In South Yorkshire a training centre had been set up at Plumtree Farm, one of the home farms of Bawtry Hall, near Doncaster. It was being run by Mrs de Wilton, who had spent twelve years farming in Canada, where she employed an almost exclusively female workforce, the *Yorkshire Post* reported. The newspaper went on: 'She is altogether an exceptional lady for the charge of such a centre as this – brimming over with life and vigour and enthusiasm, and capable of exciting a high spirit of comradeship in her pupils.' The paper's reporter described the scene of women planting a field of potatoes. '"How do you like it," was the question put to one of the pupils. "Oh," she said, "I shall be only too sorry when the fortnight is up."'[88] By November over a hundred pupils had passed through Plumtree Farm and a similar scheme was up and running at Ribston Hall, near Knaresborough.[89] The Council for Agricultural Education had given each of the three Yorkshire Ridings a grant of £100 towards training women land workers. In the North Riding this was used to set up training centres at farms and schemes were also being financed by the Yorkshire College at Leeds for 'girls and women of the working classes'.[90] In West Riding the WWAC highlighted the work of Plumtree farm and urged for similar initiatives to be established. Farmers willing to take women in and train them were offered a grant of ten shillings per week.[91] The problem of accommodating trainee land workers was also being tackled; the North Riding WWAC was fitting up disused railway carriages to accommodate women training on nearby farms. 'Painted a bright red, "The Coaches" proclaim to the travelling public passing up and down the line that the colony consists of "Women Landworkers,"' the *Yorkshire Post* observed.[92]

Training women to milk remained a priority. Louisa Wilkins told a meeting:

> *Next to soldiers and munitions, the urgent problem of the hour was our food supply, the shortage of which, especially of milk, was becoming serious. Milk could not be imported. Milk was now 6d per quart in London. It was absolutely necessary for children, invalids, and convalescent soldiers. Owing to want of milkers, farmers were giving up the farms, selling cows, even killing them for beef.*[93]

In response, dairy training continued to expand. With the support of the Board of Agriculture, scholarships were offered at Newton Rigg Farm School and at Durham's new County Dairy and Poultry School.[94] Still, for all the efforts, dairy instructress Mary Darrell would write in October 1916:

> *It amazes me to notice how few women are employed in this occupation, in spite of the war, the scarcity of men, and all that people like myself, who have devoted their lives to the work, have said on the subject. One can still go through village after village and not find a single woman milker! For this deplorable state of affairs our farmers must be blamed. They will not employ women so long as they can obtain men.*[95]

All over the country the efficacy of women as milkers was being deliberated. It was even debated in the House of Commons. Challenging the negative opinions of fellow MPs, Charles Bathurst said that he had had women milking on his own home farm for the past two months and that they had done some of the best dairy work that he had seen. 'My own experience is that a woman, when properly trained, seems to have more sympathy with the animal and is more capable of effectually milking out a cow than a man or even a capable boy.' Moreover they were willing to lend a hand to all the other jobs on the farm:

> *The operations they are conducting to-day are not confined to milking. They have been turning a separator; they have been making butter; they have been hoeing and singling the roots; they have been rolling and harrowing the land; they had been spreading manure and generally carrying out a large variety of farm processes, which leads me rather to ask, not what can women do in the way of agricultural work, but what cannot women do?*[96]

Beatrice Oaks was one of 1916's new milkers. She later recalled:

> *I had already learned to hand milk (extremely slowly), but that was about all. I knew that I loved animals and the countryside, and wanted so much to do something useful. Men were volunteering for war service, and I could think of nothing more suitable than helping to keep the country fed.*

She was sent to a farm in Hampshire, where her employer told her:

> *When I could comfortably hand milk eight cows I could think I was taking the place of one man. There was a lot to prove in that first month, and I did learn to milk many more than eight cows at a sitting. I remember a joke that was played on me when I was new, and I suppose on lots of other girls. There was one cow who was separated from the rest as she had recently calved. I used to take the calf out at intervals and milk the mother. One morning I went as usual to the box, and thought nothing of the*

tittering going on in the cowshed. When I opened the door, there, instead of the cow, was the bull. By that time I was aware of the difference, and made myself scarce![97]

Mary Lees now had twelve cows to milk. The conditions of her training obliged her to work in Devon for the next few months and so, via the Labour Exchange, she'd found a position working for Farmer Tozer, who had advertised for 'a good strong woman'. For £1 per week, Mary had to milk a dozen cows twice a day. From that she had to pay out 'seventeen bob for keep' and 'two bob for laundry'. That left her with one shilling – 'which I put in the plate on Sundays. So that was a help, wasn't it?' The living accommodation was rough ('the feather bed was just a bag with about six feathers in it') and Mary felt 'used' by the family. 'Old Mother Tozer she was a real old bitch,' she recalled. After completing her obligatory stint in Devon ('I couldn't stick any more of it'), Mary went to Pixton Park, Dulverton, in her home county of Somerset. Here she was working on the estate's home farm and conditions could not have been more different: 'The home farm had white tiles on the floor of the cow house and if the cow made a mess you had a bucket of water to clear it away!'[98]

By April 1916 Arthur Nicholson was noting in his 'Country Diary' that it was 'becoming most difficult to carry on ordinary farming.' He went on: 'If the market gardens and small, highly cultivated holdings that are so numerous in South Lancashire and North Cheshire are to continue to produce even what they have done in recent years, some prompt effort must be made to get women to volunteer for the work.'[99] By May it was getting more severe:

Great efforts are being made to get in the potatoes but labour is hard to find, for though this is work that women can do, their labour is in such demand that I know many farmers who are willing to give a good wage and yet can get no help. Matters grow worse each week, and the country districts are becoming rapidly denuded of the working population, from which agriculture must inevitably suffer.[100]

And worse was to come. The Somme offensive was in the planning and more men were needed for the army. In May 1916 the provisions of the Military Service Act were revised, extending conscription to all men aged 18 to 41. The Board of Agriculture sent a notice out to farmers informing them that certain occupations would now be removed from the certified list; these included bailiffs and foremen, if they were unmarried and under the age of 30, and stockmen, carters, horsemen, ploughmen, wagoners, if they were unmarried and under 25. It also called up all unmarried men who had not been in certified occupations before August 1915. Men appearing before the tribunals would now have to prove that they were 'absolutely undispensible'.[101]

The Board of Agriculture hadn't conceded to the army's demands lightly. Selborne spoke out at the second reading of the Military Service Bill in the House of Lords.

Agriculture has given not only its full share but more than its full share of men to the Army...We have reached a point where, unless the Tribunals are extremely careful what they do, the food production of this country will be seriously impaired. Those words are uttered with a very full sense of responsibility. Taking the farmers of the country as a whole, they have parted with almost all the skilled labour they can possibly spare.

He outlined the consequences if the indispensable men remaining were taken:

It means that more food will have to be imported, and tonnage diverted from the carriage of munitions to the carriage of food; it means that money will be spent on buying food elsewhere which would otherwise be used in supporting the finance of the Allied Armies in the field; and it means a constantly increasing cost of living—it means famine prices.[102]

'The National Food Supply' was the subject of debate in the House of Lords on 22 May 1916. 'Consider the state of the industry!' exclaimed

Francis Acland. He said that between 250,000-300,000 men (twenty-five to thirty per cent of the workforce) had now left agriculture. 'Surely it is clear that the danger point of gravely decreased production is already reached,' he remarked. Rowland Prothero was in agreement about the gravity of the situation. He estimated that the fall in numbers working on the land would have the effect of reducing the country's food production by fifteen to twenty-five per cent. With imports curbed and expensive, the reduction in food supply was likely to become serious. He went on: 'I am not a panic-monger, and I am not an alarmist, but I should be very glad if the Government would grasp this situation firmly and put us upon rations. I believe that, sooner or later, that will have to be done.' Francis Acland concluded: 'When all is said and done, it is on women's work that we must depend this year very largely, and women's work is very much the best and most hopeful way of supplementing the skilled labour still left.'[103]

The Board of Trade monitored the agricultural working population by sending out periodic surveys, which required farms to detail changes in their labour force. In the 1970s, studies by Peter Dewey called the Board of Trade's figures into question and proposed that labour was considerably more plentiful than contemporaries were claiming. On account of the insufficiency of the sample size and the fact that the surveys were only sent out to large farms, Dewey contended that the figures were 'inherently implausible'.[104] However, while historians might debate the reliability of statistics, evidence overwhelmingly suggests that in many parts of England contemporaries sensed a real labour shortage by the summer of 1916.

Selborne resigned as President of the Board of Agriculture in June 1916 because of his disagreement with the way that Lloyd George was handling Irish Home Rule negotiations. He was replaced by David Lindsay, Earl of Crawford. Histories have damned Selborne with the words '*laissez-faire*' and 'wait and see'. It is an unfair criticism, probably, as he was frustrated in what he could do. Despite repeatedly arguing that more intervention was needed, ultimately he didn't have the backing to bring his ideas to fruition. Without special powers, or the ability to offer inducements to farmers, Selborne's only resource was to construct appeals to their patriotism and their pockets. Much of the policy enacted under Prothero has its origins in the Milner committee and in Selborne's own recommendations.

Arthur Nicholson was travelling south through the country in June. Though he passed fields where the hay seemed ready, 'in no case did we see anyone busy with it.' His first sight of haymaking was in a field on the south of the Thames. There it was being done by a party of women and children.[105] And as the summer went on these 'queer teams of volunteers' would typify 1916's harvest labour.[106] The War Office had promised to make a workforce of 27,000 soldiers available to farmers for the 1916 wheat harvest and between the start of June and the end of July farmers accordingly applied to Labour Exchanges seeking 33,089 men. But, with the War Office hampered by administrative complications and the build-up for the Somme offensive under way, only 14,227 soldiers were actually made available. They wouldn't be any more plentiful later in the summer; from August to October farmers applied seeking the labour of 28,805 soldiers; only 16,690 were released.[107] Whether they wanted to or not, farmers now had to look to other labour sources. The Board of Trade estimated that in July 1916 the number of women working on the land was forty per cent higher than it had been in July 1914, with particular increases in the south-east (up seventy-eight per cent) and east midlands (up eighty-six per cent).[108]

The Co-Operative Wholesale Society's monthly magazine, *The Wheatsheaf*, carried an account of a woman's experience of haymaking ('A Lady of the Land'). Leaving behind a life of 'penswomanship', she was initially full of enthusiasm for her new occupation ('A life of adventure and achievement in the open!') but soon found that the work brought 'a different ache for every day.' She wrote:

> *I think my first morning in the hayfield was the longest and the weariest I have ever spent. I worked like a slave from 9.30 to 1, only stopping to lift my handkerchief to my face. The sun's rays beat down; my hands began to blister; my wrists felt strained; perspiration drenched my clothes; my legs seemed to give way*

beneath me. The hay was painfully dusty, and my throat and lips
so parched that the craving for water was unbearable.

She reflected that she was not quite matching up to the 'the pretty pictures of the lady farmers' that were so prolific in the newspapers. But she was sustained by patriotism and 'and the thoughts of doing one's bit; otherwise the cold rain, snow, and frost would soon thin the ranks of the lady farmers.'[109]

As in 1915, various private initiatives were endeavouring to make lady farmers of penswomen. Addressing recruiting letters to the press, the Women's Defence Relief Corps lauded its 'pioneers' of the previous summer – and made field work sound almost like a health cure:

Although they carried stout hearts, it was with some doubt as to whether being untrained and inexperienced – for they were of all sorts – schoolmistresses, housemaids, women of leisure, sick nurses, shop assistants, artists – they would be able to stand the work. For the first three days the work certainly seemed very hard. After that muscles quickly adapted themselves and in the end proved equal to any and every task. The result was delicate women came back strong and blooming, and have been immune from colds this winter, nerves vanished, and all admitted they were better in health for the experience.[110]

The Women's Defence Relief Corps would spend the summer of 1916 harvesting and hop-picking. Five hundred members of the Corps were working on the land at the end of the year.[111] The National Land Council had meanwhile focussed on recruiting women to work on the market gardens and fruit farms of Worcestershire. In June, the *Daily Mirror* carried photos of Land Council volunteers working near Evesham. 'Among them are daughters of officers, doctors and many professional women,' the paper reported. 'They are being housed in barns and huts, where they will remain for four months, and work in gangs of ten, each under a captain.'[112] By July there were 300 Land

Council women working in the district. 'They work 10 hours a day and receive a minimum of 15*s* a week,' the *Western Daily Press* reported.

> *Some weeks the workers earn more, and one girl had made 27s by picking gooseberries. The girls enjoy the life immensely, and those who have been employed in offices and drapers' stores find themselves different beings after a few weeks in the open air of this beautiful garden of Worcestershire.*[113]

The camp, with its military discipline, was the subject of some press fascination. The *Birmingham Mail* sent a journalist out too. He reported:

> *The experiment in feminine organisation on military lines has been an unqualified success. Though discipline is firm and strictly enforced, there has not been a single case for court-martial from among any of the 75 "Brownies" who inhabit the camp, "Brownies" who deserve their name not merely because of the colour of their neat and workmanlike uniform, but because of those golden-brown skins which life in the open has given them. The camp government is based, like all good governments, on the willing assent of the governed. But though the workers are all volunteers and all willing to subdue personal feelings to the accomplishment of the tasks in hand, it is not light and easy work which they have undertaken. Reveille sounds at four and work is well in hand by five o'clock, and there are only short breaks for breakfast (at 7 a.m.), dinner (at 12.30 or 1) and tea (at 5 p.m.). "Lights out" sounds at 8 every evening. Nor are the conditions too easy or pleasant, for the bedrooms are only large barns, which hold eight or nine women each, and the only method of bathing is to fill a hip bath with water for yourself. Yet the girls like it.*

The women of the camp had started their stint cutting cabbages, had picked strawberries, then raspberries and peas. They were shortly to move into woods for timber work and were later engaged for plum and apple gathering.[114] Photographs published in the *Illustrated War News* showed the 'War-Brownies' merrily watering marrows and pitching hay.[115] By October the National Land Council claimed that it had placed over 5,000 women in farm work, around ninety per cent of them from towns. They were from 'many classes', and included 'actresses, artists, business girls, the daughters of generals, colonels, naval officers, doctors, lawyers, and other professional and business men.' They had taken on all varieties of farm work and had stuck to their work 'grit and endurance', Mary Adelaide Broadhurst, Chairman of the National Land Council, told the *Sunday Mirror*. One of the girls, who had been an actress, was reported to have said: 'Well, the first week I was so tired that I was afraid I was going to die. The second week I hoped that I might die; but the third week I was glad to be alive!'[116]

Women were also employed on bracken camps in the Savernake Forest, under the direction of the War Office. Taken on for eight weeks and 'under semi-military discipline', the women worked with sickles cutting bracken for bedding army horses. The workers were accomodated in tents in 'a beautiful, bracing spot', but 'there are heavy dews (if not heavy rain) on long grass and tall fern – and reveillé is at 6.30.' Letters were sent to the press asking for donations of magazines and books for their 'mess tent' – and for work boots ('Would it be possible, she asks, to hunt up a few pairs of strong boots for those of the girls who have come ill-shod?').[117]

Many university students were spending their summer on the land via a scheme promoted by the Board of Trade. An official told the press:

The University woman has proved very promising material for training to work on the land. As a class, they are intelligent, disciplined, well-drilled, and athletic, and, being generally of social status superior to the people who are placed over them, they take little pin-pricks in a more philosophical spirit than some other women workers.

The universities participating included King's and Bedford College of London University, Girton and Newnham colleges, Cambridge, and Somerville and St Hilda's at Oxford. From the end of June the Varsity women would be picking soft fruit, then cherries and plums, haymaking and corn harvesting and hop picking.[118]

The university women might be of robust temperament, but that did not mean that they were over-delighted by their summer accommodation. Hilda Rountree was one of the Newham College women. On arrival at her billet in Norfolk she found that they were to sleep on straw-filled mattresses on the floor. If that wasn't testing enough, they also had 'company': 'I remember that by the second night there was not a shoe among the company which did not bear witness to the mortality of the usual inhabitants, the beetles.' A local doctor offered the women the use of his bath, but when the boiler burst, the workers resorted to rain water or a bicycle ride into town. 'The plan joined us with a bunch of regular village women,' Hilda recalled, 'who treated us at first with distinct caution if not actual disdain. But we wore them down with our tomfoolery, and we sang lots of songs with good choruses.' A press photographer and journalist from Cambridge travelled over and the ensuing article observed, 'their hoods were bewitchingly rural and only their speech betrayed them, for they came from Newnham.' Returning to Cambridge, Hilda was amused to see one of the photographs reproduced on a poster with the caption, 'Is this what higher education does for women?'[119]

Battling against the beetles seemed to be a recurring theme. A university student from Scotland wrote an account of her summer fruit picking in Norfolk for the *Aberdeen Journal.* In response to the 'great plea' for women workers, she and a friend had decided to work for the month of July. They joined a party of nine fruit pickers accommodated together in a house, of which she wrote: 'the entire furniture consisted of a mattress laid upon the floor of each room. The farmer expected three people to sleep on each mattress... To add to our misfortune, the house was certainly damp, as it had never been lived in, and was overrun with black beetles.' There was only a tap in front of the house to wash with, and no basin. 'This we had to do during the whole month, and we generally had a few onlookers, who seemed surprised, though also rather horrified at the performance.' But, she concluded, 'To weep would have been unpatriotic, so we made up our minds to laugh and make the best of things.' They were put to work picking strawberries. By the second day 'our aches and pains were awful and we could scarce drag one foot after another. We felt very much inclined not to work, but decided that we must not give in unless it was absolutely necessary, and so walked away wearily to the field... by the end of the week we could not have been in a more sorry state.' Occasionally there was the relief of raspberries, though:

Only three times did we pick raspberries instead of strawberries, and these days were red-letter days in our fruit-picking experiences. No stooping was required, and how happy we felt to be able to stand straight once more! We all sang gaily when we were among the rasps, and bitterly regretted that the field was not full of them.

They were paid 1½*d* for each 4lb of strawberries they picked and some weeks earned as much as 26*s*. 'It was wonderful how our aches and pains recovered after the first payment, and how much better we felt!' They got used to the work too.

We became quite accustomed to stooping all day, accustomed also to working in the heaviest of fogs with the strawberry beds simply soaking. Often, before two minutes were over, our feet and legs were as wet as possible and our shoes ankle-deep in mud. There was nothing for it, however, but to work on, to try to forget how wet and cold we were.

By the end of the month their aches and pains had 'entirely vanished' and they were 'very healthy both in mind and body (without even a wasp sting or a twinge of rheumatism, though our friends had prophesised that these would be the least of our ailments), and very much the better in every way of our work on the land and in the open air.' From the locals, with whom they were working, they received 'much kindness in every way'. She observed: 'It seems that there had been much speculation as to the capacity of University women for manual labour, and they were evidently much surprised to find out that, despite the disadvantage of higher education, we could do a good day's work as well as any of them.' Even their employer was impressed: 'Our farmer, who was of a sour and grudging disposition, actually admitted that he could not have got on without us, and he hoped that next year we would return.' On leaving they felt 'that we had done something – small and insignificant though it may be – to help our country, and that in itself was a reward.'[120]

In all, colleges and universities provided 2,890 'vacation land workers' in 1916.[121] E. N. Thomas, who was President of the University of London Vacation Land Workers, wrote: 'Its effect both on farmers and local women was not inconsiderable, and helped to foster both supply and demand in the employment of women on the land.'[122]

Mabel Smith did a nine-week stint on a Yorkshire farm during the summer of 1916 and wrote an account of it for *The Spectator*. 'I had chosen agriculture for my war work for the following reasons,' Mabel detailed:

1. Because there is a shortage of labour in this all-important industry, and, having been asked to help in organizing women's work on the land, I wished to find out from practical experience how much of such work women can and ought to do;

2. Because I think it is a mistake to allow children to leave school, in order to work on farms, before the school leaving age, and so I hoped to take the place of one such child;

3. Because there seemed to be an idea that educated women could not undertake manual labour, and would be of no use if they did, and I wanted to disprove this.

Mabel registered with her nearest Labour Exchange, but found that her desire to work was treated 'as a joke'. Eventually she was taken on by a farmer (she attributed this decision on his part simply to curiosity), but having arrived on the farm a debate ensued as to what she might be able to do. Every task that she volunteered for was met with the reply that she wouldn't be capable. Eventually she was put to work in the potato fields and, having performed adequately here, she was promoted to mangolds and eventually to haymaking. While her employer had at first considered women workers to be 'useless,' his opinion was changed by example. 'Our employer now considers that there is a great waste of woman labour in England. Is this altogether women's fault?' Mabel concluded:

> *My experience of farm life leads me to believe:*
> *1. That much, even if not all, farm work can be done by women, and that they can be trusted to go on doing even a monotonous task conscientiously without supervision;*
> *2. That farm life is not suitable for young children, and that it is in the interests of the nation to keep them at school;*
> *3. That educated women are at no disadvantage. If taught to use their tools properly, so as to produce the greatest effect with the smallest effort, they will soon achieve good results, and the intelligent interest they take in their work will enable them to appreciate the use and value of tasks which to others might appear needless and monotonous.*[123]

In addition to the challenges of dubiously enthusiastic employers, new skills to master and beetles in their beds, women coming onto the land often faced hostility from locals too. Village women sometimes saw the importation of workers as a slur on their labour and others feared that these in-comers would see them (and possibly even their husbands) out of their jobs. Rowland Prothero also suspected other motives. He told the House of Commons:

> *I do not think the movement is very popular with the wives of the farmers. I think if you could get to the bottom of it the difficulty is this, that the farmer's wife says, "I am not going*

to have any London minxes trapesing about the farmyard when you are there." I honestly believe that this prejudice, and the more serious objection amongst the agricultural labourers, in the pressure of this unexampled time, are not likely to endure.[124]

There was a big gulf in background between the women who had carried on working the land and those now coming onto it, and the imported women do seem to have landed like aliens, with their strange accents and manners and dress. Ellen Walshe had signed up for a season of fruit picking having been persuaded that she must 'come forward and save the country.' But the local women were explicitly hostile to Ellen and her breeches-wearing friends, talking openly 'of hooting us off the field.' At the end of their stint the farmer told them 'that he had never really wanted us at any time, as he had quite as many of his regular pickers as usual, but that he had been so bothered by Government officials to try us that he had consented.'[125] Other women had a less disheartening – if similarly awkward – experience. In Yorkshire Mabel Smith found herself side-by-side with women who had worked all their lives as casual farm labourers. She wrote:

They treated me at first with a kindly tolerance mixed with awe, but gradually came to look upon me as a fellow human being, and we soon became great friends, one bond of union being that we all had husbands, sons, or brothers at the war. They obligingly moderated their language in my honour, and I acquired an extended vocabulary of the finest Yorkshire.[126]

It is unfortunate that we have a one-sided body of sources for this subject. While many women wrote articles about their experiences on the land for newspapers and left behind diaries and recollections, it was the educated women, those who did not previously have experience of this type of work, who felt motivated to make a record. We can only hear the voices of the village women second-hand. This is largely the reason why the experience of these women has been 'eclipsed'. Nicola Verdon observes that the village women 'stand in the shadows, recorded and judged by others. It is almost impossible to reconstruct how village women perceived their work or understood their place in the wartime economy, as they remain largely nameless and voiceless.'[127]

The Board of Agriculture wasn't always delighted with educated women's well-meaning efforts either. The Women's Legion was established in 1915 and its Agricultural Section inaugurated in February 1916. The Legion's President was Lady Londonderry, daughter of the former President of the Board of Agriculture, Henry Chaplin.[128] The Legion managed to secure a grant of £200 from the Board of Agriculture for its work and over the summer of 1916 it canvassed the women of Rutland and staged motor ploughing demonstrations.[129] But relations with the Board of Agriculture cooled over the course of the year. While Lady Londonderry's name, money and connections were appreciated, it was felt that she was too inefficiently intrusive – that it was a pet project and not always one that was working wisely. Mr E. Cheney, Chief Agricultural Adviser to Board of Agriculture, wrote:

> *It is all very well for, say, the local duchess to be brought into a new movement on its inception, mainly because her name is of value as an advertisement and because her purse is useful to provide the necessary funds, but when the movement has once been started, unless the duchess has the good sense to efface herself as quickly as possible, and to allow the project to be carried on by people who are primarily interested in it, in nine times out of ten the scheme is bound to fail.*

Cheney concluded that the Women's Legion had 'done a little mischief to the broader interests of the movement in some localities'. And he wasn't any more complimentary about the National Land Council. He observed that it had 'pursued methods which the Board considered to be mischievous and of very little practical utility'.[130]

Women's struggles in the fields were dwarfed by the enormity of

Fig 1. 'How Women are Filling the Gaps in the Ranks'; Women sheaving corn, Missenden, Buckinghamshire. *The Sketch*, 26 August 1914.

WOMEN FARMERS TO VISIT FRANCE.

Through an enterprising scheme by the Berkshire Committee of Women and Farm Labour, a small party of selected working women left Charing Cross yesterday for a tour in France, in order to see how the French peasant women were carrying on the agricultural industries. Left to right: Miss Gladys Pott, Miss La Methe (Board of Trade representative), Mrs. Boyeo, Mrs. N. Stocks, Mrs. Saint (Staffordshire Education Committee), and Miss Chillingworth, a Berkshire farmer's daughter.

PEERESS AS PRACTICAL POULTRY-KEEPER

Lady Denman, who takes a keen practical interest in poultry-keeping, is doing very useful war-work by instructing the people round about her farm in Surrey how to keep fowls at a profit. She is seen among her own poultry. (L.N.A.)

Fig 2. Women's trip to observe French farm work. *Birmingham Daily Gazette*, 24 February 1916.

Fig 3. Lady Denman 'who takes a keen practical interest in poultry-keeping'. *Leeds Mercury*, 19 September 1916.

Fig 4. Cicely Spencer, Forage Corps, 1916. (Private Papers of Mrs C.M. Spencer – IWM Catalogue number: Documents.11603.)

Fig 5. 'The "War-Brownies" at work on a farm' ('so nicknamed because of their earth-brown breeches and smocks'). *Illustrated War News*, 25 June 1916.

Fig 6. 'The farmer's daughter, Miss Luke, is herself driving the machine, and a soldier in khaki is at the side. Mr. Luke, of Aldboro' Hatch Farm, Essex, has arranged for a number of soldier helpers. His daughter is an expert reaper and is shown cutting a large field of wheat.' *Illustrated War News*, 23 August 1916.

Fig 7. 'Picturesque War-Work: The Lady Shepherd', *Illustrated War News*, 5 July 1916.

Fig 8 and 9. Bessie ('Cuckoo') Ziman and fellow workers. (Private Papers of Miss B.A. Ziman – IWM Catalogue number: Documents.7926).

Fig 10 and 11.
'Women's War-Work
on a Royal Farm'.
Miss Hilda Hobson,
Miss Marjorie
Maxfield and Miss
Phyllis Hobson,
workers on the
Sandringham estate.
Illustrated War News,
8 November, 1916.

Fig 12. 'Girl-pupils'
spreading manure in the
snow in Nottinghamshire,
Illustrated War News, 24
January 1917.

NATIONAL **NS** SERVICE

10,000 Women
Wanted at Once
to Grow and Harvest the Victory Crops.

Send your application at once to The Director-General, National Service, St. Ermins, Westminster, S.W. 1, on a form which must first be obtained at your local Post Office or Employment Exchange.

Women who enrol to-morrow will secure :—

1. A free outfit, high boots, breeches, overall and hat.
2. Maintenance during training.
3. Travelling expenses in connection with the work.
4. Wages 18/- per week, or the district rate, whichever is the higher.
5. Maintenance during term of unemployment.
6. Housing personally inspected and approved by the Women's County Committees of the Board of Agriculture.
7. Work on carefully selected farms.
8. Promotion—good work rewarded by promotion and higher pay.
9. After the War, special facilities for settlement at home or overseas.

These are wanted :—

5,000 Milkers
4,000 Field Workers
1,000 Carters
DON'T DELAY!
ENROL AT ONCE IN THE WOMEN'S LAND ARMY.

Application Forms at all Post Offices and Employment Exchanges.

Women and Girls of England!
Golden days are passing quickly.

The
Women's Land Army
needs YOU to-day

Every day lost to England is a gift made to Germany. The girl who tills the soil helps to win the War as much as the girl who makes the shell.

To all who enlist under the NATIONAL SERVICE and BOARD OF AGRICULTURE scheme the GOVERNMENT GUARANTEES :

MAINTENANCE during training, TRAVELLING expenses, WAGES 18/- or district rate if higher, HOUSING personally inspected and approved, WORK on carefully selected farms, MAINTENANCE during unemployment up to four weeks, FREE outfit, overalls, breeches, hat, boots, and other welfare benefits.

Forms of enrolment at all Post Offices, Employment Exchanges, or from the Director, Women's Section, National Service, St. Ermin's, Westminster, S.W. 1.

Women engaged in Government Departments or controlled firms should only apply with the written consent of their employers.

**"Here and here did England help me.
How can I help England?"**

Fig 13. Initial advert for the Women's Land Army, widely placed in the press in March 1917.

Fig 14. Advert for the Women's Land Army, placed in the press in June and July 1917.

Fig 15. 'A farm wagon-load of women land-workers in Worcestershire are setting out to work', *Illustrated War News*, 25 July 1917.

Fig 16 and 17. Women working in the forests of Brent Tor, Devon. *Illustrated War News*, 8 August 1917.

Fig 18. Timber measurers working with a gang of Portuguese tree-fellers. *Illustrated War News*, 15 August 1917.

Fig 19. Beatrice Bennett and fellow Women's Land Army trainees, Kent, 1917. (Private Papers of Miss B. Bennett - IWM Catalogue number: Documents.2762.)

Fig 20. Beatrice Bennett and fellow timber workers at Chilgrove Camp, West Sussex, 1918. (Private Papers of Miss B. Bennett – IWM Catalogue number: Documents.2762.)

Fig 21. A 'wood-woman' ('Given a sound and robust physique, a woman war-worker could scarcely desire a healthier occupation than that shown in our photograph.') *Illustrated War News*, 30 January 1918.

Fig 22. Women mole catchers on an estate in the Cotswolds, *Illustrated War News*, 10 April 1918.

Fig 23. Recruiting rally for the Women's Land Army, Preston, June 1918. (Reproduced with the kind permission of Lancashire County Council and Preston City Council.)

Fig 24 and 25. Recruiting rally for the Women's Land Army, Preston, June 1918. (Reproduced with the kind permission of Lancashire County Council and Preston City Council.)

Fig 26. Flax pullers, Crewkerne, Somerset, 1918.

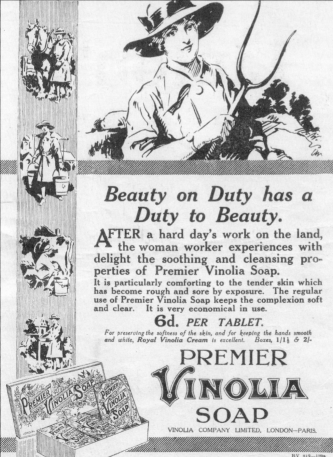

Beauty on Duty has a Duty to Beauty.

AFTER a hard day's work on the land, the woman worker experiences with delight the soothing and cleansing properties of Premier Vinolia Soap.

It is particularly comforting to the tender skin which has become rough and sore by exposure. The regular use of Premier Vinolia Soap keeps the complexion soft and clear. It is very economical in use.

6d. PER TABLET.

For preserving the softness of the skin, and for keeping the hands smooth and white, Royal Vinolia Cream is excellent. Boxes, 1/1½ & 2/-

PREMIER
VINOLIA
SOAP

VINOLIA COMPANY LIMITED, LONDON—PARIS.

RV 312—132a

Fig 27. 'Beauty on Duty has a Duty to Beauty'. Advert for Vinolia Soap, *The Landswoman*, July 1918, No. 7, Vol. 1.

Fig 28. Advert for 'Woman Power' insurance (Eagle Star & British Dominions Insurance Company, Ltd.), *The Landswoman*, July 1918, No. 7, Vol. 1. 'Woman-power throughout the British Empire stands out dominantly as the most wonderful feature of the War,' the advert stated. It suggested that women did not 'grasp the meaning of what the consequences of a serious illness or accident would be to her.' Pre-war women's labour was not considered worth insuring.

Fig 29. Cartoon by Bunty Daniel, a Land Girl, contrasting assumptions about, and the realities of, land work. *The Landswoman*, September 1918, No. 9, Vol. 1.

Fig 30. Cartoon by Bunty Daniel, *The Landswoman*, September 1918, No. 9, Vol. 1.

Fig 31 and 32. Clothing adverts from *The Landswoman*, September 1918, No. 9, Vol. 1. and October 1918, No. 10, Vol. 1.

Fig 33. Montage showing varieties of work at Great Bidlake Farm, Devon, *The Landswoman*, September 1918, No. 9, Vol. 1.

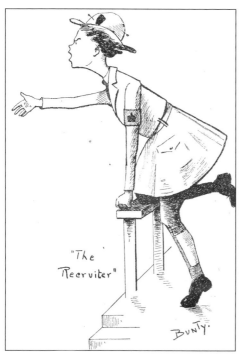

Fig 34. 'The Recruiter'. Cartoon by Bunty Daniel, *The Landswoman*, October 1918, No. 10, Vol. 1.

Fig 35. Cover for the special Christmas issue of *The Landswoman*, December 1918, No. 12, Vol. 1. The cover was designed by Land Army-member Kathleen Hale. She had studied art at Reading University College before the war and in 1917 she was painting maps for the Ministry of Food, but in 1918 she decided to join the Land Army. Kathleen spent much of the next year transporting fruit and vegetables by horse and cart from a market garden in Barnes to Covent Garden. After the war she went on to have a successful career as an illustrator.

what was going on across the Channel. The Somme offensive began on 1 July 1916. As the scale of losses started to become apparent, it seemed that women would need to step up and play their part all the more. A call-to-arms was put out to the women of Surrey – or, rather, a call to the dairies. 'The manhood of the Empire is being thrown away in the awful struggle in Europe, and it is to the women we look,' the *Dorking and Leatherhead Advertiser* wrote.

Women in their work in the dairies will do something towards that rebuilding. They will conserve the milk supplies of the country and render it possible to bring up a healthy race of men to take the places of those who are today sacrificing life on the blood-stained fields of France and Flanders. We are fighting for the upholding of great ideals, but after all there can be no nobler ideal than that of a healthy race of men, and that is the ideal we ask the women of England to keep constantly before them when we appeal to them to take their share of the work on the land upon their shoulders. [131]

By September 1916, Olive Hockin had worked on Dartmoor for nine months. Excepting one weekend and alternative free Sundays, neither she nor her co-worker 'Jimmy' had had a day off since February and it was telling on their bodies and tempers:

After the long days in the hay-fields and the long hot hours over the roots, we were both of us by this time thoroughly overworked and tired out, and the apparent hopelessness of counting on any coming respite made things worse. Our feelings of resentment were considerably enhanced when we found our Maester refusing extra help that was offered to him, thinking, apparently, that he was getting on so well as it was that to lengthen his wages bill any further would be unnecessary.

What keeps them going though, is a soldierly stoicism and sense that others were suffering more. 'Nothing, I am sure, but the feeling of urgent public necessity would have kept us going as we did all through that summer – that, and the thought of soldiers in the trenches.'[132]

In October 1916 the Earl of Crawford, President of the Board of Agriculture, told a meeting that they were 'now approaching the really critical months of the whole war.' He said: 'Those critical months will not only be settled on the plains of Flanders and in France, but will also be settled on the agricultural lands of our own country.'[133] In private he was concerned. At the end of October, Crawford addressed a memorandum to the War Cabinet. 'The outlook grows more difficult,' he began. Including the grain just harvested, supplies of wheat were now equivalent to four months' consumption, but with the crops of North America having failed, Argentina doubtful and Russian supplies unavailable, the volume of wheat on the market was contracting. 'In short,' Crawford wrote, 'there is a world's deficit'. As a result, it was now imperative that economy be exercised in the consumption of wheat. Other crops weren't looking good either. Potatoes had been planted late in cold, wet ground and then lifted in a rainy autumn with the result that the year's crop was also low in yield and quality. The shortage of labour was biting too. Crawford went on:

> *Great efforts are also being made to secure further dilution of agricultural labour and the employment of women; but unless the labour scale can be maintained at, approximately its present level—in many counties it has already been largely reduced— land will go derelict, yield will decline, and live stock must be greatly diminished.*[134]

Through the autumn of 1916 county tribunals dealing with exemptions had turned down applications from some 60,000 men working in agriculture, but they hadn't yet been called up. At the end of October it was confirmed that these men would not now have to leave until January 1917, in order to give time for ploughing and sowing winter crops.[135] Farmers were also informed that substitution would start in the spring; lists were being prepared of older soldiers, formerly farmworkers, who could be transferred from the Army to the Reserve and exchanged for young men who were presently working on farms.[136] Military Substitution Officers would now be brought in to assess whether farmers were employing any men who could be swapped for substitutes. Agriculture was being combed out.[137] With older men replacing younger men on farms, supplementary assistance from women would be all the more needed in the spring. In November an appeal from the Board of Agriculture was issued to the press:

> *The President of the Board of Agriculture desires to call public attention to the urgent need that exists for the assistance of women not already connected with the agricultural industry, in the work that is required for food production on the land, and to replace agricultural labourers who have been called up for military service... Thousands are now needed to meet the national emergency.*[138]

Meanwhile government ministers were experiencing their own personal emergency. Dissatsifaction with the progress of the war resulted in a change of leadership in December 1916. When Lloyd George replaced Asquith as Prime Minister, he quickly formed a number of new ministries and agencies and Agriculture was prominent in this show of 'new broom'. On 10 December, Rowland Prothero was appointed as President of the Board of Agriculture. He would later write:

> *The outlook in December 1916, was not hopeful. Everywhere the shortage of skilled men was acute. Considerably more than a third had already left the land for service in the navy, army or munition factories. Ploughmen were scarce. Nearly half the steam-tackle sets were out of action, either from want of repair or from the loss of drivers. Many horses had been commandeered; others were unshod. Harness and implements were out of order. Wide districts were denuded of such essential handicraftsmen as blacksmiths, wheelwrights, saddlers, and*

harness-makers. Manufacturers of agricultural machinery and implements were making munitions. Fertilisers were scarce.[139]

Prothero was an agricultural historian. He had spent years studying how the countryside worked, but he was now absolutely convinced that a breach in tradition was imperative. It was time to re-write the rules. At the end of December he addressed the CWACs. 'We are a beleaguered city,' he said, 'and we must act under the full consciousness of that fact. The reason that we have not so much food at the present time is that we are not making the best use of the land.' To that end he declared that a survey of each county must now be undertaken, analysing how the land could best be used. Prothero concluded his speech with a rousing call to arms (or maybe spades?): 'It is my sincere conviction that victory or defeat in this great war in which we are engaged may be won on the cornfields and potato lands of Great Britain.'[140]

In his first few weeks in office Lloyd George made a show of tackling the 'food problem'. Addressing the House of Commons for the first time as Prime Minister, on 19 December 1916, and with his rhetoric at full-throttle, he made it clear that food policy would be a priority. The issue was already 'undoubtedly serious', he said, 'and will be grave unless not merely the Government, but the nation, is prepared to grapple with it courageously without loss of time.' To deal with the problem, the strategy of the new government was going to be two pronged: to stimulate domestic production and to encourage more considered and measured consumption. To achieve the latter, 'men and women of all ranks and conditions' would now be required 'to play the game.' Emphasising that sacrificing on the dinner table was nothing as compared to the sacrifices of the army, Lloyd George declared, 'Let us proclaim during the War a national Lent.'[141] The man tasked with policing this was the new Food Controller, Lord Devonport.

At the end of the year, journalists were invited to the King's Sandringham estate to see the female farmworkers in action. It was reported that there was now not a single eligible man of military age employed on the Royal Farm. 'The King in his capacity as an English gentleman has set an excellent example to his neighbours,' reflected *Country Life* magazine. 'Whatever objections may be raised elsewhere to women's work on the farm, it is welcomed at Sandringham.'[142] Three women, all from London, and all of whom had taken up farm work in the spring of 1916, had been hired to look after the livestock and dairy. Wearing white smocks and khaki armlets, they were now photographed cleaning out the cow sheds. This was just the sort of image that was selling well at the time. In 1916 magazines and newspapers were full of photographs of 'the new Land-Lady'.[143] Debutantes posed with ploughs, daughters of peers and judges sported smocks, and west-end actresses modelled breeches and pitchforks. As well as being conspicuous in their numbers, the Land Ladies are also conspicuous in their 'type'. These girls in rustic uniform were held up for the public to acclaim, essentially because they were doing something to which they were not accustomed. These were nice girls from good families heroically stepping out of their 'sphere'. There was far less propaganda mileage in the image of village woman doing dirty, ill-paid and repetitive jobs that they disliked – albeit there were far more of them working than there were peers' daughters. That reality looked less pretty on the page. Other realities were distorted too. The number of photographs gives the impression of a massing army of suitably-attired Amazons. One could believe that the countryside was full of appropriately tooled-up ladies. It's a false impression, though. By the end of the year 140,000 women had registered as available to work on the land. Although that in itself was an achievement, the number was far below the 400,000 that the government had targeted to recruit. The *Board of Trade Gazette* observed that the process of substituting female for male labour on the land had been slow 'and is in no way commensurate with that achieved in industrial and commercial occupations.' It noted: 'Prejudice on the part of the farmers, reluctance on the part of the women, insufficiency of housing accommodation, lowness of wages, have all proved serious obstacles.'[144]

Some women were just struggling on through those obstacles. After an unhappy attempt at nursing, Doris Robinson had decided to volunteer for land work. ('Animals can't answer back,' she remembered as her motive). By the winter of 1916 she was working on an estate near Loughton, singlehandedly managing the home farm. Doris recalled:

> *I had seven jersey cows and about 400 hens, and a goat, and ducks – there was only me. And I had to be there at six in the morning, you see, for milking. And I had to stay until about ten at night because they had a lot of eggs in incubators which had to be turned.*

She was working seven days a week, living in a single room in a cottage and after paying board, had barely enough money left at the end of the week to buy an egg. She explained: 'If I wanted a bath, I had to take newspapers and put them all round the greenhouse and then carry the water down there. Oh, it was a very tough time in those days.' Tough indeed. When Doris asked her employer if she could go to church on Christmas Day, he refused. She recounted: '"No" he said. "You can't go to church on Christmas Day. I pay you to work."'[145]

Olive Hockin was also having a tough time on an icy Dartmoor:

> *The country lay bound in a grip of iron, silent, lifeless, and unmoving. Birds fell frozen from their perches at night, and those that survived gathered daily about our door for crumbs. From all parts came news of skating, tobogganing, and other joys – but such were not for us! Turnips, sheep, hay, cows, calves, and turnips – such was the round that filled our days.*

And for Olive too Christmas Day, 1916, was much like any other working day:

> *Milking had to be done, and all the ravening beasts must be fed… There was no holly, even, to mark the passing of Christmas, for though there had been masses of berries back in*

the autumn, by December the starving birds had eaten them every one.[146]

1916 was the first really ominous year for agriculture. The area planted with wheat had contracted by twelve per cent year-on-year and the crop would be down almost twenty per cent. The prospects for the next year were looking bleak too; as at December, on account of bad weather and shortage of labour, only around forty per cent of the usual quantity of winter wheat had been sown. Also, for the first time, the availability of foreign supplies had shrunk back this year; the harvest was poor in America and, as Turkey had now allied with the Central Powers, the Dardanelles had shut to allied shipping, cutting off Russian imports. Added to this the last few months of the year had seen the German U-boat campaign in the North Atlantic shift up a gear. At the end of the year Britain's food security looked distinctly shaky.

Chapter 6

'Our Front is Where the Wheat Grows Fair'

The men must take the swords,
And we must take the ploughs,
Our Front is where the wheat grows fair,
Our Colours, orchard boughs.

The Land Army Song.

Food prices had gone up by forty-two per cent over the course of 1916. Putting food on the table was noticeably more expensive and more difficult by the start of 1917, but the public were told that the situation was worse in Germany. Stories about famine and food riots were printed. The press said that the endurance of the German people was reaching its limit. There was some morale boost in that, but it also heightened fears that similar conditions would follow here. Those fears would increase throughout the spring of 1917.

In the last three months of 1916 alarm had been raised by the sharp increase in losses of British shipping. Things were about to get worse though as, on 1 February 1917, Germany lifted its restrictions on submarine warfare. The aim of the campaign was to inflict such great losses that it would be impossible for the Allies to carry on with the war. In the first month nearly 500,000 tons of merchant shipping was lost and British newspapers reprinted taunting reports that had been published in the German press forecasting starvation in Britain and thus capitulation. The U-boat campaign would have a 'devastating result' said a piece from the *Norddeutsche Allgemeine Zeitung,* reproduced in the *Liverpool Echo.*

'OUR FRONT IS WHERE THE WHEAT GROWS FAIR'

The sinking of 100,000 tons of shipping means for England a deficit of about 250,000 tons of corn or food for the whole population of England for twelve days… We can safely reckon that England must come to the end of her tether in a period of time that can be easily calculated.[1]

The problem of food supply was suddenly pressing. With rising food prices, food shortages and perceived unfair distribution, unrest would start to break out across the country.

Food was now 'a munition of war', in Lloyd George's words, 'and in its production the national interest was asserted as paramount.'[2] The Food Production Department, tasked with co-ordinating the use and supply of land, materials, machinery and labour, was established on the 1 January 1917, under the direction of Sir Arthur Lee. Its primary focus would be to advance a 'Plough Policy' – targeting the addition of an extra two million acres of ploughed land by 1918. In order to realise this plan the Government now asked CWACs to appoint Executive Committees. These bodies would be given the power to enforce policy, to make farmers plough, to transfer control of the land if they weren't satisfied with how it was being managed and, if necessary, to take it on and plough it themselves.

The impact of this policy wouldn't be felt evenly across the country's diverse agricultural regions. In the well-established arable counties of eastern England there were limits to how much further farmers could go; while in the grazing districts of the midlands, south-west, the north and Wales, this conversion of land-use would be a hefty ask. Here farmers lacked the equipment, the know-how and the experience of arable farming – and, crucially, the necessary labour. Fundamentally, the land was not suited to arable use; these had evolved to be pastoral districts with good reason. In upland areas of the north, fields were small and scattered and the topography just wasn't appropriate. Tractors and ploughs broke on the long laid down and well-matted grasslands. It was here, then, that the policy was most resented. An article published in the *Berwick Advertiser* gives an insight into the opinion of the Northumberland CWAC. In 1916 there were just 177,886 arable acres in Northumbria. It fundamentally wasn't arable country, but, complying with Government requirements, the CWAC had set to work surveying the land, identifying areas that could be ploughed and improved and, in August, the CWAC submitted a list to the Food Production Department detailing what it would require in order to make an attempt at the targets that it had been set. This list included (amongst other things): 10 tractors, 400 pairs of horses, 500 harrows, 400 horsemen and 200 labourers.[3] Falling labour supply and a diktat for increased productivity wasn't a happy combination.

By mid-January men were needed for the army's spring offensive and so another 30,000 male agricultural workers were called up. Rowland Prothero told the Farmers' Club in London that this was 'a staggering blow' to him (a voice in the crowd shouted 'To all of us'), but he told them that substitute labour would be arriving within days and that there should therefore be 'no gap in agricultural operations.'[4] Writing later he acknowledged: 'In exchange for the skilled sturdy men with whom they were accustomed to work, farmers were offered strangers belonging to the C III category, unaccustomed to agricultural work, and physically unfitted for active service in the Army.' He added: 'Farmers grumbled that they were asked to keep infirmaries.'[5] In February he presented a Memorandum to the War Cabinet. It stated:

The position of agriculture is serious. The confidence of the farmer has been dangerously disturbed during the last two months. Unless it is restored, and restored immediately, production will shrink, and the country will be left with a very diminished supply of home-grown food for 1917, and little effort will be made to increase production for 1918. Food is wanted, and in as great abundance as possible. A system of guaranteed prices lasting over a series of years seems to me to be the only possible means which would restore confidence to the farmer and encourage him to embark upon increased production, with its attendant initial outlay and risk.[6]

A few days later Lloyd George addressed the House of Commons. He said:

> *At the present moment I want the country to know, our food stocks are low, alarmingly low – lower than they have been within recollection… It is essential, therefore, for the safety of the nation – for the maintenance of the nation, for the life of the nation – that we should put forth immediately every effort to increase production for this year's harvest and the next, and that we should do it immediately… Now the plough is our hope. You must cure the farmer of his plough fright, otherwise you will not get crops.*

To that end, Lloyd George outlined a schedule of minimum prices.[7]

The principle of introducing a minimum price had been approved by the War Cabinet on 13 December 1916, just four days after the government had been formed, but it would be August 1917 before the Corn Production Act finally came into law. Guaranteeing minimum prices for wheat (60*s* per quarter) and oats (38½*s* per quarter) for six years, it was hoped that this sweetener would remedy all 'plough fright'. The Act also introduced, for the first time, a minimum wage for agricultural workers. Farmworkers' unions had been campaigning for this since 1912 and, in real terms, agricultural earnings had actually fallen during the war. County Wages Boards, would now determine a local rate (to be rubber-stamped by London). This did not apply to women.

In a further effort to encourage expansion of the cultivated acreage, and to compensate farmers for their loss of labour, Prothero announced that he was organising a 'fleet of motor tractors'. The War Office would undertake to man, repair, and keep these tractors running and they would be placed at the disposal of CWACs. But these promises would fall short. With British engineering companies engaged full-time in the production of munitions and military vehicles, tractors had to be ordered from America and, with the pressure on shipping, few could be transported over to Britain in time for spring ploughing. In the end a much reduced collection of government-owned and privately-hired vehicles was pulled together and farmers complained that they spent more time repairing these temperamental machines than they did actually working the land. These early tractors particularly struggled to work long-established grasslands – exactly the type of terrain that the government was now asking farmers to plough.[8]

The War Office also agreed to supply some manpower for the spring cultivation; 12,500 men from the Home Defence Forces were promised, plus a further body of 12,000, to be detached and quartered in infantry depots in different parts of the country. However, as it turned out, not more than 3,000 out of the total number of military personnel released had any experience of ploughing. Therefore, in March, all skilled ploughmen serving in the forces in the country were asked to return to their depots. Unfortunately the weather was not playing the game though, and the season was unusually late. The Army Council extended furlough until May, but 18,000 ploughmen were recalled before the job was completed.[9]

Olive Hockin would now find herself supplanted by a soldier. By the end of January 1917 she had done a year on Dartmoor. Her co-worker, 'Jimmy', suffering with appendicitis, had left the farm permanently and Olive felt isolated without a companion. 'I could have sat down by the roadside and wept for sheer lonesomeness,' she wrote. 'My spirits were about as low as the thermometer, and on the same level was my rate of energy and inclination for work.' After a long journey through the snow with her sheep, she returned to be told that the farmer's application to the military had come through and that two soldiers had now arrived. 'They be proper old varrm-'ands,' the Maester told her, 'so now us'll get along a bit more shipshape!' Instead of feeling relief, Olive felt a sense of failure. There's also a sense a disappointment and frustration that, despite all her efforts, in securing the labour of a couple of soldiers, her employer was satisfied that he'd finally managed to get hold of some 'proper' farmhands. 'So that is how the end came,' Olive wrote. 'Our responsibility was over... All our beloved animals – horses, cows, calves, and cats, we left to the care of the borrowed soldiers.' She reflected:

*We may have been failures, but we did our best. We failed,
indeed, at the end; but the task was almost super-human. It
would have taxed the strength and endurance of any man not
brought up to the work from childhood, as the hardened
labourers are. Looking around among men I know, I can hardly
think of one who would have stood one week of the work that
we did.*[10]

Things would change, though, for the women who followed. And
womanpower was still very much needed. As Olive was leaving, the
Government was working on a new scheme to bring more women onto
farms.

Around this time Miss E. Righton-Trice was just finishing a post
as well and returning to her home county of Somerset. She had been
working on the land for two and a half years and, in her own words,
had 'done the hardest and dirtiest work on a farm.' Having been taught
milking in Wiltshire, she had completed stints on farms in Essex,
Ealing and Berkshire, where she had done several months as a
stockman. As an experienced worker, she was now receiving lots of
offers of work. Within ten days of being back at home, she had already
been offered three jobs. 'I shall soon be at work again,' she said. 'I
want to get back to it, because we women workers feel something like
soldiers – directly they get leave they get bad colds. I shall be quite
happy to get back to the animals.'[11]

Skilled women were in demand now and a formula was being
developed to make them available in greater numbers. In January,
Prothero told a meeting of farmers in Hereford:

*They would not say to them, "Here is a dirty and monotonous
piece of work, badly paid, and with poor accommodation," but
the appeal would be in this form: "you will be paid a soldier's
rate of pay; you will be billeted just like ordinary soldiers. You
will be part of the army supply service of this kingdom, and you
have thus an opportunity of going into the 'trenches' on just the
same terms as your brothers are doing."*

Prothero meant to raise an 'army' of 200,000 women, the papers said, uniformed, billeted and paid like soldiers. They must be prepared to be sent wherever they were needed and were in it 'for the duration'. The intention was to put women workers on a national 'war service' basis.[12]

Behind the ideas, behind even the choice of words that Prothero was using, was Louisa Wilkins. In December 1916 there had been a meeting between Prothero and a deputation from the WNLSC. As it had become clear that another raft of men was about to leave the land, Louisa Wilkins had started working on plans for what might practically be done to counter the coming deficit of labour. In a detailed report she laid out the practical workings and ethos of what would become the Women's Land Army (WLA). With such significant input from Louisa Wilkins, it's not surprising that the arrangement that emerged owed much to earlier efforts and ideas. It took the most successful elements of the WNLSC and tailored them to meet the present need.[13]

The new Food Production Department's divisions included a 'Women's Branch'. Staffed entirely by women, this agency was tasked with increasing the number of women working in agriculture. Meriel Talbot was appointed to head the Women's Branch and would now be in charge of the recruitment and co-ordination of the Women's Land Army. Talbot had served for many years as secretary to the Victoria League and then, in 1916, had been appointed the first woman inspector with the Board of Agriculture. Nicknamed 'Slasher' Talbot on account of her prowess with a cricket bat, she was described as a giving 'the impression that she had just got off a ship after a tremendous hammering on the high seas, and is feeling all the better for that shaking up, and doesn't care a button if her hair is a little disarranged and her garments anyhow.'[14] Whatever the impression of disarray, Talbot was a focused and ambitious woman and had a long-term vision for her new role; she hoped that the WLA's impact would extend beyond the duration of the war – that this would just be the start of a permanent move for women into a revitalised agriculture. She now gathered a group of like-minded women around her, including her sister-in-law, Edith Lyttelton, who was appointed deputy director. One of the founders of the Victoria League, Lyttelton additionally served on the Executive Committee of the National Union of Women Workers and was a popular novelist.[15] Talbot also recruited Lady Gertrude Denman as honorary director of the WLA. Lady Denman was Vice-Chairman of the National Land Council, Chairman of the Women's Section of the National Poultry Society and Chairman of the Women's Institute Sub-Committee of the Agricultural Organisation Society (through which she would shortly become Chairman of the National Federation of Women's Institutes). With her hands-on commitment – and her political and social connections – Denman was an excellent appointee for the WLA. Her friend Eleanor ('Nellie') Grant became the WLA County Organiser for Dorset, and the two of them often attended rallies together. According to the biography written by Grant's son-in-law, Gervas Huxley, they would put on Land Army uniforms and tour the southern counties making speeches from their car:

> *Stopping the car in the middle of the High Street or in the Market Place of towns, one of them would attract the public's attention by rotating a policeman's very heavy wooden alarm rattle, which made an ear-splitting noise. After this, the other would make a rousing speech standing on top of the car. Sometimes they were invited to use the stage of theatres or cinemas, and once, in Portsmouth, they followed a turn by performing dogs, and had a riotous reception from a sailor audience.*[16]

The recruitment campaign for the WLA was launched in March 1917. Notices placed in the national and regional press (under the banner of the National Service Department) announced: '10,000 Women Wanted at Once to Grow and Harvest the Victory Crops.' The adverts called for 5,000 Milkers, 4,000 Field Workers and 1,000 Carters. A second raft of advertisements went out a month later, calling for '10,000 Strong Healthy Women Wanted At Once as Milkmaids'. The adverts of mid-April also appealed to candidates' families (just as army recruiting posters had appealed to men's wives and mothers): 'Mothers of England, give your girls a chance – urge them to enrol today in the Women's Land Army.' And mothers were offered some reassurance in return for letting their daughters go. 'These Land Army recruits will be sent to carefully-selected farms,' advised a Press Bureau statement, 'where they will be under the care and protection of supervisors, appointed by the Women's War Agricultural Committees. No parent need be afraid for the future of her girl.'[17]

Posters were issued ('God Speed the Plough and the Woman Who Drives It' is proclaimed beneath the image of a woman pushing a plough towards a stylised sunset) and the recruiting campaign extended on to the cinema screen as well. Film companies were commissioned to make short pieces, showing all varieties of women's work on farms. A recruiting talk usually accompanied their screening. Rallies and demonstrations, meanwhile, took the campaign on to the streets and in to parks and fields. These often showcased women carrying out traditionally 'male' agricultural tasks, like ploughing and manure spreading. Such energetic displays pulled crowds (and newspaper column inches) and allowed the message to be delivered directly and forcefully to local audiences. These were conceived as being occasions not only to recruit, but also to convince farmers, and the wider public, of the worth of women's work and also to boost the morale and camaraderie of those participating.

It was a substantial and sustained recruiting campaign. Lots of energy was applied to it. And it needed to be. The Women's Branch had to work hard as land work had so many disadvantages over other forms of war work and employment open to women. Wages were comparably poor, hours were long, accommodation often basic and in lonely remote places. It was hard, heavy, dirty work and the contribution of such labours to the war effort could feel remote. This wasn't directly, obviously war work. As Gladys Pott put it, 'Munition making, hospital nursing, canteen management, and the like all appear to be directly connected with Army organisation, and to be essential to the prosecution of the war. They therefore possess a glamour and attraction which is absent in Agricultural work.'[18] It simply was not possible to pretend that the negatives did not exist; if they were going to stick at it, women had to go into this work with their eyes open. But these very disadvantages would be spun into virtues. Yes, this work was gruelling, but it was also wholesome, healthy and self-improving, the propaganda claimed. It was also essential; that more than anything was underlined. It was imperative that someone made this effort, and the hardships along the way? Well, they were noble self-sacrifice. Duty and comradeship were emphasised. They were all bravely in it together – just like the men in the trenches. Rowland Prothero, speaking at a recruiting rally in London, said:

> *I do not pretend that work on the land is attractive to many women. It is hard work; fatiguing, back-aching work. It is for long spells monotonous. It is dirty work. Work in all sorts of weather. It is poorly paid, and the accommodation is rough, and those who undertake it have to face physical discomforts. In all those respects it is comparable to the work your men folk are doing in the trenches at the front. It is not a case of "lilac sunbonnets". (Laughter.) There is no romance in it. It is prose.*[19]

It could be made into lively prose, though. Miss May Kemble ('a land worker') told a Chelmsford rally:

> *No girl who had experience of the health and freedom of the land would go back to the cooped-up city life. Of course there were the winter mud and rain, but women did not want "soft" jobs while the men were risking their lives – (cheers) – and after seeing the pictures of the Somme battle there would be no more grousing about mud at home "for the duration."*[20]

Its strenuousness, its mundanity and its mud: taking this on was the finest form of patriotism. And the message hit its mark. By the start of May, 22,603 women had come forward and applications were now reported to be coming in 'at a rate of about 600 a day.'[21] The administration was almost overwhelmed by the response.

Volunteers for the WLA were required to be aged over 18, healthy, physically capable and of the right character; they were looking for stable, robust girls with a good constitution and a positive attitude. As had been the case with the WNLSC, there was a lot of emphasis on the latter. Land Army girls had to be 'the right sort'. At first women were required to sign on for the duration of the war, but this was amended, early in 1918, to a commitment of six months or one year. Volunteers were asked to fill in enrolment forms, which were made available in post offices and Labour Exchanges, and had to supply three character references. In need of such a statement, Annie Edwards approached the wife of her Canon. 'Do you know what it involves?' she asked Annie. 'It means that you will be dressed as a man! And I object to that. It's a disgrace to show your ankles.' Her father also evidently had some concerns about her being away from home, fearing that she might be tempted into 'loose' or 'wild' ways. Annie, who in her own words had been brought up 'strict', evidently gave the moral and religious implications of this life choice much serious thought. But she was determined that wearing men's clothes would not change her. 'God will steer me,' said Annie. 'The same as he has always done.' Thus she 'branched out for a good cause.'[22]

If an application form was successful, the woman would then be summoned to appear before a Joint Committee of the Employment Exchange and the District Selection and Allocation Committee of the local WWAC. More than 200 local Selection Committees were now set up. Candidates had to have a medical examination and their suitability would be assessed at interview. All of this was often a frustrating slow process, though, and many girls gave up part way through and secured alternative private employment.

The strictness with which selection criteria were applied is evident from the percentage of women who were rejected. Prothero wrote that, in total, 45,000 women responded to the first appeal, but only twenty-five per cent of them came up to the standard.[23] The reliability of this ratio seems to be borne out by local figures. In Devon, 329 women had applied by June 1917, but of these only ninety-six (twenty-nine per cent) were accepted. Mostly the girls who were turned down were from Plymouth and deemed 'not suited in any way for country life'.[24] In East Riding, twenty-eight per cent of women who applied were accepted and in both Berkshire and Northumberland, thirty-four per cent.[25] In Durham, only 144 of the 789 women who had volunteered (eighteen per cent) were deemed 'as physically or otherwise suitable'.[26]

By September 1917, the WLA had 6,000 'carefully chosen' (the words are Edith Lyttelton's) women in its ranks.[27] The numbers of women in the Land Army was never vast. At its peak, in September 1918, there were 16,000 members; at that same time Prothero reckoned that, 'at a conservative estimate', there were 320,000 part-time women workers in agriculture.[28] It was the village women, not the WLA, who were the mainstay of food production. The significance of the WLA was not therefore in its numbers. Rather, the Land Army was about making a statement – to other women as much as to farmers. It was about showing that women could do this work, do it well and feel proud of their contribution. In that sense, the WLA was a propaganda vehicle: it was about making an impression – and that it did. 'Breeched, booted and cropped, she broke with startling effect upon the sleepy traditionalism of the English countryside,' Lloyd George wrote of the Land Girl.[29]

While many of the initial recruits were from middle and upper-class backgrounds, it was not universally the case. As time went on, and the need for numbers became greater, so the socio-economic profile of the WLA broadened. Mary Lees, who would now find herself training WLA recruits, observed that many had come from 'slums in the city'.[30] Mary might have considered Patricia Vernon to be one of those city slum girls. Patricia, who was from Tooting, was in domestic service when the war broke out. She was still in her teens, a 'between maid', and had just been sacked for dropping a leg of lamb. Seeing an advert for the WLA she decided to take her chance.[31] Annie Edwards, from West Sussex, had also been in service as a cook. After a few months of doing voluntary work for the Red Cross, she had seen a poster which demanded, 'Join the Land Army'. 'I liked the soil,' Annie recalled. She had grown up on a farm and when she was in domestic service could not help herself from going out into the garden and weeding. Thus, with her employer's blessing (and having assured herself that she was not contravening any moral boundaries), she volunteered.[32] Helen Poulter was a machinist in a London leatherworks before joining the WLA. Her fellow forestry workers in Sussex were all Londoners, she remembered, with the exception of two titled ladies and a French governess.[33] Such mixing does not seem to have been abnormal. The East Kent WWAC reported, in October 1917, that the women who had volunteered for the Land Army in the county were a 'wonderful mixture of types'. It was observed: 'Before enrolling in the Land Army many of them had been working in munition factories; as domestic servants or in breweries, others had been school mistresses, while a considerable number had done no previous work and only came forward on the land out of patriotic desire to do useful work.'[34]

Motives for joining the WLA were varied. Aside from wanting to do their bit, land work attracted girls who liked nature or animals. Rosa Freedman had always helped her father on their allotment.[35] Annie Edwards' testimony not only conveys a love for working on the land, but also a sense of pride at working hard and well. 'I had my heart and soul in it,' she recalled. 'I liked it. The time used to go so fast. You never thought of looking at your clock, or watch, or anything.'[36] Kathleen Gilbert was working in London as a munitions worker, but her parents were country people and her father had always worked with horses on farms, so the idea appealed to her. 'I was always one for adventure,' she said. She liked the 'outdoor life' and 'I suppose it was in my blood to be with horses. That was what it was. Ever since I was a tiny dot we'd been used to horses.'[37] The *Western Daily* published an account of the experiences of a Bristol girl in the WLA. 'I was always fond of the open-air life and school games,' she told the paper, 'and I find a love of animals a help; they know, even if they are young and mischievous colts, when you are kind to them, and I am sure it is a healthy life.'[38]

For other women it was something to do while their husbands were serving in the forces. Mrs M. Bale's husband was in the RAMC. She recalled: 'As there was no hope of any home leave from then until the war was over, my sister and I joined the Women's Land Army. We enrolled at Weymouth and asked to do horticultural work.'[39] Sisters and friends often seem to have signed up together. Grace Elsey saw a poster of a Land Girl and that inspired her to want to join. She recalled her mother seeing it too and remarking, 'There is our Grace!' Her father couldn't see it, though. He wanted her to join the police and so tore up her first set of application papers. Her sister, Clara Harding, volunteered because Grace had and they usually managed to stick together on their placements.[40] Helen Poulter was living in a London flat and, prior to joining the WLA, hadn't spent any time in the country. 'I didn't know what country was,' she recalled. 'No. I was a real Londoner.' But her mother had just died suddenly and, having been told by her doctor that some time out of the city would do her good, the idea appealed. She signed-up with her friend and work colleague, Lizzie. They managed to stick together too.[41]

From 1918, if recruits were prepared to sign on for twelve months, they could choose whether to work in either: the Land Army Agricultural Section (the L.A.A.S. – generally known as 'the Lasses' – administered by the Board of Agriculture), the Forage Corps (under the auspices of the War Office) or the Timber section (the administration of which came under the Timber Supply Department of the Board of Trade). But if volunteers were only prepared to sign on for six months, they had to join either the Agricultural or Timber sections. Women must agree to work in any district where they were required and be prepared to be transferred temporarily to the other sections of the WLA if deemed necessary. This commitment to mobility differentiated the WLA from other women's labour organisations.

The Selection Committee would decide at interview if a candidate was sufficiently skilled to go straight on to a farm as a paid worker. One such was Florence Dundee, who was already working on the land at the start of the war. She decided to join the WLA, though, because she had 'had words with my dad!' Having never previously been more than half a mile from home, she now wanted to be away.[42] If women did not already have experience, they could either go to an approved farm for training under the 'bursary system' or be sent to a training farm or centre. Under the bursary system recruits worked for the farmer who would ultimately employ them. In consideration of providing some training, the farmer was allowed to have the recruit for three weeks without paying her any wages, but during this period the Land Army made an allowance for the woman's maintenance. Training farms took women on for four to six weeks, before they were moved on to paid employment elsewhere. Training centres were generally set up on farms, or in the centre of a district in which there were several farms suitable for training, or were hosted by agricultural colleges. At first the period of training at these centres was restricted to four weeks, but this was found to be insufficient and the period was extended to six weeks.[43] The Board of Agriculture stipulated that all courses must include instruction in milking, feeding calves, hoeing, haymaking and general harvesting tasks. The shortness of the courses, however, meant that training was far from comprehensive and it was usually the case that, in reality, women arrived on farms and had to learn on the job. Gladys Pott wrote:

> It is not pretended that six weeks' training can turn out a skilled worker. But it has proved successful in enabling a girl to learn to milk, and to obtain an insight into the kinds of jobs she will be expected to undertake upon a farm. It affords her the opportunity of practising her muscles in the performance of tasks to which they are unaccustomed, and which when first undertaken cause them to ache and give considerable discomfort.[44]

Annie Edwards was sent to a training farm, Drayton Manor, in Chichester, to do a six-week course. This involved doing 'a little bit of everything,' she recalled – working with horses, ploughing, hoeing and milking cows. 'I had to milk a cow and that done me. I dreaded it,' Annie confessed. 'I'm a coward of cows.' The horses, though, which she'd been around since childhood, were a pleasure to work with. 'I took to horses,' said Annie. 'I thought to myself: I'm going to make a go of it.' At the end of six weeks she had a railway warrant to go on to Hampshire, but, as she was packing to leave, the farmer asked her if she would stay on the farm.[45]

There were two other Land Girls on the Nottinghamshire farm to which inexperienced Patricia Vernon was sent for training. They said 'It's your turn to milk the bull in the morning.' Patricia hadn't been away from home long, 'and didn't know a bull from a sparrow.' She went on:

It was a blooming great thing... I wonder where I get the milk from? I don't know. All I could see was his tail. So, I thought, perhaps if I pull the tail the milk will come out. So I went pulling the tail, like this, and he let out such a roar. The whole neighbourhood woke up.

After that she was put in the piggery. Finding the piglets disagreeably dirty, she decided to give them all a wash.[46]

In June 1917 a correspondent for the *Whitby Gazette* went along to see how Land Army trainees were getting on at (the appropriately named) Intake Farm, at Littlebeck, near Whitby. He found the women 'clod-breaking', and going about this monotonous duty cheerfully. Mr Ventrees, the farmer, spoke in glowing terms of how the women had adapted and learned new tasks. 'Probably this is not to be wondered at,' the journalist observed, 'seeing they have been treated as members of the family and everything done to make their stay a profitable and pleasant one.'[47] It wasn't always quite so homely. In Northumbria, a training centre opened at Wideopen, on the land of the Cramlington Coal Company. The government contributed funds to furnish a house and paid towards the women's training, while other expenses ('cows, dummy cows, and a nanny goat for teaching the girls to milk') were met by the Coal Company. The centre was training eight girls per month.[48] Mary Lees, who had trained at Seale-Hayne in 1916, now had her own protégées. Her employer at Dulverton had set up a hostel and Mary was allocated 'completely raw' recruits to whip into shape. 'They used to talk about horses' paws!' she recalled. 'I had to kick them around.'[49]

That training methods varied so much across the country was in part to do with farmers' attitudes. While in Leicestershire more than sixty farmers offered their facilities to train Land Army recruits, in Devon not a single one came forward.[50] Many trainees in Devon were therefore sent to Seale-Hayne. In October 1917 a journalist for the *Exeter and Plymouth Gazette* visited the college and described a typical day for the students:

There may be seen women being trained in milking, in cleaning out cow-sheds, pig-styes, and calf-pens, in feeding pigs and suckling calves, in separating, in taking their share of the work in the sheep fold, or in the poultry yard, most of which is done before breakfast, and done with a smiling face and every indication that the neophyte enjoys it. After breakfast the new worker is either churning, making butter or cheese, or she has gone out to do field work, filling dung cart or spreading it, driving a pair of horses in the harrows, or roller, or during harvest she could be seen loading or pitching the sheaves, and, in her eagerness, soon putting to shame some of the sterner sex, who had been at it, not only a few days, but perhaps weeks and months, or she might be seen on the corn rick, passing sheaves to the rick builder. In non-harvest weather, she could be singling mangels and turnips, cutting thistles and weeds generally, besides ordinary hoeing, and, although her back ached, she felt she was 'doing her bit' and that she must hold out.

The journalist remarked (with some evident surprise) on how the women did not seem to mind getting dirty. One student told him, 'The dirtier the work the more I like it.' He reflected: 'To see the avidity with which one-time nurses and teachers take to sheep-washing and sheep-shearing, hunting out maggots, and applying dressings for the cure of foot-rot, fully corroborates this, yet with it all there seems to be no loss of refinement and no coarsening of their natures.' He observed that the students were drawn from 'the professional, trade, and working classes' and all seemed to be deriving satisfaction from the thought of their patriotic contribution.[51] In May 1918, Seale-Hayne College was acquired as a hospital for neurasthenic soldiers. Up to that point, 300 women had received agricultural training there.[52] With the college closing, the WLA launched a training programme at Great Bidlake, on the edge of Dartmoor, a formerly derelict farm which had been commandeered by the Devon CWAC. Over the course of the next year at least forty women would be taught to milk at Great Bidlake.[53]

Holmes Chapel was another agricultural college which took on Land Army trainees. The Holmes Chapel School of Agriculture and Horticulture had been established in 1895, by Cheshire County Council, to train young men but, since the start of the war, it didn't have enough male students to keep going. It now seemed like an ideal place to train WLA recruits and the first forty-five women began their four-week course in April 1917. The Principal of the College, Miss P. Bowen-Colthurst, reported that, though most of the girls had no prior experience, they stuck to the work:

I have not had a single case of complaint of long hours, of illness or overwork... The dairy girls have in a remarkably short time attained an intelligent knowledge of cheese and butter making and one was placed in a diary making cheese from the milk of seventy cows. All our girls have been placed.

During 1917, 199 students passed through the college. The *Cheshire Observer* applauded the successes of the Holmes Chapel alumnae:

One girl is a forewoman on a threshing machine with about eight girls under her – another a forewoman over potato pickers (soon to be made bailiff on a small farm). Another is bailiff to a farmer at Maghull. Another under-forewoman to a large buyer and seller in Lancashire. Several are driving milk carts.[54]

Holmes Chapel had experienced difficulties in training women milkers as there weren't enough dairy cows available and the same problem

111

was encountered elsewhere. Large numbers of novices couldn't be let loose on valuable, and not necessarily patient, milkers. Clara Harding recalled: 'I learned to milk a cow on an old chap's thumbs. He used to hold them up like that and he said, "Now you take my thumbs and squeeze when I tell you to." That's how I learned to milk a cow.' Grace Elsey, Clara's sister and fellow novice, added that the male farmworkers deserved a medal for putting up with women who had so little training.[55] Many women learned to milk on the 'artificial udder'. Beatrice Oaks had enrolled for land work in 1916 and was now teaching Land Army trainees on the 'automatic cow'. She explained: 'It consisted of a canvas bag on four legs, complete with four rubber teats. The bag was filled with water, and the teats adjusted by screws to allow hard or easy milking. I suspect it was as valuable in terms of merriment as it was in practical instruction.'[56] The *Illustrated War News* told its readers, 'After a certain amount of practice, the beginner is promoted to a goat, then, as her confidence increase, is allowed to get to work on a cow.'[57] Beatrice Bennett started her training on 'a rubber cow full of water.' When she was eventually allowed to get to work on a real cow her first pail 'went west'. Aside from milking, Beatrice's training involved stacking and sorting potatoes, harvesting cabbages, turnips, swedes and carrots, muck carting, and caring for horses and cattle. Everything that they did in training was muddy. 'You cannot stick a pin on my nice velvet breeches for white mud an inch thick,' she wrote. But this was all taken in good spirits. 'We laughed until tears came and all we could say was, "What would Mother say if she could see us now?"'[58]

Other women opted to pay for their own training; Betty Farquhar wanted to join the Land Army, 'but I thought I should be more useful if I had some real knowledge and training.' She therefore registered for one of the courses being offered by Reading University at the time 'to prepare girls for land work.' She detailed: 'We learned dairy work, butter and cheese making, milking cows (by hand), and received lectures on the welfare of stock.'[59] For some the training would go further; fifteen land workers were selected by the Board of Agriculture to take an advanced course, so that they could become instructors and bailiffs. The six-month course at Wye College in Kent covered 'agricultural zoology, mycology, botany, economics, surveying, building construction, soils and manures, foods and feeding, stock, dairy, veterinary science, crops, implements, book-keeping, poultry, vegetable growing and horticulture.'[60]

By 1918 the WLA was also operating Probationary Training Centres, set up for candidates who had failed the medical. Many of these were women who had been working in munitions – 'Many of these girls, too anaemic and worn-out to go on with this work, are as keen as mustard to follow their doctor's advice and go on the land'. The Probationary Training Centres gave them light outside duties and regular food and tried to get them back to health ('at the end of four weeks she feels a different creature'), at which point they would be passed on to a regular training centre.[61]

By September 1917, 247 training centres and 140 training farms were operating.[62] With much devolved to local level, training methods varied considerably across the country – as did their successes. Between March 1917 and May 1919, 23,000 women passed through the Land Army's training centres.[63]

The first recruits were informed that they would be provided with: 'a serviceable and picturesque dress made to measure which will mark them as soldiers in the Women's Land Army.'[64] The WLA uniform consisted of: boots, gaiters, clogs, overalls, breeches, hats, a jersey and a mackintosh. Though it perhaps lacked the tailored glamour of some of the other services, it gave them a collective identity. It was intended that this would make them feel like they were doing important war work and give them something to live up to. And they weren't allowed to forget that. The WLA handbook stipulated:

The Government has given you your sensible uniform and expects you to make sure that it is always treated with respect. It looks much better without jewellery or lace frills, for when you are at work the smartest thing is to look workmanlike. Keep jewellery and lace for the days when you wear your ordinary clothes. You are doing a man's work and so you are dressed rather like a man; but remember just because you wear a smock and breeches you should take care to behave like an English girl who expects chivalry and respect from everyone she meets.[65]

What certain members of the public feared most about women taking on 'man's work' is summed up by an article published in the *Sunday Mirror*. The writer of the piece recounted meeting a group of women land workers. (This he identified 'by their dusty boots, hot faces, and generally hay-bestrewn hair.') On realising that he had formerly known one of these 'Amazons', the writer was taken back – 'A girl I had known before the war! Seventeen then – very fair and fragile. Now aged about twenty-one – very firm and large and wide and stalwart.' But it wasn't just her appearance that had changed. It was her voice and manner too: 'She not only looked larger. She spoke louder. Her language was brief and vigorous. Yes – that was the general impression. She was a man. She had become a man.' When the writer suggested to her that, after the war, she would 'have to be a woman again', the land worker replied: 'I could never go back to the old life. I can't be a lily in a china vase again. I'm henceforward a wildflower.' The writer asided that she was perhaps more accurately a stinging nettle. He concluded that women were being spoilt by this 'unwomanly' work. 'It deforms their physical constitution,' he asserted. 'It is man's work. It makes women into men.'[66]

The process of 'becoming men' was sometimes, generally jokingly, referred to by the women themselves – that or becoming a third sex: 'Some time ago, as I was passing three small boys, I overheard one say: "Why, it's a man!" "Nor it ain't," said the second, "it's a woman." "It ain't neither," said the third, "it's a landworker!"'[67] But this sort of attitude, both within the organisation and externally, was something that the WLA deliberately positioned itself to counter. The women were encouraged not to be 'mannish'. At a rally in Hereford Edith Lyttelton appealed to the girls 'to uphold the dignity of the uniform'. She told them: 'When people see you go by they know you at once; they say, "There goes a Land Army girl." See to it that this phrase means, "There goes a steady, pure-minded, hard-working, yes, and *attractive* girl.'" She reminded them that they were pioneers, that in a sense the whole reputation of their sex lay on their shoulders, to make or to mar. 'Just because you are dressed like a man, just *because* you wear no skirts, we want you to behave like a woman.'[68] At a rally in Gloucester Meriel Talbot reminded the audience 'that just because they were dressed like a man, just because they wore no skirts, their friends wanted them to behave like a woman.'[69] The message was repeated: they were dressed like men, but had to counter this by spotless respectability, by retaining feminine good manners.

'There is nothing frivolous in instancing the admirable choice of the workmanlike yet becoming uniform of the Land Army,' Rowland Prothero wrote. 'Even Victorian prejudice grew reconciled to the dress or found solace in the reflection that it was very Greek.'[70] That Victorian prejudice was still around in 1917, though. Annie Edwards recalled an old lady's comments: "Hmm. Neither man nor a woman' – because I never had a long skirt on.' Annie herself didn't like wearing trousers at first – not because she felt unladylike, but because she found them uncomfortable. There were other feminine garments that she was happy to abandon, though. Wet through with sweat and sore in her steel-boned corset, Annie walked away from the summer harvesting and took her corset off in a barn. She threw it into an outside lavatory. 'I throwed them right down in there,' she recalled. 'And from that day to this I've nothing at all. Nothing!'[71] Helen Poulter was also self-conscious about her Forestry Corps uniform. In the spring of 1918 she travelled from London to Sussex to begin work in a black mourning dress, silk stockings and high-heeled shoes. She would remain in (and work in) her 'civilian' clothes for the next fortnight, as she and her fellow new recruits waited for their uniforms to arrive – and then waited again for the wrongly-sized uniforms to be replaced. Helen swapped her black cashmere dress for breeches ('thick, hard, corduroy things'), puttees and men's army boots. The boots were heavy and hurt, but it seems to have been the breeches that bothered her most. It was the first time that she had ever worn trousers, she recalled, and 'they were most uncomfortable at first.' What's more she felt 'terrible' about wearing them in public. 'We knew we were being looked at, you know, and talked about.'[72] The Bristol girl who wrote an account of her experiences for the *Western Daily* was amused to be talked about:

> *Naturally, perhaps, people stared at first to see a girl in breeches and leggings and farm overall; but their remarks, if plain, were amusing to me... One of our dairy women says she is going to wear breeches like me, and her husband says if she does he'll wear petticoats and skirts! Certainly the 'un-mentionables' are the most comfortable working costume I have discovered.* [73]

Many women appreciated the practicality of their uniform. Beatrice Bennett revelled in the freedom and the break from polite conventions of ladylike dress and deportment:

> *After dinner tonight we had some music. It is strange to see the girls dancing, breeches and jerseys, a log hut with a stove in the middle... We have not seen a soul since we arrived, outside camp people. A fire in the woods and such figures as we cut would frighten people anyway. We dress in sou'westers and short oilskin coats and no smocks. We look like Skipper Sardines.* [74]

Victorian prudery might be fading, but an Edwardian smirk replaced it. The breeches were a gift to cartoonists; images multiplied showing farmers (and menfolk in general) baffled by assertive trouser-wearing women – and also the women blithely, girlishly, getting it all wrong. The instantly-recognisable Land Girl became a *Punch* favourite and the breeches even generated their own genre of mildly risqué postcards.

During the first year of the WLA's operation the Women's Branch expended £130,037 (around £8m in 2015-terms) on clothing.[75] Uniforms worked hard and women went through them fast. Members only got one item of each piece of clothing (excepting two overalls) upon enrollment. Further items would then be issued after training and a month of satisfactory work. Four pairs of breeches could be issued within two years, but any more than that had to be bought by the girl herself.[76] It's no surprise then that WLA's magazine, *The Landswoman,* is full of adverts for clothing. That Harrods advertises a 'Land Outfit' (25*s*) says something about the social status of certain of the women, but most of them complained at the expense of renewing kit. And photographs show that, in practice, uniform really was not quite so *uniform.* There was much variation and personalisation and while 'jewellery or lace frills' might officially be outlawed, they were evidently not entirely abandoned. Reporting on a demonstration of land work in Essex a journalist for the *Chelmsford Chronicle* observed: 'Although the girls appeared in masculine attire, they remained very feminine all the same.' The 'farmer girls' had adopted various 'articles of adornment', he noted. Their jewellery choices were remarked upon and the fact that they gave off 'a faint odour of scent not usually associated with labour on the land.' The journalist obviously appreciated seeing these feminising touches. (Though it perhaps was not quite what Mmes. Talbot and Lyttelton had in mind.)[77]

When the Wages Board was set up at the start of 1917, it was suggested that 12-15*s* per week might be a suitable wage for women – but by March 1917 those volunteering for the Land Army were offered a minimum wage of 18*s*:

> As soon as the trained recruit starts her independent career on *a farm, she will receive not less than 18s a week, with the usual bonuses for special work and harvesting. Wherever the district rate is higher than 18s, the pay given to women workers recruited under this scheme will be higher also. A girl's earnings above 18s a week will depend upon her energy, intelligence, and skill. When she can rear, take to market, and sell a prize beast, or take a good crop off a piece of derelict land, she will be worth high wages to her employer, and her War Agricultural Committee will see that she gets it.[78]*

Wages were lower than in other branches of war work (by comparison, unskilled munitions workers were starting on a salary of around 25*s* per week in 1917), but it was deemed inappropriate for WLA members to be paid significantly more than local workers.[79] E. N. Thomas wrote:

The present low rate of pay militates heavily against securing a sufficient number of suitable land workers, and it is very probably one of the chief reasons why not more than half of the original volunteers follow up their cards by appearing before a Selection Committee.[80]

Thomas added that it was practically impossible to maintain 'a decent existence' on 18*s* per week. Clara Harding paid 12*s* per week for board out of her 18*s* earnings. 'It was murder!' she recalled. 'You couldn't even get to the pictures and back for that. I said to the farmer once, "This wage is enough to put a girl on the streets."'[81] The minimum rate of pay was raised, early in 1918, to 20*s* per week – and could be over 22*s* if women passed proficiency tests.

For this meagre salary they were expected to do a typical day of ten to twelve hours, according to a directory for women workers.[82] The length of the working day varied considerably though, depending on the woman's particular circumstances and the time of year, and often the hours were substantially longer. Annie Edwards, recalled working 'from dawn 'til dusk' in summer. 'We always went to work just as it was getting light, the old birds twittering about, you know – and the owls, at the night the owls started hollering as we went home from work.'[83] It's something that reoccurs in the recollections of these women – the length of the day and just how hard they were expected to work for their money.

It was often heavy work too. Traditionally women had done the lighter jobs on farms, their roles rarely extending to working with stock or machinery. Carters, shepherds, stockmen and ploughmen were just that – *men*. In August 1918 a survey of 12,657 members of the Land Army recorded their occupations: 5,734 were milkers, 3,971 field workers, 635 carters, 293 tractor drivers, 260 ploughmen, 84 thatchers, 21 shepherds, with the remaining 1,659 being in mixed roles.[84] While the majority of the women might be designated as milkers, the reality on most farms was that there was a great deal of variety to the day and a wide range of tasks would have to be learnt.

Rosa Freedman, in domestic service before the war, began her career in the Land Army going from farm-to-farm as part of a threshing gang, but soon found herself doing a bit of everything:

> *We were in a mobile group – sent where we were most needed which made the job very varied. Once we worked on a market garden picking frosted sprouts and in the spring pulling rhubarb and other produce for the market. We picked fruit at Dumpton Park, Broadstairs. The over-ripe fruit was put in barrels for a jam factory. We picked raspberries, gooseberries, blackcurrants, plums and apples, climbing tall trees with baskets tied around our waists.*

At other times she was flax pulling, haymaking, cleaning out pigsties, cow pens and stables, muck-spreading and mincing mangelwurzels for cow feed. On one of her last assignments she was attached to the Women's Volunteer Reserve near Cambridge and had to guard fodder, destined for horses in France. (She recalled, 'while on duty we would watch the Red Cross trains going through with the wounded, the railway lines being free at night.') Rosa reflected: 'The work was hard, but after the discipline and confinement of domestic service I found the work liberating and rewarding… it was a job we set out to do and I hope I did my best.'[85]

Florence Dundee worked on the estate of the Earl of Selborne. There she did milking, driving, ploughing and harvesting. In her own words she could turn her hand to 'everything' – 'and I used to love it all.' Starting as a dairymaid, she rose to stockman.[86] Some women excelled with stock and horses. Annie Edwards was quickly recognised as having 'the making of a good horsewoman' and became a skilled plough operator. Men came to watch her plough. 'Two or three farmers wouldn't believe it,' she recalled. 'And they'd come on this farm and they'd see me doing it. And one patted me on the back. They said, "It's really unbelievable."'[87] Kathleen Gilbert had the same inclinations. When the farmer on her first placement asked if any woman would be interested in working with horses, Kathleen was quick to volunteer. 'My hand shot up, quick as lightening,' she recalled. In addition to caring for horses, she would soon be carting, hoeing, harrowing and ploughing. 'I could plough pretty well a straight furrow,' she said. Her employers complimented her skill and coaches sometimes stopped on the road to watch her working the plough. She also did a lot of muck spreading. 'You didn't take any notice of the dirt,' she reflected. 'Didn't take a bit of notice of it!' When she wasn't working with the horses, Kathleen was haymaking and also did a season fruit picking in Wisbeach. 'Oh, yes, I was happy in the Land Army,' she concluded. 'It was oudoor life and I like that outdoor life and I was used to horses then. Of course that was in my blood... I was young and strong and healthy. I was country bred and born, you see. That made a lot of difference.'[88]

With motor tractor technology not yet widely adopted, horses were still the main source of power on British farms. In 1917, of the horses being used on the Western Front, only sixteen per cent were of the heavy draught type used in agriculture, but while the reduction of horse power on farms wasn't catastrophic, farmers were more stretched than formerly and horses that previously might not have been used (those that were old, or stubborn or flighty), would now find themselves in harness, and they were often badly shod. [89] As the war went on horses that had been sent back from army service were also returning to the fields. Rosa Freedman had to work with one in Hampshire:

I was driving a demobbed 'war horse' – marked by a broad arrow on his rump. He was full of nerves. While going around the large field the shrill whistle of the train at the station frightened the poor animal and he tore around the field, foaming at the mouth – and there I was pulling on the reins for dear life. I lost my hat – and with my long hair blowing in the wind I must have looked like a runaway charioteer. Suddenly he stopped and I was thrown, escaping only with bruises and a good shaking up.[90]

As large numbers of tractors were not being used on farms before 1914, many of the first drivers would be women. Farmers had expressed doubt that women were suited to the task and to counter such objections great care was taken in the selection of recruits, preference being given, where possible, to those who had 'preliminary knowledge of motors'. The WLA's magazine, *The Landswoman*, asserted that women had an aptitude for this work:

> *Experience has shown that a fair knowledge of the machinery of motors and their construction, gained in many cases in the driving of pleasure cars in less strenuous days, is by no means unusual to the sex, and with the lessened demands that the more modern models of agricultural tractors make upon the physical strength of the driver the work can be most satisfactorily accomplished by women of a normal standard of health and endurance.[91]*

Courses in tractor driving were launched at Harper Adams Agricultural College, in Shropshire, with the Food Production Department providing several makes of tractors, fuel and spare parts. Fifty-five women attended the first course in November 1917. A visiting journalist remarked that the women were 'providing continual ocular demonstrations of women's fitness for farm work, enough to convince the most stubborn unbeliever'. Two of the women trainees had already shown such skill that they had been kept on as assistant instructresses.[92] Ultimately, 415 women were trained as tractor drivers.[93] By the summer of 1918 the WLA was offering women a salary of 30s per week after they had completed their training, with a bonus per acre – the same wage, it was advertised, that was being paid to men.[94] And, in some cases, they were better at it than men. When Distinguished Service Bars were awarded to WLA members in 1919, around a quarter of them went to tractor drivers. One of these was Miss F. Bridgman, a Lancashire woman, who 'by her strenuous efforts for sixteen months had a weekly tractor average just double that of the men, and on one occasion she risked her life to deal with a tractor that was out of control on a bad hill'. Miss D. C. McCrae was awarded for ploughing land in Cumberland, 'which some men workers had refused to touch.' Another woman, who had demonstrated 'exceptional skill', had been put in charge of the tractor department for a firm of contracting engineers. Five women from Berkshire and East Kent were recognised for 'having ploughed more acres with less petrol than any men similarly employed, and having successfully ploughed difficult and dangerous ground which men refused to undertake.'[95]

There were a few farms where, radically, men were dispensed with altogether. When a staff of four women arrived at Great Bidlake Farm, on the edge of Dartmoor, in November 1917 the whole area was in a state of neglect ('it had fallen from being one of the best bits of wheatland in the district to grazing ground let annually, with little or no manuring or upkeep'). The farm had been taken over by the Devon CWAC and the women who had been tasked with managing it now set to work ploughing, 'in spite of the gloomy mutterings of all the neighbouring farmers that all the crops would be doomed to failure on newly-turned land, and, above all, "bewitched" by woman labour.' Twenty acres were now put to wheat, forty-six acres to oats, six acres to mangolds and eight to potatoes. Six cows were brought in in the spring, the number increasing to ten when, prompted by the closure of Seale-Hayne College, Bidlake began to operate as a training farm. By July 1918 the Devon WWAC reported: 'The crops were most flourishing – wheat 6ft. high, and weeds *non est*. Potatoes were excellent, and mangolds the best in the district.'[96]

Moor House Farm, Bedale, was taken over by the North Riding CWAC and placed it in the hands of an all-female team. As at Great Bidlake, the land here had 'gone back', but in four months it was transformed from a derelict farm into a 'healthy-looking holding.' In the spring of 1918, the 128 acres were being managed by four 'town lasses', all in their teens or twenties, and all new to agriculture, under the supervision of a manageress from the Northallerton training centre. The women had 're-claimed land which in normal times some farmers would have given up as hopeless,' the *Yorkshire Evening Post* reported. 'They have ploughed out 40 acres of grass land, and have got into a condition for ploughing perhaps half the acreage, which, dotted as it was with whins and other fox covers and rabbit warrens, seemed good for nothing but sheep grazing.' It was all good publicity to cure male farmers of that 'plough fright'. Though much had been achieved, the *Yorkshire Post* journalist who visited the farm observed that the women weren't exactly enamoured of their work: 'They state, frankly, that when the war is over, the land will have no further attractions for them. Girl-like, they have sometimes shed tears of regret when the tasks of the field have appeared too much for them.' On the upside the women observed:

> *They confess to a feeling of "fitness" such as they have never known in the towns, a tremendous capacity for work which develops enormous appetites, and a general satisfaction that they are 'doing their bit,' but – and here the eternal female speaks – they find the life lonely and the lack of companionship very trying.*[97]

Lord Treowen, Regional Director of National Service for Wales, set up an all-woman farm in Llanover, Monmouthshire. Photographs published in *The Landswoman* show women posing with a selection of farm animals and making a start at ploughing.[98] Similarly this had been a property which was in a 'very bad state' in 1917, but according to various press reports the 'plucky' women of the WLA had tackled the necessary work with determination.[99]

The plucky women foresters also attracted a lot of newspaper attention. When the Devon WWAC was approached with a proposal for a timber project in the Lydford district they were 'somewhat dubious' as to whether the experiment could be a success. 'Felling and barking was at first thought to be work that women could not be expected to do,' reflected Sylvia Calmady-Hamlyn. But the WWAC decided to let them have a try and, by May 1917, around fifty women were working in the Lydford Forest, felling, cross-cutting, barking the timber and coppicing. The WWAC reported:

The workers were drawn from all classes, educated ladies, factory girls, servants, etc., and they were shaping so well that in the opinion of an expert the work during the first four days was far ahead of that turned out by a novice gang of men in the same time. The girls, who were drawn from various parts of Devon, Cornwall, and Somerset, had never attempted such work before. Some of them were people who had been "turned down" for National Service because the Committee could not place them.[100]

The *Exeter and Plymouth Gazette* published photographs of the lady timber workers. It observed:

The work is not child's play by any means and many a back was sore, many a shoulder ached, and hand was scarred and galled before the workers got somewhat into the knack of doing their work. Now they are experts and talk in the phraseology of the woodman, in a manner which is somewhat puzzling to the uninitiated.[101]

It was said that Mrs Hockin, formidable forewoman of Lydford gang, 'could cut down 30 oak saplings before dinner'.[102]

The Women's Forestry Service was officially set up now, under the Timber Supply Department of the Board of Trade, and an appeal for workers was put out in July 1917. 'Accuracy and reliability are essential,' the advert for timber measurers advised, 'and some knowledge of clerical work and of accounts would be useful.' There was no age limit, but it was stipulated that applicants 'should be healthy and active, used to the country, and able to be out in all weathers.'[103] All in all, 370 women passed through the Wendover training camp, learning to measure and mark off where a tree should be sawn and how to calculate the cubic contents of the logs. Afterwards, they were put in charge of gangs of twenty to thirty cutters and, in some cases, women had the entire charge of a saw-mill, with men working under them. There were administrative responsibilities to this role and so they were also taught 'stocktaking, returns of output, pay-sheets, etc.' By 1918 the minimum wage for timber measurers was 35s per week.[104]

The Timber Supply Department also advertised for women to do felling and timber preparation and government camps were set up to train them. Over a three to four week course they learned how to cut down and stack trees; to load and transport timber; how to operate saw mill machinery; how to produce pit props and other timber products for the war and sapling cultivation and planting. The two training camps for cutters, however, were eventually disbanded, as it was found that training was unnecessary if the women were put out to work in gangs under skilled forewomen. By 1918 timber cutters were paid a minimum wage of 20s per week.[105]

Dora Budge was one of twelve women employed to prepare timber on the estate of Lord Armstrong, at Rothbury, in Northumberland. She explained:

> *The trees, after being felled by men and dressed ready for sawing, are dragged out of the wood by horses. We lift them on to a trestle, where they are measured into different lengths, according to the sizes required. The thick ends are sawn off and sent to the sawmill to be made into sleepers for use on the railways. Next there are the balks – these measure from six feet up to twelve. The remaining part of the tree is sawn into props. We use a cross-cut saw, and, as two girls use one saw, it is not heavy work.[106]*

Beatrice Bennett, meanwhile, was working in West Sussex on a clearing job, felling trees, cutting the wood into measured lengths and then stacking it. She loved the work:

> *It is great, axeing at great trees. We were given a bill hook, an axe, a saw and a cord measure… It is great to watch a grand old tree crash to the earth and feel that you did it alone… The work is grand and the life is just what I have always longed for.[107]*

Meanwhile, L. Edmiston was part of a gang of thirty women ('a very merry little party') working at Lyndhurst in the New Forest, clearing and planting trees. She wrote:

The work may seem hard at first, but one soon gets used to it. We take our lunch and midday meal out into the forest; there we have a nice big fire to sit by at meal times, so we all sit round and toast our bread on sticks. Some people would say how awful, but nothing of the sort; we think it simply grand. We enjoy it very much, it's simply ripping.[108]

Patricia Vernon was one of a party of twelve women working near Ollerton in the Sherwood Forest. There they were planting saplings to replace the trees that had been felled. 'This freedom was marvellous for me,' she recalled, 'being away from home and being able to do as I liked.'[109]

In October 1917 an arrangement was made whereby all future workers for the Forage and Timber corps would be recruited via the mechanisms of the WLA, and that labour would be interchangeable between the departments. Helen Poulter was one of these women. Volunteering for the Land Army in April 1918, she was asked whether she would like to work on a farm or in the forests and chose the latter. 'I didn't like the idea of working with cows,' she recalled and forestry work seemed worthwhile to her: 'We felt we were doing something better than picking up eggs.' Helen ended up working in a wood in West Sussex, where trees were being felled for pit props. She learned on the job. 'It just come to us, you know... it became easy.' Interviewed in the 1970s, she recalled her work with evident pride and pleasure.[110]

At its height the Women's Forestry Service had about 2,000 members. Many worked with the Canadian Forestry Corps (forty-three battalions of which came over to work in Britain's woods), and with gangs of Portuguese forestry workers. In total they were estimated to have processed 450,000 acres of woodland over the course of the war.[111] In 1918, the Women's column of the *Gloucester Journal* observed how 'fitted' women were for forestry work. 'And yet, before the war, if it had been suggested as a possible opening for us, how people would have been up in arms! What arguments we should have heard regarding woman's physical weakness and the like! The nation's extremity has been women's opportunity.'[112]

Like forestry, women's forage work was now formalised. Women had been working in forage since 1915, but a women's branch of the ASC's Forage Department – the Women's Forage Corps – was officially established in March 1917. Cicely Spencer, who had been doing this work since since the start, noted:

In the spring of 1917 great changes were to take place: all able-bodied men were to be drafted into fighting regiments. This meant that their place would be filled by women, who would have to work with the balers.[113]

The women of the Forage Corps were now entitled to a khaki uniform, with an ASC badge and a brass 'FC' shoulder title. They were also designated rank, as officers or 'industrial members', the latter being equivalent to army privates. Wages ranged from 22s to 35s per week.[114] *The Landswoman* recorded: 'The women hay-balers belong to the Forage Committee and are now under the Army. Jolly proud they are of it too, as they stand in their uniform, green hats, white overalls, green corduroy breeches and heels clicked smartly to attention.'[115] Cicely Spencer was delighted by her new Forage Corps uniform. 'It was a very neat uniform,' she wrote, 'and I always wore mine with great pride and always tried to be worthy of this.'[116]

Whatever area of work they were occupied in, accomodating women land workers remained a challenge. Many farms were remote and workers' cottages just weren't available in any numbers. In March 1917, however, prospective WLA recruits were reasurred that the WWACs would oversee their care and that adequate accomodation would be provided. An official statement promised: 'Experience in munition centres has proved the possibility of housing girls and feeding them well at 15s a week. In some cases the farmworkers' hostel may be a country mansion, in others a collection of cottages.'[117]

In practice, standards of accomodation varied considerably, depending on the area and the employer. Rosa Freedman recalled:

We met good farmers' wives and others less generous. But they were all expected to supply us with our tea during the day – but when you were given a bit of cake to go with it, it was very welcome after the hard work. One of our landladies would come out to the fields with our tea, in a pot wrapped in a towel, with some lovely thick slices of bread and butter, and she would sit down with us. Her husband was in France.[118]

Such sympathetic care was the ideal that the WLA hoped for, but circumstances were often rather rougher. Dora Brazil was living in a cottage on a Duke's estate in Buckinghamshire. She was in sight of the 'country mansion', but a long way away from its comforts and cleanliness. It 'was terrible,' she recalled. 'Only the bare necessities of life, and about ten yards from some abandoned pigsties which housed a few hundred rats! Before we could have even a cup of tea we had to collect wood to light a fire.'[119] Kathleen Gilbert was cosied up against the pigsties too: 'The farmer got us one of the sheds, close to the pigsties, we had that furnished out and we lived in there… the farmer's wife had done wonders. Rugs and everything we had in there.' She called her shed a 'homely' billet – though one girl's idea of homely was perhaps different from another's.[120] Annie Edwards might have prefered a nice clean shed. Though she felt sympathy for the hard-up family she was boarding with, she was uncomfortable with the lack of cleanliness. The girl who Annie shared a room with left because she thought it was too dirty and Annie herself soon ended up with headlice (and afraid to tell this to her mother because 'she was so particular'). 'I didn't like it,' she recalled, 'but I thought, "Well, you've joined and you've got to make the best of it."' The food provided was also less than plentiful. Annie used to buy a cake as a treat and eke it out over the week. She also recalled eating turnips in the fields and apples and berries from the hedgerows. She never let her mother know 'no hardships', though. When a better billet became available, she took it. Later on accomodation was inspected, and standards were policed more keenly, Annie recalled. WLA officers came in to examine the accommodation from time-to-time: 'Ladies, you know... dressed up, polished shoes.'[121] There were great gulfs of experience between rural and urban England in 1917. For girls from well-scrubbed suburbs, it could be like landing in another world. It was one thing to read about rural poverty in books, but quite another to be plunged into its dirt and deprivation. There's a sense of shock in the way that many of the women describe their accommodation, even at the distance of many decades.

With a lack of suitable alternative accommodation available, hostels were set up in Northumbria, at Wooler and Carham. The Wooler hostel was a bothy built for quarryman, now providing 'cubicles for twelve girls'.[122] Securing suitable accommodation was a real problem in Wales too and limited the placing of female workers there. A hostel opened in Cadoxton, near Cardiff, and a Young Women's Christian Association (YWCA) depot and hostel was established in Aberystwyth.[123] YWCA hostels also opened their doors to land workers in Bedford, Cambridge, Huntingdon, Lewes and Spalding. Forty forage-girls were accomodated in Gloucester and land workers were offered convalescent stays in Margate. The YWCA also provided canteens and recreation clubs for the camps of flax workers.[124]

Accomodation could be particularly primitive for timber workers. Beatrice Bennett worked at Chilgrove Camp, in West Sussex, where women were accommodated in huts – 'like the ordinary YMCA hut'. Beatrice recorded: 'Our beds are just off the floor on a wooden frame, a straw mattress and pillow and five blankets... the camp is miles away from anywhere, absolutely isolated. One would never imagine such a place existed.'[125] Helen Poulter considered herself to be fortunate in the billet she was allocated – excepting its outside toilet and the four-mile walk to the forest where they were working. She was living in a cottage in Singleton, West Sussex, where the owner (her husband was away in the army) was putting up five girls. Helen shared a bedroom with her friend Lizzie in which they had their own washbasin and there was a bath – a wooden tub, like a wine vat, she recalled – in the cellar of the house, with hunks of bacon hanging overhead. The family had their own allotment, and so while some food was rationed, vegetables were plentiful. 'Our food was marvellous,' she remembered. They had cooked breakfasts, took 'a jolly good bundle of sandwiches' into the forest, and then a hot meal at night. 'I put on a lot of weight', she recalled.[126]

Mildred Hodgson was shocked at quite how profoundly rural Dorset was – and, equally, Dorset seems to have been surprised to receive her. She remembered that, on arriving in the village, she was greeted with the sight of 'a row of boys and girls, all seated open-mouthed and wide-eyed.' As the Land Girls descended from their bus there were cries of 'Tis the war-workers, you!' She wrote: 'The people were nearly half a century (more in some ways, for I found that some believed in Black Magic) behind the times.' The scenery provided compensation, though. The country around was 'simply grand.' To work in those fields 'was a constant joy and delight for one could see for miles and miles.' But the war could not quite be forgotten. There were reminders here of why she was doing this work:

Those blue waters, shimmering in the sunlight held, however, a reminder that though 'God's in His Heaven' all was not well with the world. About two miles out to sea two long poles, hardly discernible to the naked eye, showed above the water. They were the two masts of a small merchant vessel which had been sunk by a German submarine – and that not much above twenty miles from our largest naval stations.

Occasionally there was another reminder in the form of a great airship shaped something like a cigar that had somehow grown fat in the middle – with one end blunter than the other. She gleamed like silver in the sun as she made her way out to sea and often we would see her poised like a hawk, above the water, watching for her prey.[127]

The war isn't actually mentioned *that* often in the women's writings and recollections. Often based on remote farms, and working hard and long hours, they didn't have much opportunity for catching up with newspapers. The Women's Branch however felt it necessary to maintain a sense that their labour *was* war work. Members of the WLA were constantly told that their work was vital to the war effort and the whole thing was dressed up in martial language. The opening paragraph of the WLA handbook stated: 'You are now in the Women's Land Army; serving your country just like the Soldiers and Sailors, though in a different way. You have to grow food for them and for the whole Country and your work is quite as important as theirs. You should always bear this in mind.'[128] Extending the military metaphors, there was a Roll of Honour for casualties in farm accidents and a whole series of decorations. After three months' good service, each woman received a Service Armlet. Stripes were added to uniforms for every six months of work. Badges could be earned for passing tests.

And, like soldiers, they must slog on. Speaking to a Hereford rally, Edith Lyttelton 'gave the girls a recipe for the moments in early morning when they feel they cannot get up, or at midday when their backs ache, or at night when evenings seem so long and dull.' She advised them: 'Shut your eyes and imagine yourselves in Flanders or Italy or Mesopotamia; think of the mud and the cold there; think of the men without any fireside to come back to facing danger and anguish and death every day.'[129] Their lot, then, was better than a soldier's, but theirs too was war-winning work – and if they let their 'front' down, the whole campaign could be sunk. Prothero told a Wiltshire rally:

> *Now you have got to hold this home front, just as your brothers and your friends are holding our various fronts by land and sea on the Continent. If you do not hold it by growing all the food you can in this country, then the line will be broken at home. If it is broken at home, in respect of food, it will break down throughout the whole of the fronts, and you will be letting down the men who are giving their lives for you on all those fronts.*[130]

Quite often the women's contribution was quantified in terms of war-winning American troops. Lieutenant-Colonel R. A. Sanders M.P. told a Taunton rally:

> *The more food they could produce in this country, the more shipping would be available for bringing over American troops, who were ready and anxious to help us. He had seen some of the American troops, and they were pretty hefty men, and, when fully equipped, weighed about two cwt. – about the same as four bushels of wheat, so that every extra four bushels of wheat that was produced meant that one extra American soldier, fully equipped, could be brought over. Every 125 or 130 extra acres cultivated meant an extra Battalion of American soldiers. He thought that that was sufficient to show them the importance of their work.* [131]

Through their labour they could determine the outcome of the war. Such sense of imperative was perceived as key to maintain discipline and focus. But WLA propaganda was as much about carrot as stick; women were also constantly told that this experience was self-improving. Working on the land, far from robbing them of their femininity and degrading them, was making them better women, improving their characters, their figures, their complexions, their after-the-war employment and marriage prospects. An appeal for recruits, in April 1918, coaxed: 'Land labour may give you a few backaches, but it will also give you health, a complexion such as a fortune spent with beauty specialists would never beget, and happiness such as only comes from the knowledge that you are doing your full share to speed the day of Victory.'[132] It seems a curious combination of motivations to a modern ear. Much is made of Land Girls' complexions (so different from the sallow cheeks of munitions workers); it seems almost obligatory for journalists to notice them. Launching its 'Women War Workers' Beauty Competition', the *Daily Mirror* observed: 'No photograph can truly disclose the perfect complexion and healthy glow of, say, most women land workers.'[133] Cosmetic companies latched on to it too; 'Beauty on Duty had a Duty to Beauty', asserts the strapline for Vinolia soap beneath the image of a girl in rustic uniform.[134] A poem published in *The Landswoman* gently parodied the advert:

> *They said when they got us to join :*
> *"It is time that each girl did her bit,*
> *By combining duty*
> *Together with beauty*
> *And putting on Land Army kit."*
> *All can see that to work in a skirt*
> *Is to gather up masses of dirt,*
> *But the leggings and breeches*
> *And smock that just reaches*
> *The knee, why no weather can hurt.*
> *And all figures this uniform suits -*
> *A fact they should tell their recruits.*[135]

Another poem penned by a WLA member sums up this brand of propaganda:

> *Daughter dear, daughter dear, where have you been?*
> *I talked to a girl with an armlet of green...*
> *Daughter dear, daughter dear, what did you do?*
> *I saw her complexion and I enrolled too.*[136]

While this was tongue-in-cheek, *The Landswoman* was absolutely earnest in its selling of the self-improving lifestyle. This is the magazine's description of life in the Forage Corps:

> *After a few months of life on a baler, travelling from village to village and living in the open, the post office clerk, the domestic servant, the typist, are very different girls. Pale cheeks have turned to a healthy glow, their features are sturdy and plump, and their eyes bright and keen. Not only have the girls altered physically but their mental outlook is different. The girls are now part of the Army, with responsibility and tradition to uphold, as*

well as the good name of their own special gang. For the first
time these girls are working with men as comrades and equals.
It is not tinsel and jewellery that will attract the man now, but
energy and stability that will awaken his admiration. These
robust qualities will be better expressed on a Sunday morning
by spotless white overalls and shining boots and gaiters than by
cheap feathers and flimsy blouses. The glow of comradeship and
esprit de corps will found a surer basis for friendship than the
giggles of flirtation.[137]

Land work is not just pinking their cheeks, its making them into
marriageable material. And, never mind a soldier, they might even
corner a squire. Lieutenant-Colonel Sanders' speech at the Taunton rally
continued: 'Their contribution on the land had inspired poets and
painters and he reminded the women workers that Ruth was one of their
early predecessors, and that she married the local 'squire and was the
great-grandmother of King David. (Laughter and applause.)'[138] The fact
that these ideas were put out to the public and press, as well as being
addressed directly to the women themselves, helped to take the sting out
of the sight of the trousered Amazons. As Bonnie White writes, the WLA
'simultaneously challenged and reinforced gender expectations.'[139]

Employment prospects could be improved by service in the Land
Army too, recruits were promised. 'After the War, special facilities for
settlement at home or overseas' would be available to women,
advertisements proclaimed.[140] Unlike in other forms of war work, they
were told that there was 'a permanent opening for a woman' here.[141]
Women were sold munitions work as a contribution that was
immediate and urgent and vital and well-paid – they were not lured
by the promise of a future career in engineering. But on the land
(largely because of the background of the personnel at the front of the
movement) this was always part of the sell. This was work with
prospects. There was a future in it – if they applied themselves. The
WLA handbook advised:

Try and learn all you can about your new industry; it is the

*oldest and the most important in the world. You have a great
opportunity now; you may, if you will, become one of the skilled
workers, who are always on request, looked up to, consulted,
and able to get a good wage... give the best of yourself, body,
heart and soul and you will have your reward.*[142]

There was also immediate reward to be had, they were told, in the
contact that this work gave them with the land. They ought to be
mindful of this and it should be making them happy. When Olive
Hockin published her account of her year on Dartmoor, *Two Girls on
the Land,* in 1918, it didn't go down well with the Land Army top-
brass because there simply was not enough happiness in there. It was
all too grumbling and grimy and defeatist for the taste of the Women's
Branch. It was not noble and positive enough. It just didn't send the
right message. The review of the book, in the August 1918 edition of
The Landswoman, directs women away from Hockin's alleged
negativity and tells them what they ought to be experiencing:

*It is the supreme joy of helping to make things grow – the love
of the animals, the sense of freedom which the close contact with
Nature brings you, the larger view of life, the realisation of the
wonderful beauty of the Lord – beauty of which we should be,
and are, a part, and which we have no more right to mar by ugly
hearts or unhappy faces than the flower or the butterfly has the
right to spoil its petals or its wings. Add to this the perfect
happiness which comes with perfect health, and you have the
secret of the mysterious fascination of work on the land. Of
course, the thought that helps most when the work is hard is the
thought that we are sharing in the much harder work which our
men are doing at this time. But even after the war is over, and
the need for this particular labour is not so urgent, many of you
will stick to it for the sheer love of it, and because the call of the
land will make it impossible for you to go back to the
confinement and triviality of town life.*[143]

That pre-war back-to-the-land spirit sings out loudly in these lines. Here, the clean God-given countryside is saving town girls, at the same time as they are saving it. But as well as that older note, there's also something intrinsically of-its-era in the tone of WLA propaganda – something akin to that idealisation that put rolling hills and thatched cottages on recruiting posters and *Country Life* and *The Oxford Book of English Verse* in officer's kitbags. There is a bit of that England-as-Arcadia sense in there – a pastoral Albion with the colour turned up – a slightly over-heated and urgent nostalgia. Crowds turned up to see the WLA parade through towns, with their smocks and hay rakes and shepherd's crooks, and it wasn't just their labour that they cheered; there was also something romantic and sentimental about the way that the Land Army was presented, and that caught the public imagination. The word that is often used to describe them on such occasions is *picturesque*. They represent a rosy-cheeked and wholesome Ye Olde England (as long as you don't concentrate too long on their trousers), where there is honey still for tea. Theirs is not the grime of a munitions factory. Theirs is not destruction. Their lot is in nurturing and preserving. This rural romanticism doesn't quite sit comfortably with the realities of manure spreading and tractor driving, but one can understand how it might have appealed both to the women themselves and to those looking on.

The Land Army was not about rolling back the clock, though. The language that surrounds the WLA is nudging at a future image of England too. There is a lot of talk about regeneration in 1918 and how women would be part of that movement – it's both about holding on to the best of older values and applying lessons learnt to make something new and better. They're spearheading a new rural reality. By 1918 we're thinking about re-colonising the land, cleansing the returning servicemen by putting a spade in their hands, reconnecting them with the good English earth and placing a good English girl at their sides.

And it was so important that they be a good English girl. While the WLA might employ much military terminology, this was not army service; it was voluntary labour and it didn't really come with enforceable rules and regulations. There was a lot of petitioning and positioning, though – much appealing to women's sensible instincts and self-discipline. There was no mechanism to punish them, but a lot of words about appropriate conduct. The WLA handbook told new recruits:

> *Noisy and ugly behaviour bring discredit, not only upon yourself but upon the whole Women's Land Army. When people see you pass they recognise you at once as one of the L.A.A.S.; they watch you and admire your pluck and patriotism. Make them also admire your independence and your modesty, your frankness and enthusiasm; show them that an English girl who is working for her country on the land is the best sort of girl.*

Every recruit was required to promise to:

    I   *To behave quietly*
    II   *To respect the uniform and make it respected*
    III *To secure eight hours sleep every night*
    IV *To avoid communication of any sort with German prisoners.*

Furthermore there was a list of behaviours to be avoided:

> *She should avoid entering the bar of a public house.*
> *She should not smoke in public.*
> *She should never wear the uniform after work without her overall, nor walk about with her hands in her breeches pockets.*
> *She should not be out too late at night.*[144]

But, often away from home for the first time, the women did not always behave like the 'best sort of girl'. Enjoyment of new freedom is a recurring theme in the recollections of the women, and sometimes that meant that best behaviour got forgotten. In June 1918 Meriel Talbot wrote to the Board of Agriculture: 'Reports of bad behaviour are becoming more frequent and we are seriously alarmed that at any moment some scandal about the Land Army may break out and the Department be blamed for its inadequate supervision.'[145] More of those negative reports would shortly follow. Lady Ada Mather-Jackson, Chairman of the Ladies' Committee of the Monmouthshire CWAC, wrote to Meriel Talbot in July, relating that women of the Monmouthshire WLA 'stay out late and do not often return to their farms until 12 and one in the morning… they are much talked about.' As a remedy Lady Mather-Jackson proposed that more women should be accommodated in hostels and stricter controls applied there ('in short being "confined to Barracks" for so many days according to their misbehaviour'). Meriel Talbot replied with great diplomacy, but concluded, 'with all young people the best results are achieved when the fewest rules are in force.'[146] For all the WLA's military trappings, Meriel Talbot was reluctant to impose military discipline, but she was evidently thinking that some action needed to be taken. Her solution was to introduce welfare officers. Eighty full-time officers were appointed to visit workers 'and check on their morals and their morale as well as to arrange carefully supervised leisure activities.'[147]

It was appreciated that the effects of boredom and loneliness needed to be addressed. To that end, *The Landswoman*, the monthly magazine of the WLA, had been launched in January 1918.[148] In an introductory piece for the first issue Rowland Prothero acknowledged that land workers 'pine for some congenial soul with whom to compare notes.' Therefore he expressed the hope that the new magazine would 'be a companion, and that women workers will talk to one another through its pages.' The Club Page of the first issue told women that the object of the magazine was to 'bind you all together into one big family – a very happy family indeed; and I want you to take me on as a friend, and to write to me, every one of you, and tell me all about yourselves and your doings.' There was to be a Sewing Club, a Knitting Club and a Correspondence Club ('Let me have your name and address, and I will put you into touch with some girl who is feeling just as lonely as you are.'), a Notes and Queries column ('This column will be devoted to answering any questions you like to ask about your farm work. They will be answered by an expert, so don't be afraid to ask') and an Employment for Winter Evenings section ('If any of you would like to get up a little play or concert, do write and ask me how to set to work.') The inaugural Competitions column offered five prizes of one shilling each for the five best hints on 'How to Cure Chilblains.'[149]

Essay competitions were very popular. A competition on the topic 'Farm Work I Like Best, and Why' received over sixty entries. 'If you girls will insist on sending in such excellent essays you will land me in a nervous breakdown once a month,' the editor complained.[150] Competitions to write WLA songs also brought in lots of submissions. The winning entry in March 1918 was written by Helen M. Lee:

All the boys have been in Flanders for the last three years or more,
All the girls are doing jobs they never did before –
All of us are working hard to help to win the war –
To help win the War.

Chorus: Come and join the Women's Army –
Come and join the Women's Army –
Come and join the Women's Army –
And carry, carry, carry, carry on![151]

It sums *The Landswoman* up pretty well. Its tone is jolly, sprightly, stalwart and full of play-the-game purposefulness and keep-calm-and-carry-on humour.

Reading *The Landswoman* gives an insight into the social life (or lack of it) of Land Girls. There are sections devoted to cooking (potato-based recipes predominate) and gardening, and articles full of thrifty and practical advice – such as 'Boot-Mending at Home by Lady Petre' ('It is my object to show how easily women can acquire the art of cobbling, and in their spare time repair their own boots and those of their children').[152] It carried serialised stories about good wholesome girls being in challenging situations which called for stamina, self-sacrifice and pluck, and there was a real all-round educational emphasis as well; girls were encouraged to put on plays and concerts, to set up lending libraries and study clubs. A note at the launch of an essay competition advised: 'Even if you don't get a prize, it is ever so good for you to learn to express yourselves on paper and to put into words the thoughts that come to you during your work.'[153] The magazine ran a series of features on the lives and work of great artists who produced agricultural subjects and there were also scientific and technical articles – on calving, thatching, cleanliness in the dairy, care of implements and preservation of farmyard manure.

The *Landswoman* was also the magazine of the Women's Institute and it encouraged co-operation between the two organisations. By 1917 the WI was bringing the government's food production and preservation message into parish meeting rooms and gardens and kitchens. From the autumn of 1917 the Women's Branch was providing financial and practical support for the WI, but the organisation technically became independent in October 1917 with the formation of the National Federation of Women's Institutes (NFWI). Lady Denman was now elected chairman and Madge Watt chief organiser. Members of the NFWI's Central Committee of Management included Meriel Talbot, Edith Lyttelton and Louisa Wilkins.[154] Over the next year membership would more than double, but it was in 1919 that it would really take off; in December 1918 there were 199 branches and by the end of 1919, there were 1,405.[155] Lady Denman wrote, 'Through their initiative more food is being grown, help is being given on the land, food is being saved both by individuals and by united action, which results in the preservation of fruit and vegetables, the provision of dinners for school children and other co-operative efforts.'[156] WI branches set up co-operative markets, jam factories and canteens. Members could attend lectures and demonstrations of food production, preparation and preservation. They could acquire new skills, learn about changing agricultural techniques and glean know-how to co-operatively sell the goods they produced. In Madge Watt's own words: 'There was in them something educational, something of recreation, and something social.'[157] The WI and WLA were pushed together for the potential of the former to maintain the morale of the latter. The WI offered both practical support to the Land Army and, with its dances and socials and educational initiatives, provided a way out of isolation and boredom.

The movement was all so full of good intentions and determination – and labour was so badly needed – but still, many farmers remained stubbornly resistant to employing women. As at mid-May 1917 it was reported that 1,200 'young, strong, trained women' were awaiting employment. 'Obstinate farmers' were causing a 'serious deadlock in the Women's Land Army scheme', said the *Cambridge Daily News*.[158] Selling the Land Army to women was going well; selling it to farmers, less so. When the Durham WWAC received a letter from the National Service Recruiting Committee, encouraging recruiting campaigns, Mrs E.W. Rowe, the Board of Agriculture's Inspector for the Northern Counties, threw up her hands. She responded: 'The very last thing wanted in Durham County was a recruiting campaign for women. There was the supply; what was wanted was a demand for workers.' The county's five training centres were already full and there were no available places on training farms, but of the 500 women who had volunteered in Durham, only seven had so far been placed.[159] In an effort to recruit employers, rather than workers, the WWAC decided to publish 'An Appeal to Durham Farmers'. This stated the terms under which women were available and, as such, it gives an insight into the objections that the WWAC was encountering. The 'Appeal' stipulated that the women were being supplied with a 'suitable outfit' by the Government and it went on: 'Any selected woman signs a written agreement that she will make her own bed, etc. And if the weather should prove unfavourable for outside work, that she will undertake to give general assistance in the ordinary domestic work of the farmer's household.'[160]

The Board of Agriculture sent inspectors out to every county in the summer of 1918 to assess the state of the agriculture labour market. Their reports show that in some of the counties where few women were employed before the war, there was still much resistance to change. In Derbyshire a Board of Agriculture investigator was told: 'Generally speaking, throughout the district there is a considerable prejudice against women's labour, and the custom of the county is against outside women's labour. The farmer (and his wife) find it undesirable to have women "living in" as well as men.' Moreover it wasn't just the farmer. He went on: 'The girl suitable for farm work, again, regards farm work as being badly paid for the long hours, compared with the money attractions and short hours of the munition factory.'[161] In counties such as Wiltshire, the custom of working in the fields had just gone and refused to return. Here women agricultural workers were 'only to be found regularly employed in quite exceptional cases.' The county's investigator reflected:

> *The low wages which prevailed for their work in former times, and, possibly, the somewhat higher wages obtained by the men in recent years, have influenced women against engaging in the field-work on farms, and it is only for work at hay and harvest in the pleasanter months of the year, and for the higher wages then offered, that women can be induced to give some assistance.*[162]

The same was true in Surrey. Here a Board of Agriculture investigator recorded: 'Some farmers are deeply prejudiced against women as workers and will not employ them if they can help it upon any condition. Others object to women working on the land at all from what may be called for brevity chivalrous feelings, except at such light work as hay-making.'[163] In other counties though, the WLA wasn't taking off simply because it was not needed. In Lincolnshire, for example, there was already an ample, able and well-organsied supply of local women. As the Board of Agriculture's investigator put it, there was a 'ready-trained reservoir upon which to draw for more continuous labour'.[164]

In several counties the investigators were told that the imported women workers were regarded as 'dear labour' by farmers.[165] After reporting positive comments about women's work in the area, the Board of Agriculture's investigator for Gloucestershire noted, 'Then, on the other hand, there was a complaint that women were expensive at 4*d* per hour; they spent their time in talking and did less than the men.'[166] 'Women's labour on field work is generally considered to be expensive,' the investigator for Middlesex wrote, 'and those farmers who can make the necessary arrangements prefer to employ German prisoners.'[167] One Oxfordshire farmer told the investigator that the imported women 'brave the elements in an heroic manner and are more dependable in that way than the village women'. He would keep them on after the war, he said, were it not that their labour was expensive. 'He regards them all as heroines,' wrote the investigator, 'but if he employed enough of them it would make him bankrupt.'[168]

There were complaints from farmers in some areas about women's attitudes too. The report of the Monmouthshire investigator brings to mind some of Lady Mather-Jackson's comments:

The opinions of farmers regarding the uniformed girls varies. Some of the girls appear to have volunteered for the work in a spirit of adventure, and not to be taking the task seriously, and this had led some farmers to condemn the women's land movement as a failure. Most of the farmers, however, speak more favourably of the development. They say that the girls can be very useful in the lighter farming operations, and that, on the whole, they are well worth the wages they earn. They are unable, however, to face the hardships of wet, cold and inclement weather.[169]

The WLA perhaps were not universally doing all that they could to win admirers. 'I have heard some farmers praise the work of the Land Army girls,' wrote the Board of Agriculture investigator for Sussex, but 'others complain that they play at work, and do not stick to it, or do it with regularity enough, and are touchy if rebuked or exhorted.' That being the case, he did not have high hopes for the movement in this county:

I am told that in East Kent many of the Land Army girls are now earning 23s, 24s, and 25s a week, and that in Hampshire they are much employed, but the movement does not seem to have made so much headway in Sussex. The Sussex farmers are, I think, less inclined to innovations or new experiments than those of Kent.[170]

Generally though, there was much positive feedback about the attitude and efforts of the WLA. 'The small body of workers of the Land Army is well thought of by those who have employed any of its members,' the investigator for Cambridgeshire was told. 'It is also stated that they can now be trusted to work without supervision.'[171] The investigator for Surrey observed: 'Most of the women of the Land Army I have met seem happy in their work, and many profess a determination to stick to the land after the war.'[172]

In some areas a preference was expressed for the 'imported' women over local women – something which occasionally provoked ill feeling among the native workers. 'Imported women are sometimes the cause of a little jealousy among the village women,' wrote the investigator for Buckinghamshire. 'It is stated that cottage women with their men-folk away prefer to take in soldiers to taking women land workers as lodgers.'[173] The investigator for Northamptonshire reported that, although more expensive, imported workers had often 'given more satisfaction than average village labour.' He continued:

The imported women workers are very plucky, and 'stick it out' in bad weather, and in winter time much better than the village women. They are always very keen and feel very patriotic, and always try as hard as they can. They are rather unpopular with the farm hands, who, probably not without some reason, think that the ladies get the softest jobs.[174]

In Staffordshire there was evidently some choosiness amongst farmers over the type of Land Girl they got. 'It is much easier to place women of really good class than the rough, industrial type,' the investigator reported. He went on:

During personal enquiry, farmers have remarked that the Land Army labour largely depends on the class of women recruited;

*the better class are satisfactory, but there are a certain number
who seem to regard a uniform as a passport for parading the
streets of the towns and "showing off," and in consequence
some farmers – and more often the farmers' wives – regard this
labour with diffidence and as likely to upset such labour as they
have retained.*[175]

It was said that village women in Staffordshire were 'working much
better than usual to prevent farmers employing the Land Army.'[176] This
is precisely what the government had wanted.

As more women came on to the land, and appeared to be making
a decent stab at the work, so resistance to employing them declined.
The War Office assisted by confirming, in January 1917, that it treated
female labour as 'supplementary to, and not in substitution for, male
labour.' There was no danger then, it underlined, that a farm
employing women would lose its male labourers to the tribunals.[177]
'You must remember this,' Prothero told meetings of agriculturalists,
'you don't run the risk of losing your man-labour because you take
women.'[178]

The *Whitby Gazette* reported that local demand for female labour
was 'continuous and insistent'. The paper quoted an official of the
Women's National Service Department, observing that there was
'much less prejudice today among the farmers against the employment
of women. A successful woman worker on a farm is a splendid
advertisement for us in the neighbourhood.'[179] Relations were thawing
further west too. In May 1917 the *Yorkshire Evening Post* carried a
headline 'Farmers now approving women labour. Change of attitude
in the West Riding.' The article ran: 'Definite indications point to the
West Riding farmer casting off his prejudice against women farm
workers.' Mrs Lane Fox, secretary of the West Riding WWAC, told
the newspaper: 'There is an immense amount of goodwill shown
towards us... If it were not for the difficulty of accommodation our
work would be much easier now that the farmer has accepted our
contention that women are valuable on the farm for supplementary
and auxiliary work.'[180]

Even in Devon, where there had been such bitter feeling between the WWAC and farmers back in 1916, things seemed to be improving. In June 1917 the WWAC reported that 'the conditions of women's employment had changed during the past month. Whereas there were formerly few applications, the committee had now difficulty in supplying the women.' Sylvia Calmady-Hamlyn said that 'For the first time the supply and demand was pretty well balanced in Devon.'[181]

In November 1917 Edith Lyttelton spoke at a meeting of the West Riding WWAC. She told them: 'When they first began their great difficulty was to persuade the farmers that the women could do the work, and they were in the position of having far more women than they could place; now they had far more places than they could find women to fill them.' In an effort to bring more women in ('to rope in as large a proportion as possible of people who had not yet been touched') the terms of enrolment were now being altered. Henceforth there would be three classes of recruit: firstly women signing on for one year who were prepared to be sent anywhere in the country; secondly workers committing for one year would remain in the county where they signed up; thirdly a group of workers who would go anywhere but who would only sign on for six months. Thus it was hoped to attract a 'good many people who had been frightened of signing on until the end of the war.'[182]

It was with pride – but also a strong sense of purpose – that members of the WLA took part in the Lord Mayor's Show, in London in November 1917. They marched with troops representing all Commonwealth nations, with displays of captured German aeroplanes and guns and alongside representatives of munitions workers. *The Landswoman* carried an account written by one of the women who marched ('One Of The Girls'). She wrote:

> *There was round after round of cheering as we passed through the streets. It did us girls lots of good, and made us feel glad that we were doing our bit... We went back to our work very proud to have taken part in such a big show, and very determined to do our level best to 'carry on.'*[183]

Other women's organisations were also 'carrying on' in parallel with the Land Army. The WNLSC continued to recruit women for seasonal work and in the summer of 1917 the Corps was particularly occupied with providing labour for flax pulling.[184] Flax had been widely cultivated in Britain in the nineteenth century – the heads pressed for linseed oil and the stems processed for linen – but since cheap imports had started to come in, principally from Russia, native production had declined. The war both diminished imported supply (Russian imports effectively ceased in 1917) and augmented the demand, as the fibre was used to make cloth for aeroplane wings. Thus, at the request of the War Office and Air Ministry, there was now a big push to re-start flax growing in the UK. In 1917, 420 acres had been sown. Flax needed to be pulled from the ground by hand (attempts at mechanisation had failed) and required a lot of labour. In July 1917, the WNLSC placed adverts in the press, seeking 200 women for five weeks' work. The rate of pay was 30*s* per acre and the women were lodged in a hostel. It would all move up a scale in 1918, when 13,000 acres were planted with flax and the WNLSC recruited 3,529 women as flax pullers.[185]

Meanwhile the women of the National Land Council were fruit picking again. Seventy women, 'mostly University and professional ladies', were on Perry Oaks Farm, Heathrow, picking Worcester apples, and accordingly calling themselves 'the Worcester Battalion'. The *Middlesex Chronicle* observed: 'They regard their stay at Perry Oaks as an ideal holiday, and the sense of the patriotic role they are playing enables them to enjoy it the more.' In September, the lady fruit-pickers of Perry Oaks Farm were reported to have written and staged a musical comedy. The local paper reported that in the play 'the farmer is adored by his lady pickers and returns the compliment by flirting outrageously with them.'[186]

The Women's Legion was making an exhibition of its work too. In September it staged an agricultural competition in Rutland. A journalist observed that the competitors, in breeches and leggings, with their hair tucked up under their caps, looked like 'farm boys', but 'their speech and style betokened breeding and refinement – just the type of country girl, in fact, that the Legion and the Women's Agricultural Committees have aimed from the first at enlisting. Jolly girls, they brought to their work a sense of zest and enjoyment that imparted its tone to the whole assembly.'[187] But not everyone was so delighted by Lady Londonderry's jolly farm girls. In October a Board of Agriculture Travelling Inspector reported that in Rutland and surrounding counties the Legion was regarded as 'anathema, and held up as an example of absolute incompetence.' The Legion seemed to have become more a frustration than an asset to the Board of Agriculture and it was in danger of being an outright embarrassment – of actually discrediting women's work. In November 1917, Lady Londonderry was stripped of her government grant and persuaded that the Legion's 'agricultural' activities should be confined to 'fruit bottling and horticulture'.[188]

Well over a million women had joined the labour force during 1917, many of them taking on what had formerly been men's jobs, doing work that was both heavier and sometimes more skilled. In July 1917, according to the *Labour Gazette*, the number of women working full-time on the land had increased by 23,000 over July 1914's figure (up twenty-nine per cent), while the number of casual workers had increased 39,000 (up seventy-seven per cent). The total number of women in agricultural work in July 1917 was 192,000.[189] In November 1917 the number of WLA members was 6,672, but their significance, in encouraging other women on to the land and winning farmers' acceptance, was greater than the sum of their numbers. By the end of the year it was reported that in every part of the country the demand for female farm labour was 'considerably greater than the supply.'[190]

In addition to increased numbers of women, 1917 saw a real mixture of labour sources on farms; 12,000 soldiers were released by the War Office for the hay harvest, and 5,000 more for the wheat harvest. Additionally, in the autumn, 1,500 former ploughmen were given furlough for three months.[191] In January the Board of Agriculture and the War Office also agreed to allow Prisoners of War to work on farms. Arrangements were made to house the prisoners in depots and they would be sent out in small guarded working parties. The scheme was extended in June, allowing larger groups to be made available, and by the end of July, fifteen camps had been set up accommodating 1,476 prisoners. In November 1917 an additional 4,000 German prisoners, who were skilled ploughmen, were transferred to Britain from France. The Food Production Department also encouraged CWACs to use civilian 'enemy aliens' and the Home Office sought to find agricultural employment for conscientious objectors. Through an arrangement with the Local Government Board, Old Age Pensioners were allowed to earn wages for doing agricultural work without forfeiting their pension, and a Central Harvest Committee was formed by the National Service Department, bringing schoolboys, teachers, Boy Scouts, the Church Lads Brigade and Cadet Corps on to the land.[192]

The ploughed acreage didn't actually increase significantly in 1917, but 1916's decline was arrested, and with less manpower. Production of cereal crops and potatoes were up year-on-year, but the change in direction, the checking of 1916's malaise, was probably more significant than the actual increases in volume achieved. Plans for 1918's harvest were being formulated in the spring of 1917. At that point, to realise its goals for the next year, the Board of Agriculture had requested that the government make 80,000 soldiers available to work on the land, 60,000 horses and 5,000 tractors. It was not to be, though. The war got in the way. The Third Battle of Ypres had launched in June. After some initial success, the weather had broken and through the autumn the campaign turned into a heavy, muddy slog against well-prepared enemy defences. The campaign had to be prioritised over agricultural plans. The Board of Agriculture got fewer men for the land than it wanted and many of those that it did get were less skilled than they had claimed to be.[193] When a conference of county representatives met in December 1917 it was acknowledged that the acreage goals for 1918 were no longer realistic.[194]

Increasing prices and shortage of food through the course of 1917 brought home the need for labour to be committed to increasing domestic food supply. It was made plain to the public in the colour of the national loaf. One of the first actions of the Food Controller had been to increase the flour milling extraction rate (conversion of grain

149

to flour) from around seventy to seventy-six per cent. 'The perceptible difference in the bread to the public might be chiefly found in its colour,' the *Liverpool Echo* advised.

> *It might be darker in tint, approaching most nearly, it is said, the colour of what is known as Hovis bread. Upon other possible differences experts are not in agreement. There are some who contend the new bread might be more palatable; while others warn the public to expect a less pleasant taste.*[195]

It was the colour that seemed to most perturb the public. The British liked their white bread and tampering with the national loaf was not welcomed. But it was very necessary. Wheat supplies were shrinking and, rather than consumption going down, the opposite trend was observed; as people economised in other areas, they were eating more bread. As at the end of December 1916, stocks of grain were sufficient for only another thirteen and a half weeks.[196] In March 1917, flour extraction rates were upped again, to a minimum of eighty-one per cent and 'admixture' was also now compulsory: five to fifteen per cent of flour extracted from other grains (rice, barley, maize, maize semolina, oats, rye, or beans) had to be added by the miller. It was estimated that over 1917–18 the increase in extraction rates saved the country five weeks' consumption of grain, while admixture saved seven weeks' supply of wheat.[197]

In February 1917, the *Labour Gazette* reported that retail prices of food were up about thirty per cent year-on-year. Compared with July 1914, prices in large towns were up ninety-three per cent and in small towns and villages up eighty-five per cent. Butter, cheese and eggs were thirty to forty per cent dearer than a year earlier and the price of potatoes had more than doubled.[198] The Ministry of Food now announced a schedule of voluntary rations, setting out the quantities of the various foods that should be consumed per head per week. The Food Controller, Lord Devonport, hoped that this would have the effect of 'putting the nation upon its honour.'[199] The schedule particularly pushed for bread consumption to come down; pre-war the average weekly consumption of bread per head was 6.9lb, but people were asked to now limit themselves to 4lb, plus 2½ lbs of meat and ¾lb of sugar per week.[200] In March 1917 the Food Control Campaign was launched in an effort to get the public to adhere to the voluntary ration scheme. This included a house-to-house canvass to induce householders to adopt the 'food pledge' ('In honour bound, we adopt the national scale of voluntary rations') and the production of a huge volume of posters ('Save the Wheat, Help the Fleet') and leaflets ('Mr Slice O'Bread', told the public, 'When you throw me away or waste me you are adding twenty submarines to the German Navy.')[201] All over the country, exhibitions and demonstrations were arranged, giving instruction in how to substitute meat, wheat, potatoes, sugar and eggs in recipes and how to avoid kitchen waste. Housewives were asked to have a 'meatless' and 'potatoless' day once a week and, in April, the public were asked to cut back further on their bread consumption – from 4lb to 3lb weekly. The office of the Food Controller warned: 'Victory for Great Britain is absolutely dependent on the maintenance of the bread supply.'[202] But, never mind cutting back, just getting hold of food was becoming a struggle. There were now bread and potato queues of such a length in London that the police had to be brought in to regulate them. At Wrexham, when a farm wagon laden with potatoes arrived, it was set upon. 'The wagon was surrounded by hundreds of clamouring people, chiefly women, who scrambled on to the vehicle in the eagerness to buy. Several women fainted in the struggle, and police were sent for to restore order.'[203]

By May, grain stocks were at a low of less than seven weeks' supply and the food control campaign was cranked up a gear.[204] The King made a proclamation appealing for economy and it was read aloud in churches and chapels across the country, in schools and at the Empire Day celebrations.[205] Attention was called to the 'thrify and intelligent' town of Keighley in Yorkshire, where the populace had achieved a 'miracle' in terms of cutting down their flour consumption. People were urged to adhere to the 'the Keighley regime'.[206] Meanwhile examples of 'bad form' were publicised too: a 75-year-old Colonel was fined for feeding pigeons and two women were penalised for throwing rice at a wedding.[207]

But proclamations and pledges and good examples did not fill bellies or negate the prevalent popular suspicion of profiteering. Starting in Manchester, a wave of strikes quickly spread across the engineering sector. 200,000 workers in forty-eight towns and cities walked out in May. That this vital industry was threatening to come to a halt, was a serious concern for the government, particularly with the newspapers full of revolution in Russia and France seized by industrial action. Commissioners investigating the source of the unrest reported, 'the question of Food Prices is the most important present cause.' Belief in profiteering and inefficient distribution was causing particular bitterness. Workers were reading reports 'of bacon lying rotting at the Port of London, or herring in the north of Scotland, or of potatoes being in some places superabundant, and in others, non-existent, and he has a deep resentment that the possibility of such things was not timeously prevented.'[208] On 1 September 1917, the average price of a 4lb loaf was 11½d – about double the pre-war cost – and overall food prices were 106 per cent above July 1914. The government needed to be seen to be addressing this issue and so it was announced that the price of bread was to be reduced to 9d for a 4lb loaf.[209] As the government was responsible for buying and selling all supplies of wheat it was effectively subsidising bread. The new Food Controller, Lord Rhondda, also published a revised schedule of voluntary rations, now weighted according to the consumer's occupation and, to back this up, a series of home economy leaflets were released and speakers were dispatched throughout the country. Nearly 1,000 demonstrations and lectures were conducted from September 1917 to March 1918. This programme was delivered by women and targeted at women.[210] But, at the end of the year, there were still queues for food. Preston butter market was 'besieged' by 3,000 housewives and long queues for butter, margarine and tea were reported in every London district.[211] 'The food queues are rapidly becoming a scandal,' wrote the *Daily Mail*.[212] In December 1917 Lord Rhondda met a deputation of 'housewives' from all over Britain. They appealed to him to immediately introduce compulsory rationing and gave evidence as to the hardships being experienced. 'In some places feeling was becoming very bitter,' the women told the Food Controller.[213] Increasingly the grievance was not so much about shortage of food, but perceived inequality in its distribution. Rationing was held off for as long as possible, but people wanted it now because it seemed fairer. Sugar rationing came in on 31 December 1917 and the public were told that rationing of other foods was likely to follow.[214]

The Food Controller was never going to be a popular figure. Mary Lees, in particular, wasn't impressed by Lord Rhondda. After leaving Somerset, she was next sent to Wales, where she was employed on Lord Rhondda's own farm, near Newport. Mary said: 'His idea of looking after agriculture was to come down and stand in a field and announce that he was there to oversee food production. He was conceited and wanted his picture in the paper, but he didn't know the first thing about working the land.' She also recalled (with a note of censure) that he collected Hereford bulls and employed several men who should have been eligible for army service to exercise them. Lord Tredegar, who owned the neighbouring estate, had Land Army girls working on his home farm and Rhondda therefore decided to do the same. Mary said:

> *Because Tredegar had got this, he had to have one. And I was the poor hooch who was sent there to look after this cottage they'd taken for these Land Girls – five of them. And naturally I thought, you see, I'll go and see the foreman at the home farm and he'll give the girls a job. Well, not a bit of it, my dear. The foreman was anti-female and, do you know, for the first ten days those girls did nothing but sweep up leaves and pick up apples.[215]*

With the great emphasis on thrift and self-reliance, allotment-keeping became a craze in 1917. When local authorities were given powers to seize vacant land and offer it for allotments, take-up was high – and was encouraged by the Archbishop of Canterbury's confirmation that it was not a sin to work an allotment on a Sunday.[216] The number of allotments would increase from 570,000 pre-war to 1,400,000 in 1918.[217] 'The enthusiasm was great,' Rowland Prothero wrote. 'Nearly a million and a half of small producers studied the vicissitudes of the climate and the capabilities of the soil with the interest of farmers. Extraordinary successes were achieved. Crops were grown on the most unpromising material: cabbages appeared out of concrete and broccoli from brickbats.' Recreation grounds and golf links were dug over. Even the flower beds of Buckingham Palace were turned over to potatoes. Prothero estimated the additional weight of food produced at not less than a million tons.[218] Even Lloyd George was 'growing his own', and the press carried reports on the progress of the Premier's potatoes. ('Mr Lloyd George's chief foe seems to be the wire-worm, but he is hoping next season to overcome the predatory attacks of this insect. In spite of these difficulties the average weight of the roots lifted on Saturday was nearly 4 lbs.')[219] Not everyone went as far as Mrs Symons of Totnes, though; she applied for permission to grow potatoes in the unused plots in the town's cemeteries. The Burial Board of Totnes would support the suggestion if the potatoes were being sold at 'such prices as may help the local market and assist the poor.' The Bishop of Exeter was reported to have conceded to the plan with some reluctance.[220]

The Department of Food Economy issued recipes to the press at the end of the year, so that housewives might make the best of the available produce over Christmas. They included 'Mince Meat for Patriotic People' and 'Patriotic Plum Puddings'.[221] The *Sheffield Independent* advised, though, that 'the real out and out patriot will have no plum pudding at all this year.'[222] One can't imagine that Meriel Talbot's thoughts were on plum pudding (patriotic or otherwise) as, at the end of the year, she circulated a letter to members of the WNLSC. It made no bones about the present dangers to food supply and the imperative of the women keeping at their work. She wrote:

The danger, therefore, of widespread famine will be a very real one for the next few years, and this is the enemy you members of the Women's National Land Service Corps have to keep at bay; you cannot afford to relinquish your efforts even for a day, for famine is a foe that wants to catch us unawares, and may even now be creeping into towns and villages. Every woman working on the land is fighting hand to hand that foe, and defending the homes of the men who are abroad. To know that so much depends upon us brings grave responsibility but we are full of courage and hope. Every fresh acre brought into cultivation is a fresh victory for ourselves and a new blow to the enemy.

She called on all members to conduct their own recruiting campaign over Christmas: 'Will every member get at least one friend to join before December 31st? In that way the Army will begin the new year with double its present membership, giving us greater security against hunger at home, and greater certainty of victory abroad.'[223]

Chapter 7

'Hold the Home Front'

Little Bo-Peep
Has all her sheep,
And knows just where to find 'em.
She's joined, you see,
Our Land Armee;
We've taught her how to mind 'em.

Verse published in *The Landswoman*,
August 1918.

'Farmers had been prejudiced and stupid about women,' Edith Lyttelton told a Land Army rally in Bristol in February 1918. ('It is a way men have,' she added as an aside.) 'They always have underrated us,' she went on, 'but they are beginning to find out about it now.'[1] It might not have been the most diplomatic boast, but there was something in it. That month some 7,000 WLA members were working on farms. They were just a small part of the whole – the Board of Agriculture estimated that there were 260,000 women working on the land at this time – but they were a conspicuous part and their industrious visibility mattered.[2]

In March the government put out an appeal for 12,000 new WLA volunteers. A Recruiting Club was launched in *The Landswoman* (every girl who brought in five new recruits would get a cockade of red and green ribbons to wear in her hat) and those rallies went into overdrive.[3] Demonstrations and parades and test meetings were put on with a view to showing the usefulness of the women, to bind them together and reward those already participating, and most importantly to attract new recruits. Widely publicised in the press, these were occasions for making statements. Meriel Talbot or Edith Lyttelton was usually on hand to make a stirring speech and a ceremony was made of awarding of stripes and badges. If farmers could be called upon to offer supportive words, that was all the better; one particularly obliging farmer told the audience (and hence the press) that the women on his farm were so successful that 'he received £5 more on each head of cattle than he had done at previous markets before the girls had invaded farm work.'[4] What more could other farmers want to hear? Local notables were welcomed on the platform too. The Lord Mayor of Birmingham told a rally, 'When the history of the war came to be written the part women had played in the national struggle would receive a prominent place.' He went on: 'What they were doing in connection with agriculture for the production and the proper organisation and distribution of food would have a considerable bearing on the result of the war.' That was just the ticket. And Edith Lyttelton was on hand to underline the theme: 'In this country they were not going to starve, they were only going to be short; and the reason they were not going to starve was in great measure because of the way women had come to the rescue.'[5]

They were going to need to come to the rescue all the more now. In the spring of 1918 the government was starting to think about its agricultural strategy for 1919, assuming that the war would be on-going and trade still restricted. A target of adding a further one million arable acres was discussed. If this was to be achieved, it would be necessary to start ploughing up more grassland in the summer and autumn of 1918 and accordingly a programme was prepared. But it would never be submitted to the Cabinet for decision. It might be desirable to have troops to help on the land, but right now they were more needed in France. Suddenly the pressure was on all the more. The German army launched its spring offensive on the Somme on 21 March 1918 and soon the allies were retreating and in urgent need of reinforcements. Shipping now had to focus on replenishing lost men and materials. Food imports would contract further. And so would labour supply. The resources of the countryside were about to be tested.

In April 1918 the CWACs had been expecting soldiers to be released for spring work on the land, but instead they found themselves asked to select another 30,000 men for the army. The Military Service Act (No. 2), raised the upper age limit for conscription to 51 and raked another comb through exemption certificates. As Prothero later put it, 'agriculture ceased to be a protected industry.'[6] The reaction from the CWACs was confusion and anger. They protested that it just could not be done. Deputations went to London and objections were voiced in both houses of parliament. As a result, on 27 June, the cabinet decided to suspend further call-up notices until after the harvest, but by that point 22,654 men had already gone.[7] 'It seems to have slipped the memory of the authorities who made this heavy call that those engaged in agriculture (at any rate I can speak for it in this north-western district) volunteered freely in the early months of the war,' Arthur Nicholson wrote in his 'Country Diary'. He forecast that the task of getting in the harvests would be 'a very difficult matter' this year.[8] Prothero faced up to farmers' complaints by asking them to compare their sacrifice with that of men at the front:

Compare for one moment what we are asking the men on the farms to do to-day and what we are asking the men at the front to do. The men at the front have every day to go down into a veritable hell and face death in its most appalling form, but whatever they are asked to do they do with a simple, unquestioning courage and self-sacrifice which would put many of us here at home to shame. Compare their conditions with the conditions of the men on the farms, working in their own familiar peaceful surroundings, not risking their lives, their limbs, their eyesight, and their health for all time.[9]

But whatever the comparative lightness of agriculture's burden, farmers needed help. The April 1918 issue of *The Landswoman* reported that due to the 'tremendous struggle' now going on in France, there would be no soldier labour to assist on the land this spring. Therefore the number of new recruits needed had increased from 12,000 to 30,000. The magazine urged, 'Let us all be full of flaming enthusiasm! Let us set fire to such a blaze of endeavour throughout England that not the smallest demand for labour on the land shall be left unsatisfied, and that every want shall be filled and well filled by women.'[10]

There were recruiting rallies all over the country in May. The martial language and sense of imperative was cranked up. The word 'starvation' got regular outings. Banners were carried displaying the legends: 'Hold the Home Front', 'England Must be Fed', 'The Lasses are Massing for the Spring Offensive' and 'Men on the Battlefield; Women in the Cornfield' (with the message on the reverse: 'Join the Land Army for Health and Happiness').[11] At a rally in Cambridge the chairman of the CWAC said that during the past fortnight, 600 men from the district had gone to the army.

Every one of these men was needed on the land in the interests of food production, but the need of the Army was so great that they had reluctantly to send these men to join the Colours, and they looked to the women of Cambs. to fill the places of those men.

Viscount Goschen, Parliamentary Secretary of the Board of Agriculture, told the Cambridge crowds that, 'At any moment the biggest battle that had ever been fought might break out' and the country needed to be self-supporting in food so as not to be 'hindered in any negotiations for peace by the fear of starvation at home.' Mrs Hobbs, travelling Inspector of the Food Production Department, said that it would now 'take very little to turn the scale of the war, and she wanted every woman to bear in mind that her efforts might turn the scale.' She added: 'The crops would not wait.'[12]

The largest rally was in London. After parading through the streets, and making speeches in Trafalgar Square, the procession of 200 Land Girls marched on to Buckingham Palace, where they were inspected by the Queen. *The Observer* carried a lengthy account of the event:

> *Some carried ducks and other farm pets; others shouldered their hoes and rakes, their forks and spades; whilst those in the forestry section, who were distinguished by pretty green bonnets, carried the woodman's axe, the measuring stick, and the cross-saw. The tall and handsome girl who marched at their head, carrying the Union Jack, is the chief tractor woman on Sir Arthur Lee's estate in Buckinghamshire, and has just been engaged with others in ploughing over fifty acres of the Chequers for planting potatoes. Wagons decorated with daffodils and laden with farm stock, and the band of the 17th London Regiment, playing cheerful music all the way, completed the picturesque procession.*

The women sang choruses of *To be a farmer's boy*. They were all a 'picture of health', the journalist observed. 'Their rosy cheeks were envied by many a young townswoman.' The city girls might not envy their clothes, though. Miss Painter, one of the land girls, told a crowd of London women 'of the fine clothes they got on the land – two beautiful smocks like this,' she said, pointing at her own white holland overall, 'and breeches' – at which all the girls in skirts laughed a little – 'and leggings, and clogs, and a mackintosh.' She concluded her speech: 'But all we ask you is to give up one year of your life – one year of your life for England!'[13] 1,000 new recruits were signed up and 5,000 copies of *The Landswoman* were sold. The editor wrote: 'Great crowds waited to receive us at Trafaglar Square. The reception they gave us when we did arrive made one feel quite choky. They were all so very friendly and so pleased to see us.'[14] One of the people who was reading about the London rally was Helen Poulter in Hendon. She'd never heard of the Land Army prior to reading reports of the London rally, but the idea suddenly appealed.[15]

There was a particular push in the north, with processions and meetings being organised in towns and temporary recruiting offices opened. In York, women were asked 'to express by further work their deep gratitude to the splendid men of the Yorkshire regiments'.[16] There was a 'picturesque procession' in Chester ('reminiscent of a pastoral pageant'). A meeting was told that 'circumstances might arise in which they would want every man. It might be a question of not who was going to sow the crops, but whether we or the Germans were going to reap. Therefore the need of more women workers was very great.'[17] The temporary recruiting office in Sheffield was inundated with enquiries. In particular it was visited by a large number of parents, the local paper noted, wanting to ascertain whether it was safe to part with their daughters. The *Sheffield Evening Telegraph* reflected, 'There is no doubt that the experience would turn them into far finer women and worthier representatives of the nation than they can ever by any possibility become by an idle life of pleasure with an occasional turn at a canteen.'[18] Members of the Land Army processed through the streets of Preston wielding hay rakes and then staged a series of 'pretty tableaux'. The *Lancashire Evening Post* reported: 'A finely-arranged living picture was that depicting harvest and the need of reapers, which had the double recommendations of beauty and appropriateness.'[19] Liverpool hosted a month-long recruitment campaign, launching with a 'rustic pageant'. Four recruiting stations were opened in the city and a recruiting tram (such as had been used to round up recruits for the Pals battalions) toured the suburbs.[20] 'Play up, Liverpool!' urged adverts placed in the local press.[21] Over the course of three days more than 1,000 recruits enrolled in Liverpool, 130 in Sheffield, fifty in Barnsley and twenty-seven in Leeds.[22]

Letters were sent out to all members of the WLA asking them to each try to find two more recruits. The editor of the July edition of *The Landswoman* wrote with confidence, 'By the time you read this number over 10,000 new members of the Land Army will have joined our happy family.' An address from Lloyd George added some rhetorical canonry to the call:

The fields are ripening for the sickle; the toil of the winter and the spring is earning its reward. This is no ordinary harvest; in it is centred the hope and faith of our soldiers that their own heroic struddle will not be in vain. In the days before the war

161

the whole world was our granary. Now, not only are thousands
of men fighting instead of tilling our own fields, but the German
submarines are trying to starve us by sinking the ships which
used to carry to our shores the abundant harvests of other
lands.Women have already served the Allies by their splendid
work upon the farms, but the Army in France has asked for still
more men from the land to come and help their brothers in the
desperate battle for Freedom. These men must go; women will
be first to say it. But the harvest is in danger for want of the
work these very men would have done.Once again, therefore, as
often before, I appeal to women to come forward and help. They
have never failed their country yet; they will not fail her at this
grave hour. There is not a moment to lose.[23]

The fields were indeed ripening and the prospects for the wheat harvest
seemed excellent. Sir Arthur Lee, Director-General of the Food
Production Department, said that the country was 'well on the road to
becoming self-supporting in some important products.' He added: 'For
forty weeks out of the fifty-two constituting the year the entire
population could be fed on the anticipated harvest.' The wheat crop
was expected to be the largest since 1882, and oats the highest on
record by twenty per cent. The potato crop was expected to be fifty
per cent up on 1917 and the highest on record by twenty-seven per
cent. 'The total acreage under wheat, barley, and oats is the highest
ever achieved in the history of British agriculture,' Lee said.[24]

Prothero afterwards quantified 1918's harvest labour as being made
up of 72,246 men from the Agricultural Companies of the Labour
Corps, 30,405 prisoners of war, 3,904 War Agricultural Volunteers and
15,000 public school-boys. In total an additional 121,986 men were
found for the land. And, for women's part, in Prothero's estimation they
contributed 300,000 local workers plus 16,000 members of the Land
Army.[25] The women were 'doing good work, too.' Prothero told the
press. 'Every day their services, becoming more experienced, better
equipped, grow in usefulness. The successful woman land worker must
have a back of iron, hinged with steel, and the production of such backs

takes time, but we are producing them under the spur of necessity.'[26] The Board of Trade estimated that in July 1918 the number of women working on the land was was nearly sixty per cent higher than it had been in July 1914, with particular increases in the south-east (up ninety-four per cent) and east midlands (+157 per cent).[27]

The prospects were good, but the harvest wasn't an easy one. While the weather held in the south, in the north the rain arrived – and stayed. The incessant downpours through September and October damaged crops and made the harvest a long, wet slog. It took fifty-four days to get the wheat it (in 1911 it had taken twenty-eight days), sixty-seven days to get the oats in (thirty days in 1911) and sixty days to bring in the barley (twenty-seven in 1911). Five per cent of the crop was a total loss and seven per cent of the wheat was not fit for milling. But crucially, overall yields were good; in terms of volume per acre all crops were up on the averages realised in 1907–16.[28]

Historians have debated how significant an achievement the harvest of 1918 was, at what cost the production of cereals and potatoes was bulked and whether it could have been sustained. The bare facts are though, that it did what was needed as far as 1918 was concerned. Overall the acreage of arable land increased from 11.06 million acres in 1913 to 12.40 million in 1918. Alun Howkins writes:

In more direct terms the policy of food control, both rationing and raising the extraction rate of flour from wheat by about twenty per cent were probably more significant. However, the fact that bread remained un-rationed throughout the war was widely believed inside and outside government to be a result of the policy, and the farmers were seen as 'Britain's saviours'.[29]

Rationing was introduced in London and the Home Counties in February 1918 and was then extended nationwide. In July 1918 ration books were issued for the first time, with coupons for meat, fats and sugar. The flour extraction rate was increased again, to ninety-one per cent, in April 1918. It did not go down well with consumers or bakers, but bread was never rationed. When the idea was discussed by the War

Cabinet in October 1918 J.R. Clynes, by then Food Controller, cautioned that 'this would be a very dangerous measure.'[30] Bread, whatever its colour, was too fundamental. Some control over food prices was wrestled back over the course of 1918, but still at the end of the war retail prices were 133 per cent higher than they had been at the start.[31]

Forestry Corps worker, Helen Poulter, recalled eating well in her Sussex billet, despite some items being rationed. The five Land Army boarders all had their allocations of sugar and butter for the week laid out on a cruet stand. 'Mine used to go before everybody else's,' Helen recalled. 'I used to say, well, let's have one good feed and blow the rest!' When she returned to visit her sisters in London, there were police-monitored queues outside the grocer's. Even though rationing had now come in, she recalled women in the queues accusing each other of trying to get more than their fair share. On another trip back from Sussex to London, her landlady had filled her suitcase with vegetables. When she got home she told her sisters it was full of her dirty washing, but 'when they opened it, it was all these lovely turnips and carrots, real good stuff that was off the land – and flowers!'[32]

It was held up as a success that the calorie intake of the 'average man' only declined slightly over the course of the war: from 3,442 calories in 1909-13, to 3,418 in 1916, and 3,358 in 1918.[33] But the seemingly stable headline figures mask significant changes. Diet altered substantially for most people – and not generally in a healthy direction. As prices rose, so choices shifted and generally carbohydrates were bulked up. Ian Gazeley and Andrew Newell have made a detailed analysis of how working class diet changed over the course of the war; consumption of bread, potatoes, processed/preserved meat and offal, margarine and condensed milk increased, while consumption of sugar, butter, fresh meat, cheese, fruit, and vegetables fell.[34]

The Battle of Amiens launched in August 1918 and broke through the German lines. At home there was a sense that, at last, the tide might be turning. A rallying call was published in *The Landswoman* in September 1918. There was a feeling that things were coming to an end. But there was also a next stage in which women would need to play a vital part. Every woman had the 'opportunity and the responsibility' of helping in the work of national reconstruction that lay ahead, *The Landswoman* reflected:

> *The national life that has to be reconstructed will not be a replica of the old edifice; wiser, graver men and women are the builders; economy not alone in name but in deed, will have to be exercised by every citizen; but if all work together for the common good, a newer, better life will evolve, sounder, broader and more truly beautiful because the people as a whole will put their best into the making of a nation that will be worthy of those that died to save it.*[35]

Grace Elsey was potato picking on 11 November 1918, working in the same field as a gang of prisoners of war. Bells began ringing in nearby churches and, realising suddenly what this signified, one of the Germans shouted: 'No work. Plenty beer!' Grace went into Woking in the evening to celebrate. There was a big procession, she recalled, and an effigy of Kaiser Bill was burned on a bonfire.[36]

A celebratory double issue of *The Landswoman* was printed in December 1918. It carried contragulatory messages. 'No Christmas Day, except the first, at all resembles that of 1918,' wrote Rowland Prothero. 'It gives peace in a world of war.' He went on to deliver a message of appreciation to the Land Army - but also made it clear that their work was by no means over yet:

> *Women of the Land Army have helped the Allies to win the war, not in the limelight, but in the sequestered nooks of the countryside, on the wide solitudes of the land, in the obscurity of the manger and the stall. They are setting an example. They are treading that path of self-sacrifice which all must follow who would save the nation from the perils of peace. For months to come the end of the war will not substantially ease the situation. Food will still be scarce; the need of help in its production will*

continue urgent. I hope, and I believe, that, in the true spirit of Christmas, the Women's Land Army will persevere, neither failing in its high courage nor slackening in its efforts, nor weakening in its resolution.

'We feel almost stunned by the wonder of it all,' wrote Meriel Talbot. She went on:

We seem so small individually, and our part in it all feels insignificant; but we know that the whole is made up of all the different parts, and that every bit of honest work has helped to set free the forces of liberty and righteousness for which the Allied countries have been striving. Every member of the Land Army, every worker for a Women's Institute, has borne her part in this great campaign. Let her continue to give of her best to the country, and to keep high her courage for whatever the future may have in store.

The magazine's editor encouraged the women to throw themselves into Christmas celebrations:

Enter into the life of the village this Christmas, even if you never have before; insist on getting up a concert or entertainment, make it a howling success, bustle up everyone till they realise that it is Christmas time, and a time for great rejoicing; sweep away the difficulties with a real Land Army breeze, and if you will do this you will not only give others a happy time, but I know you will enjoy it so much.

They might, for example, put on the 'charming little play', which had been written for the magazine by Edith Lyttelton. (The editor guaranteed that it would delight any audience.) For the first time adverts in the magazine included those for civilian clothes and gowns for peace celebrations.[37]

An exhibition was being hosted in London's Whitechapel Art

Gallery through 1918, highlighting some of the 'Women's War Work' collection that was being gathered for the new Imperial War Museum. Among the items catching visitors' interests was a collection of plaster models illustrating women doing war work (girls working on aeroplane fabrics, filling TNT containers at Woolwich Arsenal and Land Army girls ploughing). Mannequins also displayed the uniforms associated with the various branches of women's work. Particularly popular, it was said, were the figures of 'uniformed lasses of the Land Army' and the 'stuffed farm animals in their charge'. The stuffed cow was so heavy that it had to be carried in by ten soldiers, but it proved to be a great draw for children. The exhibition was attended by 82,000 visitors, including the Queen and Princess Mary.[38] The fact that this was all now about to be put into a museum both gave the work of women on the land an official stamp of significance, and also underlined that this was soon to become part of history. This was war work, and if the war was now being consigned to the past tense, well, what next for the Land Army?

In January 1919 members of the WLA were told that no obstacle would be placed in the way of women who wanted to withdraw from the service. Thousands, however, chose to stay. There was no obvious cut-off point for their work and many faced the prospect of leaving with 'unfeigned reluctance.'[39] The *Yorkshire Evening Post* reported:

> *Something like fifty per cent of the women and girls engaged in agriculture and dairy work are prepared to remain on the land. Whether they will be able to do so for any length of time will depend upon the time occupied in the demobilisation of agricultural labourers from the Army. It is recognised, however, that many of the women for whom the land possesses attractions will be needed because of the many hundreds of thousands of extra acres which have been put under cultivation.*[40]

It would be months before army demobilisation was completed and, in many cases, their employers still needed the women. Thus, while other women's organisations were disbanding, their war work done, for the women of the WLA it didn't feel like it was really finished yet. Once again, they had to 'carry on'. In January 1919 Meriel Talbot told the Kesteven WWAC:

The coming season was likely to be one of the most difficult ones as regarded agricultural labour. Owing to weather conditions, the season was already a good deal behindhand. The men were not yet back in any large numbers, and it was possible the German prisoners might be withdrawn – a very large and valuable source of agricultural labour – though no decision had yet been made in that direction. Therefore, the need for every helping hand in farm work continued to be urgent and very pressing.[41]

They would not only need the present members of the WLA to stay on, but they would also need more of them. In March, Meriel Talbot told a WLA gathering in Oxford 'that so great was the demand for labour at this present time that 5,000 new recruits were to be added to the existing army.'[42] The WLA training centres were re-opening and the minimum wage was raised.[43] By June such was the demand from farmers for WLA workers that applications were being turned down.[44]

But some women were choosing to go. By March, 3,300 members of the WLA had indicated that they meant to withdraw.[45] One of these was Mrs M. Bale. She carried on working until March and remained in Dorset to see the July 1919 Peace Celebrations. That was long enough to see some of her work there reversed. She wrote: 'When the men returned from the war the market garden that we made was grassed down again after all our hard work.'[46] Cicely Spencer, who had been in the Forage Corps since 1915, was sent to Cambridge to work on the demobilisation of personnel. ('I was kept busy signing passes, travel warrants and pay slips.') She was now a Major in the ASC and wrote: 'Glad as we were that the war was finished, we wondered how we were going to adapt our lives with the civilian background.'[47] Other women were starting to think about a long-term future on the land; it was reported that a farmer in Ely was advancing capital to his women workers to enable them to develop smallholdings. Elsewhere several WLA workers were said to have been offered administrative agricultural roles by local authorities, while in East Riding an ex-WLA girl had been appointed as a Milk Recorder on a salary of £140 a year.[48]

Even to those who wanted to stay on in the Land Army it was clear that they wouldn't be able to do so indefinitely. In April 1919 *The Landswoman* published details of a scheme to help women save up for a demobilisation outfit. 'There will be quite a large number of girls who, having parted with their civilian clothes, will have no ordinary garments in which to seek for fresh employment,' the magazine stated. It urged 'every girl who has no "civies"' to join the saving scheme '*at once.*' An example was given of a girl saving a shilling per week for the next twenty-five weeks. By October she would have saved enough for an outfit in which she might be able to attend job interviews. The end was obviously coming, but no clearer indication as to a likely demobilisation date was yet given.[49]

Peace Day was marked throughout the country in July 1919. In Devon there was a celebration at 'Great Bidlake Women's Farm'. A 'Victory March' featured women in costumes representing Famine, War and Pestilence, Peace, Patriotism and 'Dora' (the Defence of the Realm Act, under the compulsory powers of which the women's farm had effectively been brought into being). Miss Molly Hockin was dressed as a land worker of 1914, while Sylvia Calmady-Hamlyn represented the Women's Land Army in 1919. The march concluded with 'an impressive scene, representing handing over the land from the women of the land army to the men, the latter represented by three soldiers and a marine.'[50]

Whether they had finished saving up for their civvy suits or not, in October the remaining 8,000 Land Army members were told that the service would be disbanding at the end of November, after the potato harvest had been gathered in.[51] Farewell parties were now organised throughout the country. The women of the West Riding WLA, which had recruited 4,000 members since its formation, processed through the streets of Leeds before retiring for tea and dancing.[52] At a 'farewell' in East Sussex a local farmer, Mr W. H. M. Killick, told the gathering that the women had 'helped us out of very serious and grave difficulties. They came to our rescue, and I do not know how we should have carried on a good many farms without them.' One of the women leaving the East Sussex WLA now was Peggy Fisher, who had been awarded the Distinguished Service Bar for rescuing a man who was being gored by a bull (she 'kicked the bull so violently on the nose that the animal backed, giving the man time to rise; and, as a result, both escaped.') She was now marrying the man whom she had rescued. The story caught the imagination of the press and the nuptials of 'the plucky bride' were widely reported ('The bride drove to the church in a gaily decorated farm wagon, drawn by six horses and accompanied by twelve land girls in uniform, who formed an archway of farm pitchforks as the pair left the church.')[53]

A final Farewell Rally was held in London at the end of November 1919. At this event fifty-five members of the WLA were presented with the Distinguished Service Bar by Princess Mary, an award which had been inaugurated to recognise 'acts of courage and unselfish devotion in the service of others and also for special skill in the course of their employment.' The press carried detailed accounts of the occasion and highlighted some of the particular achievements. One woman had been looking after a flock of 200 sheep, 150 of them breeding ewes, on a hill farm in Cornwall since 1917. Another had done a long stint as shepherdess 'in an exceedingly lonely and inaccessible part of Exmoor.' Eleven of the women recognised were tractor drivers. Several awards were 'for rescuing fellow-workers from boars and bulls, stopping runaway horses, and saving the lives of valuable stock.'[54]

Lord Lee, the new Minister of Agriculture, conveyed official thanks in a piece published in *The Landswoman* in December: 'Without the aid of women the manhood of the nation could not have withstood the attacks of our enemies,' he said, 'and the Women's Land Army is entitled to a specially honoured place among the various bodies into which the women were organised.' Meriel Talbot penned her own message: 'While we are sad at the breakup of the Land Army we are grateful, deeply grateful, for the opportunity for service it has given us, for the manifold experience gained, and for the door opened to women to take their place in the agricultural life of the country.'[55]

Some would take advantage of that opened door. It was reported that at least three-quarters of the women who were still in the Land Army on demobilisation were intending to remain on farms. In Surrey, of 299 members still working at this time, 212 said that they intended to stay on the land, thirty-three were applying for settlement in the colonies and ten wished to set up smallholdings. The *Cambridge Independent Press* went on:

> *Two of the most successful in the county were servants in a flat in Victoria-street, and one of these has recently taken first prize in the milking competition at the National Dairy Show. One admirable worker was previously a waitress in an underground restaurant in the city. The 'cockneys' have often been among the quickest and best of the farm hands, and have developed a love of open spaces and country pursuits which makes it impossible for them to return to town life.*[56]

Annie Edwards was one of those women who couldn't bear to leave the land. She ended up staying on at Drayton Manor farm – and would remain there until 1945.[57]

Chapter 8

Legacy

No other Rose is half so sweet
As she who milked our cow;
In fancy still I hear her feet –
I would she were here now...

Opening stanza of a verse ('Good-bye, Girls!'),
published in the *Essex Newsman*, 6 December 1919.

Bonnie White writes, 'The demobilisation of the Land Army represented the actualisation of the return to normalcy.' This was the 'value of victory' made manifest.[1] God was back in his heaven, man was back on the land and woman was returned to her domestic sphere. But not everyone was willing to be put back. And, after all, they had been told that it didn't have to be that way.

Right from the WLA's launch, back in March 1917, recruits were assured that this was an investment for their future. 'There will be co-operation with the Dominions,' they were told, 'so that women who have done well and found that farm life suits them will be given opportunities of taking up land. There will be a special register formed of such women and also of women who may wish to farm on their own account at home. This is as it should be.'[2] The idea that this work was training for a post-war career was regularly repeated over the next two years. Sometimes it was positioned in conventional terms – that they would be on the land as one half of a couple; this is an account of Edith Lyttelton addressing a WLA rally in Bristol in February 1918:

She did not think the work of women on the land was going to
be a temporary thing, but a permanent part of the country's

172

industry. The Government knew they would have to organise big settlement schemes for the soldiers coming back from the war; they had to arrange for establishing communities of married people on the land, and the woman of the future on the land was going to be the farmer's wife as well as the farm girl.[3]

Elsewhere, a more independent future on the land was mapped out; this is Edith Lyttelton at a rally in Sleaford in March 1918: 'The Government was considering all kinds of schemes for women to take up as their work for life, and a register was kept at headquarters for those who wanted to settle on the land and make a career for themselves there.'[4] Either way, the women were lead to believe that this was going somewhere – and that was a prospect that had appealed to many of them.

By 1918 there was much talk of post-war rural regeneration and the role that woman could (and should) play within that. In May 1918 a meeting of the Farmers' Club in London discussed the future position of women in agriculture. 'There was now a golden opportunity to re-populate the rural districts of England,' said Mr J. C. Newth. He went on:

The girls on the land were being endowed with that physical strength which in the future should prove an important part in regenerating the human race. They were becoming accustomed to the environments of country life, and were acquiring new interests which they were not likely to lose. Many would marry men associated with agriculture and settle down to rural life. It was this sympathy and mutual interest towards country life and the industry of agriculture that would most tend to strengthen the nation after the war.[5]

There is a conservative pull to an idealised past, a harking back to a healthy rural England (that same England that existed on recruitment posters, with its rolling hills and thatched cottages, and the question *'Isn't This Worth Fighting For?'*), but this movement was also about making rural living better than it had been pre-war. 'Regeneration' and 'reinvigoration' and 'healthiness' were the watchwords. And 'repopulation'. The born-again countryside needed women. In November 1918 the *Western Mail* reported:

> *The authorities, it is understood, are anxious to encourage rural romances. It is hoped that many of the young land workers and farmers will on their return from the Army marry the land girls who have been 'carrying on' in their absence. This, it is claimed, will mean that the skilled farmer will have a skilled wife to manage the dairy, and, incidentally, one who can take her turn at the hardest work. It will also mean fit parents to raise healthy families, and thus improve the standard of rural population.*[6]

Olive Hockin now re-emerged as one of these rural renaissance voices. *Two Girls on the Land* had some success and it's evident that her year on Dartmoor (and the act of writing about it) had a big influence on her future. Through the 1920s Olive regularly had articles published in the press on the subject of nature, on folklore and farming. Most often she was to be heard advocating the healthiness of rural life. In November 1920 she wrote:

> *Surely it will not be long before the reaction comes! The well-to-do are already turning their backs on the smoke and noise of towns and are creeping away into the remote places. Soon the workers will do likewise. The country needs them, and surely – with all that she has to offer; beauty of surroundings, clean air, wholesome food, work full of interest and variety, and a healthy-living outdoor life – is the country to call in vain for labour? Now that working hours are reasonable and wages good, will not working men and women forsake the towns that are slowly reducing their vitality and ruining our race, will they not soon come back to the earth that bore them, and get their living from the fields as their forefathers did of old?*[7]

Others saw a professional future for women on the land. In 1918 the London University Land Workers were debating what agriculture might look like after the war. Speakers forecast that the 'old, slow-moving type of agricultural labourer' would now disappear:

It was pointed out that the old condition of agriculture, with the farmer, or farm bailiff, at one end, and the agricultural labourer at the other, must disappear too, and there must be intermediate grades. Women would be able to supply these grades, especially if fruit canning and similar factories were erected. At present the only women on the land were wives; there was nothing to encourage the daughters to remain.[8]

Motive had to be found for the daughters to remain (more motive than marriage). In December this was the talk of Leeds University too. At a conference convened by the Women's Branch, Thomas Middleton, Deputy Director of the Food Production Department, urged that 'it was essential, for educational and economic reasons, that woman should take a more active part in the development of agriculture than she had done in the last fifty years.' The conference passed a resolution: 'That facilities for the education of women in practice and theory of agriculture and horticulture both at colleges and farm institutes, and by means of local classes, should be greatly extended.'[9]

In 1919, a government report looked at employment opportunities for women on the land 'in the light of experience gained during the war'. The committee which produced the report was chaired by Louisa Wilkins and its secretary was Gladys Pott. It opened with an observation – that women were now in a position 'entirely different from that held by them prior to 1914.' It went on:

In particular, the failure of men to return to employment in the industry in numbers comparable to those that left to join the Services or seek other employment during the war, combined with the continued shortage of foodstuffs in the markets of the world may ensure the employment of large numbers of women who have been emergency workers, and will firmly establish the idea of employing women for jobs which they are competent to perform. Perhaps the greatest change which occurred was that in the mental attitude of persons concerned, especially that of women in the areas in which their labour has been little used in the past. Patriotism, some economic pressure, and the re-discovery of the advantage of work in the open air (on some jobs) broke down many of the former prejudices of women. They no longer felt that work on the land was derogatory to their social standing. The permanency of this change will largely depend upon the conditions governing this work in the near future.[10]

In the opinion of the report, what was most needed in order to make a future for women in agriculture realistic was education. This was the overwhelming conclusion: that the government needed to provide (and to continue to provide) training for women. And it wasn't just higher education that was needed. Training had to be provided in a way that made it accessible to rural women. There must be local demonstrations, itinerant instruction, farm schools, scholarships and social enterprise.[11]

One organisation that was in agreement with these conclusions was the National Association of Landswomen (NAL). This organisation had been formed as the Land Army was disbanding and it was very much the WLA's privately-administered, peace-time successor. Meriel Talbot championed the NAL at Land Army 'farewell' meetings, explaining that its purpose was to 'carry forward that spirit of comradeship and mutual help which had been so marked a feature of the Land Army.' Its aim was to provide advice and information on facilities for training and employment openings, opportunity for co-operative purchasing (particularly of clothing suitable for farm work), and it would work to maintain the status and morale of women in agriculture.[12] County associations were formed, county committees elected and delegates chosen to attend a council to be held in London. This council met in December 1919 and decided to form a national headquarters, to be based at the offices of the WFGU, to which the NAL was affiliated. It aimed to attract a membership of 8,000 (each paying a penny per week); by December 1919, 6,000 women had already joined.[13]

In February 1919, a meeting of the Devon WWAC was told that the Board of Agriculture would ensure that some of the facilities being offered to ex-servicemen would be made available to the ex-Land Army woman as well. 'The ex-Army man was to have a cottage and ground, and work as an agriculturalist,' they were informed, and there were also going to be 'profit-sharing farms and there would be smallholdings too, administered by the Local Authority, when the necessary legislation had been passed.'[14] The Land Settlement (Facilities) Act, passed in 1919, allowed county councils, with financial support from government, to buy land and to lease it to ex-servicemen who wished to work smallholdings. In May, when the Bill was at the committee stage, an amendment was passed stating that the offer should be extended to 'women who have served on the land for six months.'[15] On the basis of this understanding, the Devon WWAC began to investigate the possibility keeping on Great Bidlake 'as a women's profit-sharing farm'. The plan was, however, eventually rejected because the farm was so remote and judged to be unlikely to yield a profit. The crops, livestock, implements and furniture were thus auctioned off and the WLA accordingly (with 'a feeling of sadness') gave up possession of Great Bidlake Farm at Christmas 1919.[16] A lack of financial confidence, and just simple want of capital, kept back other women too. By 1922 16,500 ex-servicemen had been settled on the land under the government scheme, but there's no evidence that women took up the offer in any significant numbers.[17]

There were some independent experiments, though. As early as 1917 the WFGU was looking at the possibility of a women's smallholding colony as a future project and benefactors were eventually found in the form of two previously prominent suffrage campaigners. Thus in 1920, having assessed and rejected a number of other properties, the WFGU purchased the 'Lingfield Colony' in Surrey, an estate which had originally been set up by the Christian

Social Service Union to provide occupation for paupers.[18] Candidates for the plots were carefully selected, preference being given to 'women with a good knowledge of horticulture or agriculture, who possessed a small private income in addition to capital invested in the undertaking.'[19] It was a difficult time to be launching such an enterprise. The government's smallholding scheme for ex-servicemen was losing money and many who had launched ventures were now throwing in the towel. Speaking at the Women's Farm and Garden Association's 1925 annual meeting (the WFGU became the WFGA in 1921), held at Lingfield, Charles Bathurst wasn't overly confident about the Colony's prospects. He was reported to have told the meeting:

> *Since the war it had been scarcely possible to run small holdings on an economic basis, and he wished the colony every success… Whether women's smallholdings would prove a success was a debatable matter, but it afforded to educated women, with a love of the countryside, a life which presented opportunities for happiness and contentment which were not open to those who rushed so madly after the hectic and artificial life indulged in so much nowadays by educated women.*[20]

The press picked up on the fact that Bathurst offered a suggestion to the land workers at Lingfield – that they should marry and introduce men into their community. The suggestion was declined: 'They said that their Eden is perfect as it is, and that they want no Adam to spoil its harmony.'[21]

By this time there were eleven holdings at Lingfield, two being mixed farms and the rest focussing on fruit, market gardening and poultry. In all there were thirty-six acres of pasture, six acres of arable land and eighteen acres planted with fruit. One of the tenants was running a successful Angora rabbit farm, another was breeding Alsatian dogs, another keeping horses and giving riding lessons and another had established a tea shop in an army hut. There was also a produce hut selling the collected output of the Colony ('during the summer months a good trade is done with fruit, flowers, vegetables, and farm produce.') Each tenant had her own house on the site.[22]

An Eden it may have been in many ways, but it was an Eden in the red. The Colony made a financial loss in every year apart from 1926 and so, in 1929, the WFGA reluctantly recommended that the land be sold. There may have been some faults in the way that it was first set up, but fundamentally, the negative financial climate of the time crushed the Colony's chance of success. Some of the residents left and went on to have their own farms, while others went to work overseas. Several bought their holdings from the WFGA, though, and clung on through the 1930s. The last smallholding at Lingfield was sold off to its tenant in 1938. A small group of women stayed together, working their plots and bartering their produce. Anne Meredith's study of the Lingfield Colony shows that there was both a real sense of community here and a pride in the women's independence. 'It was a mutually supportive rural community where single women were able to lead satisfying and secure lives,' she writes.[23] The WFGA carried on working to improve the status of women in agriculture, directing them to training opportunities and helping them to secure employment. The Association claimed to have placed 3,000 women in posts between the wars. It continued (and continues) to promote agriculture and horticulture as a skilled and scientific profession.[24]

The village women, who had made up the vast part of the workforce in 1918, simply went back to their domestic lives after the war and the trend of young rural women seeking better-paid employment in towns resumed. The 1921 census recorded 85,472 (1911: 94,722) women as working in agriculture, representing eight per cent of the agricultural workforce. Although, as pre-war, female employment was not necessary captured by the census methods, this is a significant decline from the figure of 300,000 female agricultural workers that Prothero had cited just three years earlier. There is potentially some shift detectable in the wage-earning status of women on the land in the decade bookending the war; twenty-three per cent of the total number of women working in agriculture were now returned as farmers (1911: twenty-one per cent), thirty-nine per cent as labourers (1911: fourteen per cent) and nineteen per cent as farmers' relatives assisting in farm work (1911: sixty per cent). The regional variations hadn't changed, though. In fact they'd become more engrained. The counties that had employed most women in 1911 generally had higher concentrations in 1921 (in Northumberland women represented thirty-seven per cent of the agricultural labour force, Durham thirty-three per cent, Carmarthen twenty-five per cent, Middlesex seventeen per cent, Lincs. Holland fifteen per cent, Pembroke twelve per cent, Kent eleven per cent, and Cardigan eleven per cent).[25]

In 1922 Rowland Prothero wrote: 'British agriculture is not a cheerful topic; on the contrary, it is gloomy and depressing... Corn growing is on the rocks; its S.O.S. signals are flying in all directions; no life-boats are yet in sight.'[26] With worldwide wholesale prices for agricultural produce falling sharply in the spring of 1921, the Agriculture Act, which had renewed the government's wartime guarantees of minimum prices, was repealed. Prices fell sharply between 1921 and 1923. Cheaper foreign produce now flooded back in and pushed English agriculture into decline. Small farms paired back their costs and, if family could be employed instead of paid workers, they were let go. Moreover returning veterans, particularly those who could not find employment themselves, did not believe that women ought to still be occupying men's jobs. In 1922, the National Union of Agricultural Workers passed a resolution stating that 'where male labour is available female labour should be discouraged.'[27] Women should be making way. The exodus of the rural labour force, postponed by the war, now resumed, and, once again, more women left than men; while the number of male agricultural labourers declined by fifteen per cent between 1921 and 1931, the number of women went down by forty-five per cent. Between the wars the total population employed in agriculture shrank by thirty per cent and the area under plough by twenty-five per cent. The cities grew, country estates were sold off and Britain again looked across the seas for her bread and butter. By 1939, seventy per cent of Britain's foodstuffs were imported.

In 1920, a scheme was proposed to amalgamate the National

Association of Landswomen with the Women's Institute, the two organisations having similar aims and functions.[28] The WI continued to champion the interests of women who lived and worked in the country, repeatedly bringing their wages and employment conditions, amongst other issues, to the attention of government through the 1920s and 1930s. In 1934 F*armers' Weekly* magazine stated that the 'rise of the WIs is the most important event in rural England since the dissolution of the monasteries'. By 1938 the organisation had 318,000 members.[29]

In May 1938, Lady Denman, still then Chairman of the NFWI, was approached by the Ministry of Agriculture and agreed to become honorary director of a new Women's Branch, if the need arose. It did. In December 1938, the Minister for Labour announced the government's intention to recruit a Women's Land Army again, 'the members of which would be available for land work in time of war.' Many of those who served in the last war had already indicated their preparedness to serve again. In February 1939 Lady Denman offered her home for the WLA headquarters as recruitment began. The WLA was officially re-formed on 1 June 1939 and women were already helping to bring in the harvest before war was declared on 3 September.[30] For all of the doubts as to the worth of women on the land in 1917, when it looked like Britain's food supply might again be threatened, government instantly resorted back to this model and the women once again responded.

Over the past century there has been a change in terms of how the impact of the First World War on women's lives has been presented. While earlier historians showed the war having a liberating influence, being a great watershed, the women's effort resulting in the happy ending of the extension of the franchise, in more recent years the emphasis has been on how there was a reversal after the war, women reverting to domestic roles, retreating from the workplace to the home, effectively being put back in their boxes.

In terms of agriculture, it is true that most women who had entered the workforce during the war had left it again by the mid-1920s, their lives shifting into marriage, motherhood and domesticity. Moreover, particularly for rural women, the experience did little to change their social or economic status, or their fundamental attitude towards agricultural work. For many who had not previously worked on the land the experience was significant, though, and had a long-term impact. For lots of them this had been a period of liberation – away from home for the first time – and self-discovery. Many of them were doing tasks that they would never have previously imagined and their own opinion of their capabilities was being challenged. It should be said that women's experiences varied considerably and, accordingly, so too did the way that this impacted their future; but, in general terms, for women who had not worked on the land before, this episode was formative. 'You can take the girls out of the Land Army, but you'll never take the Land Army out of the girl,' Second World War veteran Iris Newbold told the BBC recently.[31] And that's true of the women who served in the First World War too. There was a shift in mind-set, an expansion in aspiration, and an enduring interest in the land. It left them with a greater sense of self and sense of their worth. That is something that's not necessarily visible in statistics; but it is powerfully present in the way that these women spoke and wrote about their own experiences.

Notes

Introduction

1 The Women's Land Army's magazine in the First World War was entitled *The Landswoman*. The Second World War equivalent publication was *The Land Girl*.

2 *Chelmsford Chronicle*, 28 June 1918.

3 House of Commons Debate, 18 July 1918. *Hansard*, vol. 108 cc. 1264-336; *War Memoirs of David Lloyd George,* Volume I (1938 edition) p. 755.

4 *Birmingham Daily Post*, 17 May 1917.

Chapter 1

1 *Liverpool Daily Post*, 15 February 1915.

2 Rowland E. Prothero, *English Farming Past and Present* (1912), p. 378.

3 Benjamin H. Hibbard, *Effects of the Great War upon agriculture in the United States and Great Britain* (1919), p. 225.

4 Prothero, *English Farming Past and Present*, p.383.

5 *Report of the Sub-Committee Appointed to Consider the Employment of Women in Agriculture in England and Wales* (1919), p. 27.

6 Of the 244,000 women recorded as working in agriculture in this report, 144,000 were members of farming families, 68,000 were regularly employed labourers and farm servants and 32,000 were temporary workers. *Report of the Sub-Committee Appointed to Consider the Employment of Women in Agriculture*, p. 28.

7 While census enquirers after 1881 had not recorded farmers' wives and daughters as agriculture workers, in 1911 instructions were revised and this category was recognised again. *Census Returns of England and Wales, 1911, General Report with Appendices, Section IV. Occupations and Industries.*

8 *Census Returns of England and Wales, 1911, General Report with Appendices, Section IV. Occupations and Industries.*

9 Board of Agriculture and Fisheries. (1919). *Wages and Conditions of Employment in Agriculture, Vol II, Reports of Investigations*, pp. 413, 424, 425, 453, 467.

10 *Women in industry. Report of the War cabinet Committee on women in industry* (1919), p. 60.
11 Quoted by Nicola Verdon, 'Agricultural Labour and the Contested Nature of Women's Work in Interwar England and Wales', *The Historical Journal*, 52 (2009), p. 125.
12 Quoted by Nicola Verdon, 'The 'Lady Farmer': Gender, Widowhood and Farming in Victorian England', Richard W. Hoyle (ed.) *The Farmer in England, 1650–1980,* p. 241.
13 *Reports of the Special Assistant Poor Law Commissioners on the Employment of Women and Children in Agriculture* (1843), p. 216.
14 IWM interview: Gilbert, Kathleen - Catalogue number: 9105.
15 Viscountess Frances Garnet Wolseley, *Women and the Land* (1916), pp. 183, 207.
16 *Essex Newsman,* 1 August 1914.

Chapter 2
1 *Cambridge Independent Press*, 29 April 1910.
2 *Daily Record*, 20 March 1914.
3 Carrie de Silva, *A Short History of Agricultural Education and Research* (2015), p. 110.
4 *Essex Standard*, 22 July 1899; *London Daily News*, 6 July 1899.
5 *Sheffield Evening Telegraph*, 17 July 1899.
6 *Leeds Mercury*, 18 July 1899.
7 *Coventry Herald*, 21 July 1899.
8 *Northants Evening Telegraph*, 13 October 1900.
9 *Manchester Courier*, 21 May 1904. When Lady Warwick's students moved to Studley, agricultural education for women continued at Reading, with two new hostels opening (St George's and St Andrew's).
10 *Northampton Mercury*, 22 July 1904.
11 *Yorkshire Post and Leeds Intelligencer*, 22 January 1912.
12 de Silva, *A Short History of Agricultural Education*, p. 123.
13 *Sussex Agricultural Express*, 22 April 1905.
14 Wolseley, *Women and the Land*, p. 19.
15 *Bury and Norwich Post*, 15 May 1900.
16 *Framlingham Weekly News*, 11 March 1911.
17 *Gloucester Journal*, 29 October 1910.
18 Quoted in Peter King's *Women Rule the Plot: The Story of the 100*

Year Fight to Establish Women's Place in Farm and Garden (1999), pp. 19-20.

Chapter 3

1 Edith H. Whetham, *The Agrarian History of England and Wales*: Volume VIII (1978), p. 70.
2 *Bath Chronicle and Weekly Gazette*, 15 August 1914.
3 *Sussex Agricultural Express*, 13 August 1914.
4 *Northampton Mercury*, 21 August 1914.
5 *Yorkshire Evening Post*, 6 August 1914.
6 *Hull Daily Mail*, 10 August 1914.
7 *Birmingham Daily Post,* 13 August 1914.
8 *Western Gazette*, 14 August 1914.
9 The *Chester Chronicle* observed that, despite 'highly coloured' stories in the press, Cheshire farmers anticipated 'no difficulty whatsoever' in getting the harvest in. *Chester Chronicle*, 15 August 1914.
10 *Newcastle Journal*, 11 August 1914; *Derbyshire Courier*, 22 August 1914.
11 Caroline Dakers, *The Countryside at War 1914-18* (1987), p. 24.
12 *Portsmouth Evening News*, 22 August 1914.
13 *Western Daily Press*, 29 August 1914.
14 *Manchester Guardian*, 17 August 1914; Arthur Marwick, *Women at War, 1914-18* (1977), p. 27.
15 *Manchester Guardian*, 21 August 1914.
16 *Daily Record*, 31 August 1914. Mary Mason was the retired Senior Inspector of Boarding Out for the Local Government Board.
17 *The Sketch*, 26 August 1914.
18 Dakers, *The Countryside at War*, p. 27.
19 House of Commons Debate, 28 August 1914. *Hansard*, vol. 66 cc. 274-6.
20 *Yorkshire Post and Leeds Intelligencer*, 13 November 1914.
21 Irene Osgood Andrews, *Economic Effects of the War upon Women and Children in Great Britain* (1918), p. 147.
22 House of Commons Debate, 17 June 1915. *Hansard*, vol. 72 cc. 777-8.
23 Pamela Horn, *Rural Life in England in the First World War* (1984), p. 90.
24 House of Lords Debate, 27 August 1914. *Hansard*, vol. 17 cc. 520-31.

25 *Yorkshire Post and Leeds Intelligencer*, 1 September 1914.
26 For the period of 1909–13 the average person in the UK was consuming 3,091 calories, of which thirty-five per cent was derived from cereals, seventeen per cent from meat, sixteen per cent from dairy produce and thirteen per cent from sugar. *The food supply of the United Kingdom. A report drawn up by a committee of the Royal Society at the request of the President of the Board of Trade* (1917), pp. 3, 6.
27 Hibbard, *Effects of the Great War upon Agriculture*, p. 225.
28 *Manchester Guardian*, 2 January 1915, 10 February 1915.
29 *Liverpool Daily Post*, 4 December 1914.

Chapter 4
1 Quoted in the *Western Daily Press*, 16 February 1915.
2 Nicholson reported that, with the assistance of old men, women and children, preparation of the land was well ahead in Lancashire and Cheshire. The weather was seasonally mild, wheat crops were coming on, pastures were 'wonderfully green and fresh' and livestock was fetching good prices. Thus, despite worries over labour, he concluded: 'The agricultural outlook is one of good promise'. *Manchester Guardian*, 2 January 1915.
3 *Leamington Spa Courier*, 29 January 1915.
4 *The Spectator*, 23 January 1915.
5 *Gloucester Journal*, 13 February 1915.
6 *Western Daily Press*, 26 February 1915.
7 *Western Times*, 19 March 1915.
8 *West Briton and Cornwall Advertiser*, 12 April 1915.
9 *Exeter and Plymouth Gazette*, 6 August 1915.
10 June Purvis, *Emmeline Pankhurst: A Biography* (2003), p. 276; *West Briton and Cornwall Advertiser*, 22 July 1915.
11 *Nottingham Evening Post*, 2 July 1915; *Western Times*, 2 July 1915.
12 Montgomery, *The Maintenance of the Agricultural Labour Supply*, p. 22.
13 House of Commons Debate, 22 May 1916. *Hansard*, vol. 82 cc. 1831–952.
14 *Coventry Herald*, 18 June 1915.
15 *Manchester Guardian*, 31 May 1915.
16 *Aberdeen Journal*, 12 June 1915.

NOTES

17 *West Briton and Cornwall Advertiser*, 1 July and 22 July 1915.

18 *Manchester Guardian*, 2 August 1915.

19 Quoted in the *Manchester Evening News*, 16 September 1915.

20 *Western Daily Press*, 26 February 1915.

21 *Western Times*, 16 November 1915.

22 Montgomery, *The Maintenance of the Agricultural Labour Supply*, pp. 62-3.

23 *Yorkshire Post and Leeds Intelligencer*, 23 February 1915.

24 *Report of sub-committee appointed to consider the employment of women in agriculture*, p. 64.

25 *The food supply of the United Kingdom. A report drawn up by a committee of the Royal Society*, p. 7.

26 Whetham, *The Agrarian History of England and Wales*, pp. 11, 22, 42.

27 *Gloucester Journal*, 24 April 1915.

28 *Manchester Courier and Lancashire General Advertiser*, 2 September 1893.

29 *Carlisle Patriot*, 12 February 1897; *Yorkshire Post and Leeds Intelligencer*, 3 November 1896, 9 November 1916.

30 *Tamworth Herald*, 27 February 1915; *West Briton and Cornwall Advertiser*, 12 July 1915; *Birmingham Daily Post*, 3 November 1915.

31 *Gloucestershire Chronicle,* 5 June 1915; *Cheltenham Chronicle,* 5 June 1915.

32 *Sussex Agricultural Express*, 26 March 1915.

33 *Cornishman*, 15 April 1915; *West Briton and Cornwall Advertiser*, 1 July 1915.

34 *Western Daily Press*, 16 December 1915.

35 *Board of Agriculture and Fisheries. (1919). Wages and Conditions of Employment in Agriculture*, p. 135.

36 Quoted in Marwick, *Women at War*, p. 79.

37 Private Papers of Miss B.A. Ziman – IWM Catalogue number: Documents.7926; Wendy Davis, *Dal & Rice* (2009), pp. 5-6. Every reasonable effort has been made to obtain the necessary permission to reproduce this source.

38 It was set up by the National Political League, a society founded by Mary Adelaide Broadhurst which supported the cause of women's suffrage. *Newcastle Journal*, 28 October 1914.

39 Lady Cowdray was vice-president of the National Political League. *Aberdeen Evening Express*, 12 July 1915.

40 *Aberdeen Journal*, 12 June 1915.

41 *The Sketch*, 21 July 1915.

42 *Reading Mercury*, 30 October 1915.

43 *Sheffield Independent*, 23 June 1915.

44 *Western Daily Press,* 17 March 1916.

45 Quoted in *Bucks Herald*, 26 February 1916.

46 *War Memoirs of David Lloyd George,* Volume I, p. 772.

47 *Gloucestershire Chronicle*, 5 June 1915.

48 *West Briton and Cornwall Advertiser*, 12 April 1915; *Cornishman*, 15 April 1915.

49 E. N. Thomas wrote: 'In agriculture, ridicule replaces regulations, and is frequently more potent; custom controls action and is difficult to evade. In the most conservative of all industries, there are many who do not "hold with women," as there are some who do not "hold with the war."' 'Women Workers in Agriculture', Adam W. Kirkaldy (ed.), *Industry and Finance. War Expedients and Reconstruction: Being the Results of Enquiries Arranged by the Section of Economic Science and Statistics of the British Association, During the Years 1916 and 1917* (1917), p. 152.

50 *Sussex Agricultural Express*, 18 February 1916.

51 *Manchester Guardian*, 8 April 1915.

52 *Whitby Gazette*, 30 July 1915.

53 *Yorkshire Evening Post*, 22 October 1918.

54 *Sussex Agricultural Express*, 28 May 1915.

55 Private Papers of Mrs C.M. Spencer – IWM Catalogue number: Documents.11603. Every reasonable effort has been made to obtain the necessary permission to reproduce this source.

56 *Cambridge Independent Press*, 7 May 1915; *Liverpool Daily Post,* 16 June 1915; *Chelmsford Chronicle*, 13 December 1918; For a full account of the formation of the WI see: Jane Robinson, *A Force To Be Reckoned With: A History of the Women's Institute* (2012), pp. 29-81.

57 *Manchester Guardian*, 24 November 1915.

58 *Birmingham Daily Post*, 25 November 1915.

59 This letter (dated 27 December 1915) was reproduced in Viscountess Wolseley's *Women and the Land,* pp. 65-66. Wolseley set this out as a good example of what women ought to be doing.

60 *Birmingham Mail*, 31 December 1915; *Buckingham Advertiser and Free Press*, 8 January 1916.

Chapter 5

1 *Yorkshire Post and Leeds Intelligencer*, 28 January 1916.
2 The press reported that the court of the Old Bailey was littered with the 'munitions of war' recovered by the police from Olive's 'studio arsenal.' *Yorkshire Post and Leeds Intelligencer*, 5 April 1913.
3 Olive Hockin, *Two Girls on the Land, War-Time on a Dartmoor Farm* (1918), p. 8.
4 *Ibid.*, p. 9.
5 *Ibid.*, pp. 10, 11, 12, 16.
6 *Ibid.*, p. 132.
7 *Ibid.*, p. 33.
8 Wolseley, *Women and the Land,* pp. 12, 22, 63, 66, 178, 179, 180.
9 *Daily Mirror*, 20 July 1916.
10 *Newcastle Journal*, 9 June 1916.
11 Thomas George, 'Female Agricultural Workers in Wales in the First World War,' Maggie Andrews and Janis Lomas (eds.) *The Home Front in Britain: Images, Myths and Forgotten Experiences Since 1914* (2014), p. 97.
12 'Lincolnshire Home Front' (on-line paper), Dr Katherine Storr, p. 16.
13 *Huddersfield Daily Examiner*, 15 February 1916.
14 *Lincolnshire Echo*, 9 March 1917.
15 *Wells Journal*, 11 February 1916.
16 *Hertford Mercury and Reformer*, 8 April 1916.
17 *Western Times*, 28 January 1916.
18 *Daily Mirror,* 31 August 1916.
19 *Sunderland Daily Echo and Shipping Gazette*, 13 September 1916.
20 Montgomery, *The Maintenance of the Agricultural Labour Supply*, p. 56.
21 *Bath Chronicle and Weekly Gazette*, 13 May 1916; *Birmingham Daily Post,* 8 June 1916. Wilkins tended to emphasise her practical experience more than her academic achievements, but she was also the first woman to be awarded a Diploma in Agriculture (at Newnham College, Cambridge, in 1897). de Silva, *A Short History of Agricultural Education*, p. 116.

22 Letter from Louisa Wilkins quoted in King, *Women Rule the Plot*, p. 71.
23 Quoted in King, *Women Rule the Plot*, pp. 75-76.
24 *Sussex Agricultural Express*, 28 July 1916.
25 'A Lady of the Land' wrote an account of her experiences with the WNLSC for the Co-Operative Wholesale Society's monthly magazine, *The Wheatsheaf*, December 1916.
26 King, *Women Rule the Plot*, pp. 56-57; *Exeter & Plymouth Gazette*, 28 November 1916.
27 *Lichfield Mercury*, 10 March 1916; *Western Times*, 30 March 1916.
28 Carol Twinch, *Women on the Land: Their Story During Two World Wars* (1990), pp. 48, 49.
29 Thomas, 'Women Workers in Agriculture', Kirkaldy, *Industry and Finance*, p. 149.
30 *Bucks Herald*, 3 June 1916.
31 *Gloucestershire Chronicle*, 27 May 1916.
32 *Manchester Evening News*, 28 June 1916; *Sussex Agricultural Express*, 15 September 1916.
33 *Illustrated War News*, 2 August 1916.
34 *Kent & Sussex Courier*, 18 February 1916.
35 *Chelmsford Chronicle*, 18 February 1916.
36 *Reading Mercury*, 25 March 1916.
37 *Western Times*, 6 May 1916.
38 *Manchester Guardian*, 18 February 1916.
39 House of Commons Debate, 22 May 1916. *Hansard*, vol. 82 cc. 1831-952.
40 *Board of Agriculture and Fisheries. (1919). Wages and Conditions of Employment in Agriculture*, p. 48.
41 *Newcastle Journal*, 21 April 1917.
42 Quoted in Andrews, *Economic Effects of the War upon Women and Children,* p. 65.
43 *Lincolnshire Echo*, 1 January 1916; *Buckingham Advertiser and Free Press*, 8 January 1916.
44 Hockin, *Two Girls on the Land*, p. 89.
45 *Hull Daily Mail*, 23 February 1916.
46 *West Briton and Cornwall Advertiser*, 16 March 1916.
47 The quote is Rowland Prothero addressing the Farmer's Club. *Wells Journal,* 25 February 1916.

48 *Lichfield Mercury*, 25 February 1916.

49 *Reading Mercury*, 11 March 1916.

50 *Ibid.*

51 *Manchester Guardian*, 13 March 1916.

52 *Reading Mercury*, 1 April 1916; *Hertford Mercury and Reformer*, 20 May 1916.

53 *Yorkshire Post and Leeds Intelligencer*, 29 March 1916; *West Briton and Cornwall Advertiser*, 1 May 1916; *Bath Chronicle and Weekly Gazette*, 13 May 1916.

54 *Cornishman*, 20 April 1916.

55 *Cornishman*, 4 May 1916.

56 *Buckingham Advertiser and Free Press*, 12 February 1916.

57 *Yorkshire Post and Leeds Intelligencer*, 10 March 1916.

58 *Bucks Herald*, 25 March 1916.

59 *Sussex Agricultural Express*, 7 July 1916.

60 IWM interview: Lees, Mary - Catalogue number: 506.

61 *Chelmsford Chronicle*, 24 March 1916.

62 *Sunday Mirror*, 29 October 1916

63 *Hastings and St Leonards Observer*, 4 November 1916.

64 James McDermott, *British Military Service Tribunals, 1916-18: A Very Much Abused Body of Men* (2011), p. 101.

65 *Aberdeen Weekly Journal*, 23 June 1916.

66 *Stirling Observer*, 18 April 1916.

67 Hilary Crowe 'Keeping the Wheels of the Farm in Motion: Labour Shortages in the Uplands during the Great War', *Rural History*, 19 (2008), p. 210.

68 *Yorkshire Post and Leeds Intelligencer*, 10 May 1916.

69 Crowe, 'Keeping the Wheels of the Farm in Motion', p. 211.

70 *Exeter and Plymouth Gazette*, 12 January 1916.

71 *Western Times*, 2 February 1916.

72 *North Devon Journal*, 10 February 1916.

73 *Exeter and Plymouth Gazette*, 16 February 1917.

74 House of Commons Debate, 22 May 1916. *Hansard*, vol. 82 cc. 1831–952.

75 *Western Times*, 24 October 1916.

76 *Western Times*, 5 December 1916.

77 *Yorkshire Post and Leeds Intelligencer*, 27 May 1916.

78 *Yorkshire Post and Leeds Intelligencer*, 17 May 1916.

79 *Chester Chronicle*, 18 March 1916.

80 House of Commons Debate, 22 May 1916. *Hansard*, vol. 82 cc. 1831–952.

81 E. N. Thomas, 'Women Workers in Agriculture', Kirkaldy, *Industry and Finance*, p. 149; Montgomery, *The Maintenance of the Agricultural Labour Supply*, p. 64.

82 IWM interview: Lees, Mary - Catalogue number: 506. In this interview Mary Lees states that she volunteered for farm work as soon as the war began, but as Seale-Hayne did not start taking on students until 1916 the chronology of her recollections is presumably a bit out.

83 *Exeter and Plymouth Gazette*, 18 March 1916.

84 *Western Times*, 9 January 1917.

85 *Yorkshire Post and Leeds Intelligencer*, 22 February 1916.

86 *Newcastle Journal*, 24 March 1916.

87 *Lincolnshire Echo*, 24 May 1916.

88 *Yorkshire Post and Leeds Intelligencer*, 10 May 1916.

89 *Yorkshire Post and Leeds Intelligencer*, 25 November 1916.

90 *Daily Gazette for Middlesbrough*, 25 April 1916; *Yorkshire Post and Leeds Intelligencer*, 7 December 1916.

91 *Yorkshire Post and Leeds Intelligencer*, 17 May 1916.

92 *Yorkshire Post and Leeds Intelligencer*, 2 March 1917.

93 *Bath Chronicle and Weekly Gazette*, 13 May 1916.

94 *Yorkshire Post and Leeds Intelligencer*, 26 May 1916, 4 August 1916, 9 November 1916; *Newcastle Journal*, 29 June 1916, 20 July 1916, 21 December 1916.

95 *Daily Mirror*, 25 October 1916.

96 House of Commons Debate, 22 May 1916. *Hansard*, vol. 82 cc. 1831-952.

97 Twinch, *Women on the Land*, p. 44.

98 IWM Interview: Lees, Mary - Catalogue number: 506.

99 *Manchester Guardian*, 12 April 1916.

100 *Manchester Guardian*, 10 May 1916.

101 *Western Times*, 2 May 1916; Montgomery, *The Maintenance of the Agricultural Labour Supply*, p. 9.

102 House of Lords Debate, 18 May 1916. *Hansard*, vol. 21 cc. 1071-123.

103 House of Commons Debate, 22 May 1916. *Hansard*, vol. 82 cc. 1831-952.

104 P. E. Dewey, 'Agricultural Labour Supply in England and Wales during the First World War', *Economic History Review*, 2nd ser., XXVlll, 1975, pp. 100–109; P. E. Dewey, 'Government Provision of Farm Labour in England and Wales, 1914-18', *The Agricultural History Review,* Vol. 27, No. 2 (1979), p. 120; Peter Dewey, *British Agriculture in the First World War* (1989) pp. 42-56.

105 *Manchester Guardian*, 21 June 1916. In May Francis Acland restated the government position on the use of child labour in agriculture in the House of Commons: they should only be used as 'a large resort'. He emphasised: 'It is an emergency thing, an exceptional thing, a thing which ought to be circumscribed in every possible way, and ought never to be resorted to unless local authorities are satisfied that neither by the operations of the Labour Exchanges nor by the increased employment of female labour the gap can be made good.' But despite these words, 15,753 school children were released to work on farms in May, and, on the last occasion that a count was taken, October 1916, 14,915 children were still being used in fifty-seven counties. House of Commons Debate, 22 May 1916. *Hansard*, vol. 82 cc. 1831-952; Andrews, *Economic Effects of the War upon Women and Children*, pp. 147, 148, 149.

106 *Manchester Guardian*, 23 August 1916.

107 Montgomery, *The Maintenance of the Agricultural Labour Supply*, pp. 23, 40.

108 Nicola Verdon, 'Left out in the Cold: Village Women and Agricultural Labour in England and Wales during the First World War', *Twentieth Century British History,* 27.1 (2016), p. 15.

109 'A Lady of the Land', *The Wheatsheaf,* December 1916.

110 *Cambridge Independent Press*, 3 March 1916.

111 *Illustrated War News,* 16 May 1917.

112 *Daily Mirror*, 20 June 1916.

113 *Western Daily Press*, 8 July 1916.

114 *Birmingham Mail*, 28 July 1916.

115 *Illustrated War News*, 28 June 1916.

116 *Sunday Mirror*, 29 October 1916.

117 Andrews, *Economic Effects of the War upon Women and Children*, p. 66; *Western Daily Press*, 1 September 1916; *Sussex Agricultural Express*, 15 September 1916; *Coventry Standard*, 6 October 1916.

118 *Yorkshire Post and Leeds Intelligencer*, 15 June 1916.

119 Twinch, *Women on the Land*, pp. 43, 44.

120 *Aberdeen Journal*, 11 and 12 October 1916.

121 Andrews, *Economic Effects of the War upon Women and Children*, p. 66.

122 Thomas, 'Women Workers in Agriculture', Kirkaldy, *Industry and Finance*, p. 148.

123 *The Spectator*, 22 September, 1916.

124 House of Commons Debate, 22 May 1916. *Hansard*, vol. 82 cc. 1831-952.

125 *Sunderland Daily Echo and Shipping Gazette*, 13 September 1916.

126 *The Spectator*, 22 September, 1916.

127 Verdon, 'Left out in the Cold', pp. 1-25.

128 *Grantham Journal*, 12 February 1916.

129 *Grantham Journal,* 3 and 24 June, 4 November 1916.

130 PRO MAF 59/1 First World War 1916. Women's County Committees. File note by Mr E Cheney, 29.9.1916 quoted by Margaret Hilary Bullock, 'The Women's Land Army 1939 – 1950: a study of policy and practice with particular reference to the Craven district', PhD thesis, University of Leeds, 2002, p. 79.

131 *Dorking and Leatherhead Advertiser*, 22 July 1916.

132 Hockin, *Two Girls on the Land,* p. 109.

133 *Yorkshire Post and Leeds Intelligencer*, 20 October 1916.

134 Cabinet Memorandum. Food prospects in 1917. Memorandum by the President of the Board of Agriculture and Fisheries. 30 October 1916. National Archives, CAB/24/2.

135 *Yorkshire Post and Leeds Intelligencer*, 23 October 1916.

136 McDermott, *British Military Service Tribunals*, p. 110.

137 Montgomery, *The Maintenance of the Agricultural Labour Supply*, pp. 10, 11.

138 *Newcastle Journal*, 25 November 1916.

139 Prothero, *English Farming Past and Present*, p. 414.

140 Speech reported in the *Western Mail*, 21 December 1916.

141 House of Commons Debate, 19 December 1916. *Hansard*, vol. 88 cc. 1333-94.

142 *Country Life*, 11 November 1916.

143 The term was used by the *Graphic*, 4 August 1917.

144 Quoted in the *Whitby Gazette*, 22 December 1916.

145 IWM interview: Robinson, Doris - Catalogue number: 12582.
146 Hockin, *Two Girls on the Land,* pp. 140, 144.

Chapter 6
1 *Liverpool Echo*, 20 February 1917.
2 *War Memoirs of David Lloyd George,* Volume I, p. 762.
3 *The Berwick Advertiser*, 17 August 1917.
4 *Exeter and Plymouth Gazette*, 25 January 1917.
5 Rowland E. Prothero, *The Land and its People; Chapters in Rural Life and History* (1925), p. 125.
6 Minutes of War Cabinet meeting, 14 February 1917. 1. Agriculture: Guaranteed Prices for Wheat, Oats and Potatoes. National Archives, CAB/23/1.
7 House of Commons Debate, 23 February 1917. *Hansard*, vol. 90, cc.1591-649.
8 Prothero, *The Land and its People*, p. 131.
9 Montgomery, *The Maintenance of the Agricultural Labour Supply*, pp. 24, 40; *Birmingham Daily Post*, 16 February 1917; Prothero, *The Land and its People*, p. 126.
10 Hockin, *Two Girls on the Land*, pp. 147, 156, 157.
11 *Bath Chronicle and Weekly Gazette*, 7 April 1917. In 1918 Miss Righton-Trice had been appointed Group Leader of the WLA in Wiltshire. *Bath Chronicle and Weekly Gazette*, 22 June 1918.
12 *Birmingham Daily Post*, 18 January 1917; *Biggleswade Chronicle*, 19 January 1917.
13 For details of Wilkins' report see King, *Women Rule the Plot*, p. 83.
14 King, *Women Rule the Plot*, p. 59; Bonnie White, *The Women's Land Army in First World War Britain* (2014), p. 65.
15 Edith Lyttelton wrote under the pseudonym G. B. Lancaster. She published eleven novels, most of them adventures and romances set in the colonies, and over 250 short stories for magazines. See Terry Sturm, *An Unsettled Spirit: The Life and Frontier Fiction of Edith Lyttelton* (2013).
16 *Lady Denman, G.B.E: For home and country* by Gervas Huxley quoted in Twinch, *Women on the Land*, p. 16.
17 Reported in the *Daily Record*, 26 March 1917.
18 Gladys Pott, 'Women in Agriculture', H.M. Usborne (ed.), *Women's Work in War Time: A Handbook of Employments* (1917), p. 125. This

publication was a directory providing details of employment opportunities available to women. Gladys Pott was appointed as a travelling inspector for the Board of Agriculture in February 1917.

19 *Birmingham Daily Post*, 17 March 1917.

20 *Chelmsford Chronicle*, 28 June 1918.

21 *Cambridge Daily News*, 4 May 1917; *Reading Mercury*, 12 May 1917.

22 IWM interview: Edwards, Annie Sarah - Catalogue number: 740.

23 Prothero, *The Land and its People*, pp. 128, 173.

24 *Exeter and Plymouth Gazette*, 22 June 1917.

25 *Hull Daily Mail*, 10 November 1917; *Reading Mercury*, 25 August 1917; *Newcastle Journal*, 31 July 1917.

26 *Reading Mercury*, 17 November 1917.

27 *Gloucestershire Chronicle*, 22 September 1917.

28 Prothero, *The Land and its People*, pp. 128, 177.

29 *War Memoirs of David Lloyd George,* Volume I, p. 773.

30 IWM interview: Lees, Mary – Catalogue number: 506.

31 IWM interview: Vernon, Patricia – Catalogue number: 3075. At one point in the interview Patricia indicates that she was only fifteen when she joined the WLA and that she lied about her age. However, later, she mentions being eighteen when she was undergoing her training.

32 IWM interview: Edwards, Annie Sarah – Catalogue number: 740.

33 IWM interview: Poulter, Helen Beatrice – Catalogue number: 727.

34 *Whitstable Times and Herne Bay Herald*, 6 October 1917.

35 Private Papers of Mrs R. Freedman – IWM Catalogue number: Documents.10983. Every reasonable effort has been made to obtain the necessary permission to reproduce this source.

36 IWM interview: Edwards, Annie Sarah – Catalogue number: 740.

37 IWM interview: Gilbert, Kathleen – Catalogue number: 9105.

38 *Western Daily Press*, 17 November 1917.

39 Private Papers of Mrs M. Bale – IWM Catalogue number: Documents.10774. Every reasonable effort has been made to obtain the necessary permission to reproduce this source.

40 IWM interview: Elsey, Grace and Harding, Clara – Catalogue number: 3073.

41 IWM interview: Poulter, Helen Beatrice – Catalogue number: 727.

42 IWM interview: Dundee, Florence – Catalogue number: 7438.

Every reasonable effort has been made to obtain the necessary permission to reproduce this source.

43 Montgomery, *The Maintenance of the Agricultural Labour Supply*, p. 65.

44 Pott, 'Women in Agriculture', Usborne, *Women's Work in War Time,* p. 122.

45 IWM interview: Edwards, Annie Sarah – Catalogue number: 740.

46 IWM interview: Vernon, Patricia – Catalogue number: 3075.

47 *Whitby Gazette*, 8 June 1917.

48 *Newcastle Journal*, 1 September 1917.

49 IWM interview: Lees, Mary – Catalogue number: 506.

50 White, *The Women's Land Army*, p. 36.

51 *Exeter and Plymouth Gazette*, 20 October 1916.

52 *Exeter and Plymouth Gazette*, 3 May 1918; *Board of Agriculture and Fisheries. (1919). Wages and Conditions of Employment in Agriculture*, p. 66.

53 *The Landswoman,* September 1918, No 9, Vol 1; *Exeter and Plymouth Gazette*, 24 January 1919.

54 *Nantwich Guardian*, 17 July 1917; *Cheshire Observer,* 17 November 1917.

55 IWM interview: Elsey, Grace and Harding, Clara – Catalogue number: 3073.

56 After the war she continued her own training and became an instructress at Swanley College. Remaining a lifelong member of the WFGU, she also trained girls during the Second World War. Twinch, *Women on the Land*, p. 45.

57 *Illustrated War News*, 25 April 1917.

58 Private Papers of Miss B. Bennett – IWM Catalogue number: Documents.2762. Every reasonable effort has been made to obtain the necessary permission to reproduce this source.

59 Twinch, *Women on the Land*, p. 39.

60 *The Landswoman,* August 1918, No. 8, Vol 1.

61 *The Landswoman,* October 1918, No. 10, Vol 1.

62 Andrews, *Economic Effects of the War upon Women and Children ,* p. 77

63 Prothero, *The Land and its People*, p. 183.

64 Published in the *Daily Record*, 26 March 1917, amongst other publications.

65 WLA, LAAS Handbook, 1919 edition, p. 5. Women's Land Army Documents 1918–1919 – IWM Catalogue number: Documents. 8783.

66 *Sunday Mirror,* 14 July 1918.

67 *The Landswoman*, November 1918, No. 11, Vol. 1.

68 *The Landswoman,* January 1918, No. 1, Vol. 1.

69 *Gloucestershire Chronicle*, 19 January 1918.

70 Prothero, *The Land and its People*, p. 173.

71 IWM interview: Edwards, Annie Sarah – Catalogue number: 740.

72 IWM interview: Poulter, Helen Beatrice – Catalogue number: 727.

73 *Western Daily Press*, 17 November 1917.

74 Private Papers of Miss B. Bennett – IWM Catalogue number: Documents. 2762.

75 House of Commons Debate, 18 July 1918. *Hansard*, vol. 108 cc. 1264-336.

76 'Instructions and advice to members of the WLA' published by the West Kent Women's Agricultural Committee in 1918. Women's Land Army Documents 1918 – 1919 – IWM Catalogue number: Documents. 8783.

77 *Chelmsford Chronicle*, 27 July 1917.

78 Press Bureau statement in the *Daily Record*, 26 March 1917.

79 Pott, 'Women in Agriculture', Usborne, *Women's Work in War Time,* p. 48.

80 Thomas, 'Women Workers in Agriculture', Kirkaldy, *Industry and Finance*, pp. 156-7.

81 IWM interview: Elsey, Grace and Harding, Clara – Catalogue number: 3073.

82 Pott, 'Women in Agriculture', Usborne, *Women's Work in War Time,* p. 15.

83 IWM interview: Edwards, Annie Sarah – Catalogue number: 740.

84 *Western Morning News*, 4 February 1941.

85 Private Papers of Mrs R. Freedman – IWM Catalogue number: Documents. 10983.

86 IWM interview: Dundee, Florence – Catalogue number: 7438.

87 IWM interview: Edwards, Annie Sarah – Catalogue number: 740.

88 IWM interview: Gilbert, Kathleen – Catalogue number: 9105.

89 Whetham, *The Agrarian History of England and Wales*, p. 73.

90 Private Papers of Mrs R. Freedman – IWM Catalogue number: Documents. 10983.

91 *The Landswoman*, March 1918, No. 3, Vol 1.

92 *Gloucester Journal*, 2 February 1918.

93 *Sussex Agricultural Express*, 28 November 1919.

94 *Northampton Mercury*, 3 May 1918.

95 *Sussex Agricultural Express*, 28 November 1919; *Taunton Courier, and Western Advertiser*, 26 November 1919; *Gloucestershire Echo*, 27 November 1919.

96 *The Landswoman,* September 1918, No. 9, Vol. 1.; *Western Times*, 20 July 1918.

97 *Yorkshire Evening Post*, 1 March 1918.

98 *The Landswoman*, July 1918, No. 7, Vol. 1.

99 *Hull Daily Mail*, 18 February 1918.

100 *Exeter and Plymouth Gazette*, 19 May 1917; *Western Times*, 19 May 1917.

101 *Exeter and Plymouth Gazette*, 25 May 1917.

102 *Exeter and Plymouth Gazette*, 7 February 1919.

103 *Yorkshire Post and Leeds Intelligencer*, 11 July 1917.

104 *Hull Daily Mail*, 22 March 1918.

105 *Yorkshire Post and Leeds Intelligencer*, 11 July 1917; *Hull Daily Mail*, 22 March 1918.

106 The *Landswoman,* February 1918, No. 2, Vol 1.

107 Private Papers of Miss B. Bennett – IWM Catalogue number: Documents.2762.

108 The *Landswoman,* February 1918, No. 2, Vol 1.

109 IWM interview: Vernon, Patricia – Catalogue number: 3075.

110 IWM interview: Poulter, Helen Beatrice – Catalogue number: 727.

111 Emma Vickers, "The Forgotten Army of the Woods': The Women's Timber Corps during the Second World War', *Agricultural History Review*, 59, I (2011), p. 103.

112 *Gloucester Journal*, 2 February 1918.

113 Private Papers of Mrs C.M. Spencer – IWM Catalogue number: Documents.11603.

114 *Daily Mirror*, 4 November 1918.

115 *The Landswoman,* April 1918, No. 4, Vol 1.

116 Private Papers of Mrs C.M. Spencer – IWM Catalogue number: Documents.11603.

117 Press Bureau statement in the *Daily Record*, 26 March 1917.

118 Private Papers of Mrs R. Freedman – IWM Catalogue number: Documents. 10983.
119 Twinch, *Women on the Land*, p. 46.
120 IWM interview: Gilbert, Kathleen – Catalogue number: 9105.
121 IWM interview: Edwards, Annie Sarah – Catalogue number: 740.
122 *Newcastle Journal*, 1 September 1917.
123 Thomas George, 'Female Agricultural Workers in Wales in the First World War,' p. 98.
124 *Lincolnshire Echo*, 28 August 1918; *Sussex Agricultural Express*, 13 June 1919; *Surrey Mirror*, 20 June 1919; *Cambridge Daily News*, 14 November 1919; Twinch, *Women on the Land*, p. 62.
125 Private Papers of Miss B. Bennett – IWM Catalogue number: Documents. 2762.
126 IWM interview: Poulter, Helen Beatrice – Catalogue number: 727.
127 Private Papers of Miss M. Hodgson – IWM Catalogue number: Documents. 2764. Every reasonable effort has been made to obtain the necessary permission to reproduce this source.
128 WLA, LAAS Handbook, 1919 edition, p. 5. Women's Land Army Documents 1918–19 – IWM Catalogue number: Documents. 8783.
129 *The Landswoman*, January 1918, No. 1. Vol 1.
130 *The Landswoman*, February 1918, No. 2. Vol 1.
131 *Taunton Courier, and Western Advertiser*, 30 January 1918.
132 *Hamilton Advertiser*, 13 April 1918.
133 *Daily Mirror*, 9 and 28 December 1918.
134 The brand's toothpaste carried the rhyming slogan: 'To plough and sow, to reap and mow,/And be a farmer's girl,/With skin so soft, and white as snow/And teeth as pure as pearl.' *The Landswoman*, January 1918, No. 1, Vol. 1 and March 1918, No. 3, Vol. 1.
135 *The Landswoman*, December 1918, No. 12, Vol. 1.
136 *The Landswoman*, August 1918, No. 8, Vol. 1,
137 *The Landswoman*, April 1918, No. 4, Vol. 1.
138 *Taunton Courier, and Western Advertiser*, 30 January 1918.
139 White, *The Women's Land Army*, p. 8.
140 See, for example, *Sunday Mirror*, 1 April 1917.
141 *Hawick News and Border Chronicle*, 19 July 1918.
142 WLA, LAAS Handbook, 1919 edition, p. 5. Women's Land Army Documents 1918–1919 – IWM Catalogue number: Documents. 8783.

143 *The Landswoman,* August 1918, No. 8, Vol. 1. 'The whole book
left behind it a feeling of utter disappointment and bewilderment,'
The Landswoman's editor complained. It 'dwells so persistently on
the hardships'. The only bright side identified in the review was that
the book showed 'the difference which the organisation of the Land
Army has made in the conditions of employment of women in
agriculture.' Olive Hockin acknowledged that much had improved
since she had arrived on Dartmoor in January 1916 and the Land
Girls of 1918 wouldn't necessarily share the poverty, privation and
loneliness that she had endured. There was now a 'vast network' to
train and place and care for women – 'to stipulate for holidays and
decent wages; who shop for them, hunt up local friends for them,
and even publish a magazine solely to keep in touch with them'.
Hockin, *Two Girls on the Land*, p. iv.

144 WLA, LAAS Handbook, 1919 edition, p. 5. Women's Land Army
Documents 1918–19 – IWM Catalogue number: Documents. 8783.
Women could be 'induced to withdraw' from the WLA if they were
deemed unsuitable for the work 'owing to health or temperament'.
To dismiss a woman for misconduct required an official
investigation of the case and a report from an Inspector. The overall
percentage of women withdrawing or being dismissed from the
WLA was about fifteen per cent. Thomas, 'Women Workers in
Agriculture', Kirkaldy, *Industry and Finance*, pp. 157-8.

145 PRO MAF 42/8, First World War, Letter from Miss M. Talbot to
Registry, BoA, 18 6 1918. Quoted in Bullock, 'The Women's Land
Army 1939–1950', pp. 136, 137.

146 Lady Mather-Jackson added that the women in Monmouthshire
were 'an absolutely different class' from members of the WLA in
country districts. These were girls from the industrial centres and
colliery districts, 'where they have been under no control or
discipline whatever, and have been brought up to do practically
nothing.' Marwick, *Women at War*, p. 104.

147 King, *Women Rule the Plot*, p. 96.

148 Initially started by private enterprise, *The Landswoman* was taken
over as the official publication of the WLA and was edited within
the Women's Branch of the Board of Agriculture. Prothero, *The Land
and its People*, p. 186.

149 *The Landswoman*, January 1918, No. 1, Vol. 1.

150 *The Landswoman*, March 1918, No. 3, Vol. 1.

151 *Ibid.*

152 *The Landswoman*, April 1918, No. 4, Vol. 1.

153 *The Landswoman*, August 1918, No. 8, Vol. 1.

154 Whetham, *The Agrarian History of England and Wales*, p. 131; www.thewi. org.uk

155 www.thewi.org.uk

156 *The Landswoman*, March 1918, No. 3, Vol. 1.

157 *Surrey Mirror,* 21 July 1916.

158 *Cambridge Daily News*, 12 May 1917.

159 *Yorkshire Post and Leeds Intelligencer,* 12 May 1917.

160 *Newcastle Journal*, 19 May 1917.

161 *Board of Agriculture and Fisheries. (1919). Wages and Conditions of Employment in Agriculture*, p. 57.

162 *Ibid.*, p. 367.

163 *Ibid.*, p. 334.

164 *Ibid.*, p. 158.

165 *Ibid.*, pp. 14, 236, 259, 322, 354.

166 *Ibid.*, p. 93.

167 *Ibid.*, p. 217.

168 *Ibid.*, p. 259.

169 *Ibid.*, p. 467.

170 *Ibid.*, p. 344.

171 *Ibid.*, p. 27.

172 *Ibid.*, p. 334.

173 *Ibid.*, p. 14.

174 *Ibid.*, p. 236.

175 *Ibid.*, p. 259.

176 *Ibid.*, p. 309.

177 Prothero, *The Land and its People*, p. 128.

178 *Exeter and Plymouth Gazette*, 23 June 1917.

179 *Whitby Gazette*, 23 March 1917.

180 *Yorkshire Evening Post*, 24 May 1917.

181 *Western Times*, 16 June 1917.

182 *Yorkshire Post and Leeds Intelligencer*, 7 November 1917.

183 *The Landswoman*, January 1918, No. 1, Vol 1.

184 Members of the WNLSC who wanted to join the WLA were permitted to enrol directly, without having to appear before a

Selection Committee, and many senior members moved over.

185 *Wells Journal*, 20 July 1917; *Taunton Courier, and Western Advertiser*, 25 July 1917 and 27 August 1919.

186 *Middlesex Chronicle*, 25 August and 15 September 1917.

187 *Yorkshire Post and Leeds Intelligencer,* 28 September 1917.

188 King, *Women Rule the Plot*, p. 90.

189 Andrews, *Economic Effects of the War upon Women and Children*, p. 41.

190 *Sussex Agricultural Express*, 23 November 1917.

191 Montgomery, *The Maintenance of the Agricultural Labour Supply*, pp. 26, 40; *Western Times*, 29 June 1917.

192 Montgomery, *The Maintenance of the Agricultural Labour Supply*, pp. 42, 43, 70, 74; Prothero, *The Land and its People.*, pp. 127, 129, 145.

193 Prothero, *The Land and its People*, pp. 142, 143, 144.

194 Whetham*, The Agrarian History of England and Wales*, p.107.

195 *Liverpool Echo*, 30 January 1917.

196 Cabinet Memorandum, 11 January 1917. Report by the Food Controller on Bread, Meat and Sugar. National Archives, CAB/24/3. In December 1914 stocks of wheat and flour had been seventeen and a half weeks' worth.

197 Olsun*, The economics of the wartime shortage*, p. 28.

198 *Birmingham Daily Post*, 16 February 1917.

199 Cabinet Memorandum, 11 January 1917. Report by the Food Controller on Bread, Meat and Sugar, p. 4. National Archives, CAB/24/3.

200 P. E. Dewey, 'Nutrition and living standards in wartime Britain', Richard Wall and Jay Winter (eds.) *The Upheaval of War: Family, Work and Welfare in Europe, 1914–1918* (2005), p. 200.

201 *Coventry Evening Telegraph*, 24 April 1917.

202 *Western Daily Press*, 16 April 1917.

203 *Birmingham Daily Post*, 9 April 1917.

204 Michael Dennis Buckley, 'Recipe for Reform: The Food Economy Movement in Britain During the First World War', PhD thesis, University of California, Berkeley (2009), p. 105.

205 *Yorkshire Post and Leeds Intelligencer*, 5 May 1917.

206 *Burton Daily Mail*, 2 May 1917; *Hull Daily Mail*, 2 May 1917; *Gloucester Journal*, 5 May 1917; *Reading Mercury*, 19 May 1917; *Yorkshire Post and Leeds Intelligencer*, 2 June 1917.

207 *Cambridge Daily News*, 21 May 1917; *Hull Daily Mail*, 26 August 1918.
208 *Industrial Unrest: The Reports of the Commissioners* (July 1917), pp. 12-13.
209 *Liverpool Daily Post*, 17 September 1917; *Western Daily Press*, 16 November 1917.
210 *Cheshire Observer*, 17 November 1917; Buckley, 'Recipe for Reform', pp. 116-117.
211 *Liverpool Daily Post*, 17 December 1917; *Liverpool Echo*, 18 December 1917; *Taunton Courier, and Western Advertiser*, 21 November 1917.
212 *Liverpool Echo*, 17 December 1917.
213 *Liverpool Daily Post*, 5 December 1917; *Yorkshire Post and Leeds Intelligencer*, 5 December 1917.
214 *Yorkshire Post and Leeds Intelligencer*, 1 December 1917; Cabinet Memorandum, 11 January 1917. Report by the Food Controller on Bread, Meat and Sugar, p. 4. National Archives, CAB/24/3.
215 IWM interview: Lees, Mary – Catalogue number: 506.
216 *Surrey Advertiser,* 21 March 1917.
217 House of Commons Debate, 18 July 1918. *Hansard*, vol. 108 cc.1264-336.
218 Prothero, *The Land and its People*, pp. 137, 152.
219 *Daily Record*, 4 September 1917.
220 *Western Morning News*, 2 March 1917.
221 *Bury Free Press*, 24 November 1917.
222 *Sheffield Independent*, 6 November 1917.
223 Private Papers of Miss B A Ziman – IWM Catalogue number: Documents. 7926.

Chapter 7
1 *Western Daily Press*, 8 February 1918.
2 *The Landswoman,* February 1918, No. 2, Vol. 1.
3 *The Landswoman,* March 1918, No. 3, Vol. 1.
4 *Bedfordshire Times and Independent*, 14 June 1918.
5 *Birmingham Daily Post*, 30 January 1918.
6 Prothero, *The Land and its People*, p. 162.
7 Whetham, *The Agrarian History of England and Wales*, p. 112; Montgomery,

The Maintenance of the Agricultural Labour Supply, pp. 19, 20.

8 *Manchester Guardian*, 10 July 1918.

9 House of Commons Debate, 1 July 1918. *Hansard*, vol. 107 cc. 1493-533.

10 *The Landswoman,* April 1918, No. 4, Vol. 1.

11 *Bedfordshire Times and Independent*, 31 May 1918; *Lincolnshire Echo*, 17 May 1918; *Cambridge Daily News*, 27 May 1918; *Liverpool Daily Post*, 13 May 1918.

12 *Cambridge Daily News*, 27 May 1918.

13 *The Observer*, 21 April 1918.

14 *The Landswoman,* April 1918, No. 4, Vol. 1.

15 IWM interview: Poulter, Helen Beatrice – Catalogue number: 727.

16 *Yorkshire Post and Leeds Intelligencer,* 6 May 1918.

17 *Chester Chronicle*, 4 May 1918.

18 *Sheffield Evening Telegraph*, 15 May 1918.

19 *Lancashire Evening Post*, 22 June 1918.

20 *Liverpool Daily Post*, 13 May 1918.

21 *Liverpool Echo*, 4 June 1918.

22 *Newcastle Journal*, 4 June 1918.

23 The *Landswoman,* July 1918, No. 7, Vol. 1.

24 *Western Times*, 31 May 1918.

25 Prothero, *English Farming Past and Present*, p.414; Whetham*, The Agrarian History of England and Wales*, p. 113; Montgomery, *The Maintenance of the Agricultural Labour Supply*, p. 47. The Agricultural Companies were formed of men judged to be physically unfit for active service and farmers were not delighted by what they were now being offered. From July onwards, as the allies began to push back, more German prisoners appeared on the land. By October 1918 there were 330 depots throughout the country from which prisoners were sent out for daily agricultural work. Rules on supervision were relaxed in the last months of the war and prisoners were finally permitted to be accomodated on farms, greatly increasing the convenience for farmers. The War Agricultural Volunteers were men aged over 45, and liable for service in the Forces, but who had opted to work in agriculture instead. The figure of 300,000 part-time women workers, though repeated several times by Prothero, seems to have been more of an estimate than anything based on collection of statistics.

26 *The Observer*, 2 June 1918.

27 Verdon, 'Left out in the Cold', p. 15.

28 Prothero, *The Land and its People*, p. 157.

29 Alun Howkins, *The Death of Rural England: A Social History of the Countryside Since 1900* (2003), p. 34.

30 War Cabinet Minutes, 1 October 1918. 6. Food Imports. National Archives, CAB/23/8.

31 *Western Daily Press*, 17 December 1918.

32 IWM interview: Poulter, Helen Beatrice – Catalogue number: 727.

33 Dewey, *War and Progress: Britain 1914–1945*, p. 36.

34 Ian Gazeley and Andrew Newell, 'The First World War and working-class food consumption in Britain', *European Review of Economic History* 17, 1 (2013), pp. 71-94.

35 *The Landswoman,* September 1918, No. 9, Vol. 1.

36 IWM interview: Elsey, Grace and Harding, Clara – Catalogue number: 3073.

37 *The Landswoman*, December 1918, No. 12, Vol. 1.

38 *Daily Mirror*, 8 October 1918; *Newcastle Journal*, 15 October 1918; Alyson Mercer, 'The Changing Face of Exhibiting Women's Wartime Work at the Imperial War Museum', *Women's History Review*, 2013; Mary Wilkinson, 'A Closer Look At The Women's Work Collection', *Imperial War Museum Review*, No. 6 (1991).

39 *Yorkshire Evening Post*, 8 January 1919.

40 *Ibid.*

41 *Grantham Journal*, 1 February 1919.

42 *The Landswoman*, April 1919, No 16, Vol 2.

43 *Bucks Herald*, 22 March 1919.

44 *Surrey Mirror*, 20 June 1919.

45 *Gloucestershire Chronicle*, 15 March 1919.

46 Private Papers of Mrs M. Bale – IWM Catalogue number: Documents.10774.

47 Private Papers of Mrs C.M. Spencer – IWM Catalogue number: Documents.11603.

48 *Surrey Mirror*, 20 June 1919.

49 *The Landswoman*, April 1919, No. 16, Vol. 2.

50 *Western Times*, 18 July 1919.

51 Montgomery, *The Maintenance of the Agricultural Labour Supply*, p. 60.

52 *Yorkshire Evening Post*, 22 November 1919.

53 *Sussex Agricultural Express*, 14 November 1919; *Kent & Sussex Courier*, 14 November 1919; Prothero, *The Land and its People*, p. 191.

54 Montgomery, *The Maintenance of the Agricultural Labour Supply*, p. 60; Prothero, *The Land and its People*, p. 189; *Gloucestershire Echo*, 27 November 1919; *Taunton Courier, and Western Advertiser*, 26 November and 3 December 1919.

55 *The Landswoman*, December 1919, No. 24, Vol. 2.

56 *Cambridge Independent Press*, 12 December 1919.

57 IWM interview: Edwards, Annie Sarah – Catalogue number: 740.

Chapter 8

1 White, *The Women's Land Army*, p. 8.

2 *Western Times*, 10 April 1917.

3 *Western Daily Press*, 8 February 1918.

4 *Grantham Journal*, 2 March 1918.

5 *Liverpool Daily Post*, 7 May 1918.

6 *Western Mail*, 20 November 1918.

7 *Lichfield Mercury*, 12 November 1920.

8 *Yorkshire Post and Leeds Intelligencer*, 2 May 1918.

9 *Yorkshire Post and Leeds Intelligencer*, 4 December 1918.

10 *Report of the Sub-Committee Appointed to Consider the Employment of Women in Agriculture*, p. 39.

11 *Ibid.*, pp. 107, 109.

12 *Sussex Agricultural Express*, 14 and 21 November 1919; *Cambridge Daily News*, 26 November 1919.

13 *Morpeth Herald*, 12 December 1919; *Western Gazette*, 19 December 1919; *Essex Newsman*, 7 August 1920.

14 *Western Times*, 22 February 1919.

15 *Western Daily Press*, 30 May 1919.

16 *Western Times*, 22 February 1919; *Exeter and Plymouth Gazette*, 18 July 1919; *Western Times*, 23 and 26 September 1919.

17 *Gloucester Citizen*, 5 October 1922.

18 Anne Meredith, 'From Ideals to Reality: The Women's Smallholding Colony at Lingfield, 1920–39', *The Agricultural History Review* 54.1 (2006): 105-121; Harold E. Moore, *Our Heritage in the Land* (1906), pp. 38, 48, 131, 132.

19 *Gloucester Citizen*, 25 August 1926.

20 *Gloucester Journal*, 30 May 1925.

21 *Lincolnshire Echo*, 27 May 1925.

22 *Gloucester Citizen*, 25 August 1926.

23 Meredith, 'From Ideals to Reality', pp. 105-121.

24 Verdon, 'Agricultural Labour and the Contested Nature of Women's Work in Interwar England and Wales', p. 124.

25 1921 Census of England and Wales. General Report with Appendices, Part VII.—Occupations and Industries. 5. Occupations of Females and 9. Industries.

26 Prothero, *The Land and its People*, p. 216.

27 Horn, *Rural Life in England in the First World War*, p. 136.

28 John William Robertson Scott, *The Story of the Women's Institute Movement in England & Wales & Scotland* (1925), p.134. In 1922 delegates of the NFWI voted against a union, but though a combination was formally rejected, it seems to be the case that members of the NAL in practice shifted over to the WI.

29 Nicola Verdon, "The Modern Countrywoman': Farm Women, Domesticity and Social Change in Interwar Britain', *History Workshop Journal,* 70, 1 (2010), p. 102; www.thewi.org.uk.

30 *Western Times*, 3 February 1939.

31 BBC 'Heir Hunters', Series 10, Episode 7, 8 March 2016.

Index

HOLDING THE HOME FRONT